LEBANESE CINEMA

TAURIS WORLD CINEMA SERIES

Series Editor: Lúcia Nagib, Professor of World Cinemas, University of Leeds
Advisory Board: Laura Mulvey (UK), Donald Richie (Japan), Robert Stam (USA), Ismail Xavier (Brazil)

The aim of the **Tauris World Cinema Series** is to reveal and celebrate the richness and complexity of film art across the globe. A wide variety of cinemas will be explored, both in the light of their own cultures and in the ways they interconnect with each other in a global context.

The books in the series will represent innovative scholarship, in tune with the multicultural character of contemporary audiences and designed to appeal to both the film expert and the general interest reader. It will draw upon an international authorship, comprising academics, film writers and journalists.

Prominent strands of the series will include **World Film Theory**, offering new theoretical approaches as well as re-assessments of major movements, filmmakers, genres, technologies and stars; **New Cinemas**, focusing on recent film revivals in different parts of the world; and **new translations** into English of international milestones of film theory and criticism.

Books in the series include:

Brazil on Screen: Cinema Novo, New Cinema, Utopia
By Lúcia Nagib

East Asian Cinemas: Exploring Transnational Connections on Film
Edited by Leon Hunt and Leung Wing-Fai

Lebanese Cinema: Imagining the Civil War and Beyond
By Lina Khatib

Contemporary New Zealand Cinema: From New Wave to Blockbuster
Edited by Ian Conrich and Stuart Murray

Queries, ideas and submissions to:
Series Editor, Professor Lúcia Nagib – l.nagib@leeds.ac.uk
Cinema Editor at I.B.Tauris, Philippa Brewster – p.brewster@blueyonder.co.uk

LEBANESE CINEMA
Imagining the Civil War and Beyond

Lina Khatib

I.B. TAURIS
LONDON · NEW YORK

Published in 2008 by I.B.Tauris & Co Ltd
6 Salem Road, London W2 4BU
175 Fifth Avenue, New York NY 10010
www.ibtauris.com

Copyright © 2008 Lina Khatib

The right of Lina Khatib to be identified as the author of this work has been asserted by the author in accordance with the Copyright, Designs and Patent Act 1988.

All rights reserved. Except for brief quotations in a review, this book, or any part thereof, may not be reproduced, stored in or introduced into a retrieval system, or transmitted, in any form or by any means, electronic, mechanical, photocopying, recording or otherwise, without the prior written permission of the publisher.

ISBN: (HB) 978 1 84511 627 9
ISBN: (PB) 978 1 84511 628 6

A full CIP record for this book is available from the British Library
A full CIP record is available from the Library of Congress

Library of Congress Catalog Card Number: available

Designed and typeset by 4word Ltd, Bristol, UK

This book is supported by

To Hikmat and Maha

CONTENTS

	List of Illustrations	ix
	Acknowledgements	xi
	Preface	xiii
	Introduction: Lebanese Cinema and the Civil War	xvii
Part I	**Contexts**	**1**
Chapter One	On Lebanese National Identity	3
Chapter Two	A Brief History of Cinema in Lebanon	21
Part II	**Representations**	**55**
Chapter Three	Imagining Beirut	57
Chapter Four	Social and Religious Breakdown	83
Chapter Five	Violence and Masculinity	105
Chapter Six	Mothers, Fighters and Taboo Breakers	129
Part III	**Reflections**	**151**
Chapter Seven	War and Memory	153
	Epilogue: On National Cinema	185
	Bibliography	191
	Filmography	207
	Index	209
	Index of Films	213

ILLUSTRATIONS

When Maryam Spoke Out	43
Little Wars	62
Little Wars	63
To you wherever you are	64
Around the Pink House	64
In the Battlefields	67
Letter from a Time of Exile	69
Beirut, The Encounter	73
Around the Pink House	77
The Belt of Fire	87
Zozo	88
The Explosion	94
The Tornado	98
Little Wars	109
Land of Honey and Incense	116
Outside Life	119
The Shelter	131
Martyrs	139
In the Battlefields	141
Kite	146

The Veiled Man	156
Al-Sheikha	159
Bosta	161
Terra Incognita	163
Beirut Phantoms	167

ACKNOWLEDGEMENTS

This book would not have been written without two grants from the Arts and Humanities Research Council in the United Kingdom: a Small Grant in the Creative and Performing Arts given in 2005; and a Research Leave award in 2006. I am also indebted to the Department of Media Arts at Royal Holloway, University of London, for granting me sabbatical leave in Autumn 2006 to write up the book.

I would like to thank two people whose support has been priceless. My father Hikmat El-Khatib, for the invaluable help with the process of collecting films and reference material in Lebanon, and for hunting down contacts. I am eternally indebted to your tireless support and your belief in my work. And Rana Issa, who has played an instrumental role in keeping me updated about developments in the film and cultural scene in Lebanon, for sharing valuable contacts and for crucial moral support.

I would like to thank Mr. Ghassan Abu Chakra at the National Cinema Center at the Ministry of Culture in Beirut for providing me with access to key films I would not have been able to obtain elsewhere, and for copies of reference material. Thanks to Hania Mroueh and the Beirut DC team for assisting me with the process of contacting filmmakers and for the copy of *Terra Incognita*. Philippe Aractingi and Bahij Hojeij: thank you for giving me copies of otherwise inaccessible films and valuable reference material. Ziad Doueiri: thanks for helping with the cover image and the contact at 3B Productions.

I would like to thank everyone who was interviewed for this book (in alphabetical order): Ibrahim Al-Ariss, Borhan Alawiyeh, Philippe Aractingi, Danielle Arbid, Roger Assaf, Leyla Assaf-Tengroth, Bshara Atallah, Randa Chahal, Jean Chamoun, Jean-Claude Codsi, Ziad Doueiri, Assad Fouladkar, Samir Habchi, Joana HadjiThomas, Bahij Hojeij, Mahmoud Hojeij, Jocelyne Saab, Ghassan Salhab and Mohamad Soueid. I am grateful for your generous time and for your belief in this book.

Thanks also to Souraya Baghdadi, Hassan Ni'mani, Moustapha Kassem and Elie Adabashi for their time and for giving me an insight into the life and films of Maroun Baghdadi (special thanks to Hassan Ni'mani for finding me material I had no other way of obtaining). The following people have also contributed to this book through sharing contacts, resources and time: Zahia Salhi, Isolde Standish, John Hill, Stella Bruzzi, Patricia Godfrey, Nadim Jarjoura, Christine Tohmé, Ghassan Makarem, Zeina Sfeir, Neil Smith, Maha Issa, Laury Haytayan, Rifa't Tarabay, Akram Zaatari, and Rana Imam – thank you all.

Finally, I cannot thank Philippa Brewster at I.B.Tauris enough for her support, hard work and enthusiasm.

A version of chapter three appeared as 'The Contested City: Beirut in Lebanese War Cinema' in *Visualizing the City*, edited by Dietrich Neumann and Alan Marcus (London: Routledge, 2007). A version of chapter five appeared as 'Violence and masculinity in Maroun Baghdadi's Lebanese war films' in *Critical Arts: A Journal of South-North Cultural and Media Studies* 21 (2007). Part of chapter six appeared as 'The voices of taboos: women in Lebanese war cinema' in *Women: A Cultural Review* (2006), volume 17, issue 1, pp.65–77.

PREFACE

How do you write about Lebanese cinema when its existence is still contested? Like most Lebanese people, I did not grow up watching Lebanese films. Cinema for me meant either Hollywood or Egyptian cinema, but mainly the latter, seen on television rather than in film theaters. However, in the early years of the Lebanese Civil War, Lebanese cinema did occasionally feature in my life. My earliest memory of Lebanese cinema is of my parents dressing up smartly as they prepared to attend the premiere of Mohammad Salman's film *Man Youtfi' An-Nar* (*Who Puts Out the Fire*) in 1982. I was too young to accompany them at the time, but I remember their excitement as they spoke about their delight at watching Raghda and Walid Toufic in a musical about the war. The premiere they went to was at Cinema Edisson, owned by our neighbor who lived on the floor above us in a Beirut suburb. I never made it to Cinema Edisson. Like the few other cinemas scattered in Beirut's Southern Suburb, the cinema died a slow, painful death. After *Man Youtfi' An-Nar*, all that was shown in such cinemas was a combination of Asian martial arts films and pornography. Cinema Edisson opted for the former, until – like the others in the area – finally closing down in the late 1980s.

Cinemas suffered all over the country, however. Mohammad Soueid's book *Ya Fouadi* offers a rare, evocative account of the lives and fate of film theaters in Beirut during the war. One by one, they would see their audiences decline, the regular attendants replaced with bored militiamen, until most of them could bear it no more and closed down. Walking down Hamra Street in the 1980s, I was used to seeing the cinemas' colorful, often garish, posters of tired Egyptian films and Bruce Lee features. Occasionally, a Lebanese film would be advertised. All the Lebanese films at the time, it seemed to me, were poor imitations of Hollywood action films and South-East Asian martial arts films. The names of the directors – Samir al-Ghoussaini, Youssef Sharaf Ed-Din – symbolized the dream that Lebanese cinema existed. Little did I know that, at the time, other Lebanese films were being made, or had been made, but were never shown. Behind the action films existed a cinema trying to come to terms with the present. Unlike the films of Ghoussaini and Sharaf Ed-Din, this cinema did not aspire to escapism. Nor did it aspire to Hollywood-esque standards. It was a quiet cinema, though not always because it intended to be so.

My most vivid memory of Lebanese cinema in the immediate postwar period is of seemingly endless television advertisements for *Al-I'sar* (*The Tornado*) by Samir Habchi (1992). I had no idea who Samir Habchi was, but the country was hyped up with news of real-life explosions being staged for the filming of *The Tornado*. The television adverts for the film presented it as a bleak take on the Civil War. It was the first Lebanese film to be made in the postwar period. Two years later, Maroun Baghdadi died by falling down a stairwell. He was only 37, and was Lebanon's most prominent filmmaker of his generation. I had not seen any of Baghdadi's films, but the newspapers were full of praise for them. He was mourned as a lost potential for Lebanese cinema. I stopped thinking about Lebanese cinema and moved to the United Kingdom.

Five years after Baghdadi's death, I found myself doing a PhD where I researched Egyptian cinema. I was surprised at the reaction I got from people when they found out what I was researching. 'Are you Egyptian?', some would ask. To me, it was natural to choose Egypt as the focus of a study partly addressing Arab film. I did not question my choice of researching Egyptian cinema, for it was, and still is, the biggest film industry in the Arab world. However, as the years went by, I knew that I wanted to write about Lebanese cinema too. I was a bit scared at the prospect. Egyptian cinema was familiar. I knew all the stars. I could mimic the accent to perfection. I grew up with it in all its forms: the romances, the comedies, the tragedies and the melodramas (I was not a fan of the musicals). I had a certain nostalgia for the early black-and-white Egyptian films that I had watched endlessly in my childhood. Egyptian cinema was part of me. Lebanese cinema, on the other hand, felt foreign. I thought hard, but I could not come up with a single Lebanese film I knew like I did an Egyptian one. I had seen some films in passing: *Bayya' al-Khawatem*, with Fairuz; some of the action films of the 1980s ... but that was it. Like many other Lebanese people, I had merely heard of the titles of some Lebanese films. And my mother's comments that Lebanese films were difficult to watch because acting in the Lebanese dialect made the delivery of lines 'heavy' further discouraged any curiosity I may have had about Lebanese cinema as I was growing up.

There was another reason why I found it difficult to acquaint myself with Lebanese cinema. As soon as I got over my apprehension about the use of the Lebanese dialect and started investigating what Lebanese cinema might be, it struck me that – with the exception of the commercial films of the 1980s – all Lebanese films seemed to be about the Civil War in one way or another. I do not remember the precise day the Civil War ended. I do not think many Lebanese people do either. People in Lebanon are well aware of when the war started: 13 April 1975. But no one seems to agree on when the war ended. The Taef Agreement of 1989 is often cited as the reason behind the ending of hostilities; however, there is no mutually agreed on date commemorating the beginning of the postwar period. The war seemed to have fizzled out gradually, rather than coming to a defined end. Like many fellow Lebanese, I was keen to move on after the war ended. I remember the 1990s as a good-time decade. The country was being rebuilt, and so were people's lives. Those of us who were lucky not to have lost our homes or loved ones embraced the decade's promises of prosperity and peace. We did not talk about the war. We behaved as if it had not existed. We tried our best to enjoy our present and look forward to the future. So the prospect of facing the war again in a mediated form, through Lebanese cinema, was frightening. I simply did not feel I was ready to go there again. It was too painful.

But something magical had happened. In 1998, a new Lebanese filmmaker called Ziad Doueiri made a film called *West Beyrouth*. Never before had I heard so much hype about a Lebanese film. The Lebanese critic Ibrahim al-Ariss recalls being in London at the time of the film's release, and collecting 64 newspaper articles from the British press about the film in two weeks (al-Ariss, 2006). Watching *West Beyrouth* for the first time, I felt proud. Here was a Lebanese film where the characters resembled me. They spoke in the Lebanese dialect but sounded natural. And the film was entertaining. The film marked a new era in Lebanese cinema, which I choose to call the renaissance period. Lebanese cinema had been through two different phases since 1975: the first is the wartime period, where filmmakers struggled to make films and struggled even more to distribute them; the second is the period immediately after the war, where a number of interesting art house films were made that were still haunted by the war. The year 1998 was the year Lebanese cinema began to operate on a mass – though still limited – scale. *West Beyrouth* was the first Lebanese film many young Lebanese people had seen in the cinema. It attracted a relatively high number of viewers in Lebanon, and worldwide attention, winning several awards at different film festivals. The idea of 'Lebanese cinema' became more tangible.

As the years went by, the number of Lebanese films seeing the light grew. The seeds of an industry were being sown in Lebanon, although until today cinema in the country still operates as a collection of individual efforts. As I forced myself to face the demons of the war and confront it through watching Lebanese cinema, the films themselves lured me into their world, away from the distractions of 'peacetime' Lebanon. I began to realize that Lebanese cinema was one of the few arenas where the ugliness of the war was confronted. It was a place where history was chronicled, questioned and sometimes condemned. It was a necessary reconciliatory space. Ten years have now marked the beginning of the cinema renaissance in Lebanon, and filmmaking in the country is going from strength to strength, despite ongoing problems. Films that I never thought would be seen by the public when I started the research for this book in 2003 are now being sold on DVD in Beirut. Film festivals around the world continue to screen Lebanese films, to the extent that I have come to expect to watch a Lebanese film at the London Film Festival every year without thinking twice about this expectation.

The journey that this book has taken me on has been a fascinating, illuminating and sometimes painful one. What I did not expect was the twist in the story that started in February 2005, and that gave me a fresh perspective on postwar Lebanese films. I was in the process of writing this book when Lebanese ex-Prime Minister Rafic Hariri was assassinated on 14 February 2005. His assassination triggered a wave of changes in Lebanon, both on the political and social levels. Scenes of exhilaration and patriotism dominated the country for months after his death, but were fast replaced with scenes of terror as more political assassinations took place. The dream of a new, free Lebanon was beginning to fade. And then in the summer of 2006, conflict between Hizbullah and Israel escalated into a full-out war, killing more than 1000 Lebanese civilians and destroying much of Lebanon's infrastructure. No sooner had that war ended than intra-Lebanese tensions began to resurface. Traces of the Civil War became obvious. Sectarianism showed its ugly face again. The thirst for violence overcame some Lebanese people. And suddenly I realized that Lebanese cinema's obsession with the war was more than simply that. It was as if the cinema was warning us against the inevitability of what was to come. Postwar Lebanese cinema, in particular, had been consumed by a feeling of loss and emptiness, where violence lurks at every corner.

As I sat in Beirut on 25 January 2007 as a state of emergency had been declared, watching militarized riots in the streets on television, I thought of Borhan Alawiyeh's 2001 film *To you wherever you are*, where an ex-militiaman called Mohammad Atwi recalls his wartime experiences, and declares 'I get happy when I see blood ... There's going to be war soon (again). Not now, later, in a year and a half maximum'. I wondered whether Atwi was among the rioters that day. The night ended with an army-imposed curfew in Beirut – the first since the end of the Civil War – and a new-found belief in me in the prophecy of cinema.

Introduction

LEBANESE CINEMA AND THE CIVIL WAR

Lebanon is a country with a yet undefined identity. This ambivalence has been reflected in much contention ever since the State of Lebanon was conceived. Today, Lebanese national identity is still a contested notion. What does it mean to be Lebanese? There is no direct answer to this question; however, to get a better understanding of what national identity may mean in Lebanon, one has to look at the country's history, politics, social construction, and cultural expressions. Much has been written about Lebanon's formation, its link with the rest of the Arab world, and its diversity. However, most studies of Lebanon refrain from tackling the concept of national identity in the country, especially over the last three decades. It is as if the idea of national identity is a taboo: addressing it would mean unearthing much of Lebanon's past and present that is too painful, or perhaps too shameful.

However, one arena in which 'being Lebanese' is addressed is Lebanese cinema. Lebanese cinema is a small cinema, and does not constitute an industry in the common definition of the word. It is a collection of films by independent filmmakers, both in Lebanon and in exile, that often defies conventions by representing issues Lebanese history books dare not address. Over the last 30 years, Lebanese cinema has acted as a commentator on the development of sectarian conflict in Lebanon; on the normalization of war; on the reconstruction of Lebanon in the postwar period; and on the way the war still lurks in every corner in today's Lebanon. Reading the history books that have examined the same period is important and revealing. Having to do that for the purpose of researching this book indeed brought back painful memories that I, as a Lebanese citizen who lived there through the Civil War period, would rather have forgotten. But while the history books reveal – in much detail – who did what to whom during the war, for what reason, and with what outcome, they do not comment on the everydayness of the war experience from the point of view of people. Where history fails, the arts triumph. Lebanon has seen a surge in novels and biographies that address the everydayness of the war. The late Mai Ghoussoub's book, *Leaving Beirut*; Jean Said Makdissi's

Beirut Fragments: A War Memoir; Youssef Bazzi's *And Arafat Looked at Me and Smiled*; and many, many others – they all challenge the dominant representation of the war through presenting stories of how the authors lived the war, how the war became a defining element of themselves. The books vary in stance from total detachment (in the case of Said Makdissi), to total immersion in the war's atrocities (in the case of Bazzi). In this sense they mirror Lebanese cinema – another arena where Lebanon's past, present and future are confronted and interrogated, but also ignored.

So why study cinema? Sharon Willis puts it eloquently:

> cinema is not imposed from without on a passive public, but... [is] responsive to certain collective demands or desires ... We need to analyze a cinema that responds to, reads and maps collective fantasies, utopian and anxious, a cinema that is always reading us – reading our social configurations of power and desire, pleasure and violence. This is part of film's allure: as we read it, it also reads us.[1]

While Lebanon's literary tradition is well established academically, its cinema has always been relegated to the margins. The mere fact of writing this book was often met with expressions of surprise from different Lebanese people, who would comment with questions like 'is there a Lebanese cinema to study to start with?' But the status of Lebanese cinema is changing. The process of researching this book started in 2003, and it is truly fascinating to witness the vast developments that have occurred since. In the span of a few years, Lebanese cinema has become a regular presence at international festivals. Lebanese films would appear on DVD. And the Lebanese audience would become more used to the idea of watching a Lebanese film, to the extent that the marketing of the musical *Bosta* (2005) relied on the tag '100% Lebanese film'.

But Lebanese cinema is not an innocent cinema. Running parallel to the confrontation of society's ailments is its presentation of the Civil War as a process of victimization of the Self by an unknown – or known – Other. Lebanese cinema also sometimes hides the realities of wartime Lebanese society by presenting the war as a shared condition while shying away from representing the society's inherent fragmentation. Studying Lebanese cinema is therefore double edged: the cinema is as much concealing as it is revealing. In this way, Lebanese cinema plays a role in the writing of Lebanese history.

There is no consensus on the nature of Lebanese history; as Studlar and Desser argue, 'contemporary history has been the subject of an ideological battle which seeks to rewrite, to rehabilitate, controversial and ambiguous events through the use of symbols ... what is being rewritten might justifiably be called a "trauma", a shock to the cultural system'.[2] Lebanese cinema reflects the tension between revealing the ugliness of the history of Lebanon in the Civil War period, and the yearning to gloss over the trauma. When it conceals, cinema becomes part of the war machine, a silencing mechanism that stands in the way of achieving national reconciliation. When it reveals, it serves a role in national therapy:

> Psychoanalytic therapy maintains that to be healed, one must recall the memory of the trauma which has been repressed by a sense of guilt. Otherwise, a 'faulty' memory or outright amnesia covers the truth, which lies somewhere deep in the unconscious. The more recent the trauma, the more quickly the memory can be recalled; the more severe the original trauma, the more completely it is repressed. In this respect, cultures can be said to act like individuals – they simply cannot live with overwhelming guilt. Like individual trauma, cultural trauma must be 'forgotten', but the guilt of such traumas continues to grow. However, as Freud notes, the mechanism of repression is inevitably flawed: the obstinately repressed material ultimately breaks through and manifests itself in unwelcome circumstances.[3]

I was in Beirut in April 2005, at the height of the Cedar Revolution, and I was surprised to find a re-run of Lebanese films at Espace Cinema's Screen 6 in Achrafieh. The films that were shown all dealt with the topic of the Civil War. They ranged from the popular (*West Beyrouth*), to the arty (*The Tornado*), to the in-between (*The Belt of Fire*). The impression I got from the re-run is that the films had been excavated to retell the story of the war to the audience as a cautionary measure. One of the slogans of the Cedar Revolution period – that appeared on billboards, T-shirts and television adverts – was '*tinzakar ta ma tin'ad*' (remember it so it won't be repeated). I felt that Lebanese cinema was used as a process of remembering and warning. The critic Ibrahim al-Ariss disagreed when I put my theory forward to him. His response was, 'I don't think that the film distributors and cinema owners can be given such a dimension of responsibility. Maybe it was because of the longing among citizens to hold on to something Lebanese'.[4] Studlar and Desser coin the term 'will to myth' to refer to 'a communal need, a cultural drive ... for a reconstruction of the national past in light of the present, a present which is, by definition of necessity, better'.[5] Perhaps Lebanese films were used as an expression of this 'will to myth', with the myth transforming from a nation in denial of the Civil War, to alleviate guilt, into a nation with a high degree of self reflection, a nation recognizing the necessity of healing, a nation full stop.

The Directors' View: Why the Civil War?

The Lebanese Civil War started in 1975 and ended in the early 1990s. Over the course of a decade and a half, the war slowly descended into an irrational state where differences between the warring factions, be they religious or political, ceased to be clearly defined. The war became a series of overlapping conflicts about a myriad of matters that went beyond internal Lebanese politics to include issues overarching the Middle East region, such as the Arab-Israeli conflict, inter-Arab political rivalry, and American and European military intervention. From its inception, Lebanon has been a country where outside involvement has politically undermined its very existence; this was carried over during the war from its beginning, when Lebanon became a playground for external as well as internal battles. In those internal battles, the war came not to have defined parameters of good and evil, or of heroes and villains. It became a case of mutual Othering by Lebanon's many factions, where each side was at once victim and victimizer. Lebanese cinema has been occupied with depicting the Lebanese Civil War over the last 30 years. From the advent of the war in 1975 and until today – more than 15 years after its end – the war has become a central theme for Lebanese filmmakers across generations. This does not simply apply to films representing the Civil War; it also applies to films where the Civil War inhabits their stylistic elements. From the openendedness of *A Perfect Day* to the darkness of *Falafel*, the Civil War still casts a shadow on films made in the post-Civil War era.

What the war films focus on are issues of social fragmentation, sectarian animosities, class divisions, and individual devastation. Only *West Beyrouth* and *In the Battlefields* represent another side to the war, that of the possibility of having fun under difficult conditions. The other films about the Civil War, whether made during the war period or after, are more concerned with revealing its dark side. The films differ in the genres in which they present the war: while some, like *In the Shadows of the City*, take a realist angle on the war, others like *The Tornado* and *A Suspended Life* choose a more fantasy-based method of addressing it. However, what the films have in common is that none of them justifies the war as they all take part in condemning it in different ways.

This book is based on first-hand research of Lebanese films, the circumstances of which are discussed in chapter two. One of the most valuable sources of information for this book is interviews with filmmakers, critics and actors who have commented on various aspects of Lebanese cinema. What is of interest here is a question I have asked the filmmakers I interviewed for this book: why have you made a film about the war? It is interesting that virtually no filmmaker contested the notion that their film is about the war (the only exception is Assad Fouladkar, who expressed his frustration at being asked why his feature film *When Maryam Spoke Out* is *not* about the war). The directors' answers reveal the reasons behind this lack of contestation.

Filmmakers who had made films while the Civil War was on seemed to be influenced by the circumstances surrounding them, and the impact they had on their individual psyches which got reflected in their films. Jocelyne Saab said about *A Suspended Life*:

> My first feature film was inspired by the siege of Beirut in 1982. I encountered the internal destruction and so I wrote the story of this little girl who was of the war generation. It was a story of the violence I was fighting and of the tolerance I was advocating. We filmed it under bombings. Cinema is life and I wanted to make a film that reflected the reality around me.[6]

Samir Habchi took an even more personal view on the impact of the war on his artistic creation, even hinting at his inevitable seduction by the war:

> We do not always choose what films to make. Sometimes the films impose a subject on you. Cinema is a means of expression, a message. I don't remember a time in my childhood or teenage years where there was no war. There was a certain 'type' of life called Lebanon, even now when you say 'Lebanon' people say war. There was one idea that overwhelmed me. It's like falling in love with one woman even though there are many beautiful women around.[7]

Habchi's pronouncement of a lack of choice in terms of representing the war was echoed by Borhan Alawiyeh, who believes that this condition still applies to Lebanese films made today:

> When there is a war going on, how can you not make a film about it? 'Why choose the war as a subject?': Because it is *the* subject. It's normal to live with the war as you do with your wife and kids. When the war ended, it occupied our memory, and our memory is unable to express itself about it. I can devote the whole of my life to writing about this topic. The war has inhabited all the Lebanese films that have been made since its start. The reasons that catalyzed the war have not disappeared. We're now going back to the prewar terms to try to build our society, but those terms were what started the war. I haven't yet seen a film that has not been touched by the war in its dramatic structure, its characters. I wonder how there can be a film or a work that has escaped from this memory. All our memories are linked with the war.[8]

Ghassan Salhab agreed, saying that the Civil War 'is not part of our memory, it *is* our memory'.[9]

Other filmmakers who have made films about the Civil War in the postwar period confirm those statements as they reveal how they are haunted by the war. Bahij Hojeij said of *The Belt of Fire*:

> I had not grieved over the war until I made this film; I could not conceive of making my first film without it being about my experience during the war and what we had to endure during the war. It was very difficult for me to talk about something else. I wanted to exorcise the war from within me. War is imprinted on our memories, and it's difficult to erase. You have to talk about it to get out of it. The Lebanese society is only recently getting over it, with all the movements about independence in the post-Hariri assassination period.[10]

Philippe Aractingi acquiesced in terms of the necessity of exorcism:

> The war is an essential part of our identity today. My identity as a 42-year-old is 10 years without war, and 32 years within war, for example. It's hard for us not to talk about ourselves in our first films. After that you can move on to other themes. The first thing you talk about is your wound. But then, I had to think of how to present a different film, because I wanted to have a unique vision as a director. So I wanted to go beyond the wound, and into the healing process.[11]

Joana HadjiThomas on the other hand addressed the latency of the war in her and Khalil Joreige's films:

> Our films talk about the present and how we can live in it. This present is linked to the past and to memory. How come we are not able to live in the present? Maybe we are severing our relationship with the past in a way that is too artificial. It's like being on a treadmill, you run and you run and you are not progressing. When we wrote the film [*A Perfect Day*], we felt that we are dead in this city and are not having much influence on the society around us or on the city. Maybe the relationship with the past is what is preventing us from moving on … The fact that the war *happened*, means that the problems were there *before* the war. For us, the problems are still there. It's the same social formation.[12]

Some filmmakers however have tried to break away from the hegemony of the war by transforming it into a background whilst acknowledging its impact.

Danielle Arbid said of *In the Battlefields*:

> The war is not the focus of the film, and was not the motive behind making the film. The story is a personal one which could have occurred without the war. The film could have been set in a country where there is peace. My relationship with the war is that when I was twelve, I thought war was normal and that the whole world was going through war. Only when I grew up did I discover that war was not the norm. I wanted the film to be harsher than the war that surrounds the characters; the society in the film is harsher than the war. The Lebanese have good qualities, but at the same time the society is harsh. Even today, in 'peace' time, everyday life in Lebanon is harsh. You can hide from missiles, but not from internal problems.[13]

A similar focus on internal conflict and dilemmas was reflected by Ziad Doueiri in his comment on *West Beyrouth*: 'The war was just a background. The focus of the film is on how you survive in a difficult environment, how you establish friendship, how people behave under extraordinary pressure; how you can still have fun under extraordinary pressure'.[14]

But the war remains a primary, if not the only, concern for the future. Jean Chamoun believes that talking about the war would work as a precautionary measure: 'We should talk about the war and make films about it. Memory is important in the life of societies. Memory is what drives people. It teaches them to learn from their mistakes'.[15]

Jean-Claude Codsi agreed but added other dimensions:

> The war should be remembered so it won't be repeated. Representing the war would also help us get over it and move on. I imagine that every Lebanese filmmaker who lived through the war would want to make a film about it, because everyone in Lebanon was affected by the war, we all suffered from it. But the war built Lebanon in a way. Lebanon has remained after the war, which means there *is* something called Lebanon. We should represent the war because it is a crucial part of our history.[16]

Randa Chahal also said:

> I will go back to making films about the war, whether fiction or documentary. Nothing has really been spoken about the war. We should talk about the past when talking about the present. If we don't talk about the war, what else are we going to talk about? The French, Germans and Americans all talk about their wars. There are books

that talk about the war, the press does and art does. But those who complain about talking about the war just want to be entertained. But of course we should not have a fixation with the war.[17]

In 2001 Kiki Kennedy-Day commented on the obsession with representing the Civil War that permeates postwar Lebanese cinema. She wrote: 'It will be interesting to see what the film-makers turn to as the war fades from memory and new concerns overtake them'.[18] The instability that has plagued Lebanon since the assassination of Rafic Hariri poses a challenge to Kennedy-Day's statement. If the statements of the directors on their relationship with the Civil War are representative of a wider one between filmmakers and socio-political conditions in Lebanon, then it will be difficult to imagine a future where Lebanese films are not concerned with the representation of conflict. Of course, Lebanese films not dealing with this issue are emerging, one example being Nadine Labake's debut feature *Caramel* which screened at Cannes in 2007. However, it seems that Lebanese cinema is condemned to act as a socio-political commentator in a country where the shadow of the war – it seems – still lurks in the corner.

This book is divided into three parts. Part I: Contexts sets the scene with a chapter interrogating the concept of national identity in Lebanon, and another giving an overview of the history of cinema in Lebanon and an account of how this book was researched. Part II: Representations deals with the four main themes in which the Civil War has been represented in Lebanese cinema, from the representation of space (focusing on Beirut), to the representation of social breakdown and sectarianism, and the representation of gender (where men and women play different, but sometimes overlapping, roles). Finally, Part III: Reflections concludes the arguments of the book and reflects on the relationship between Lebanese cinema and war memory, with a focus on postwar Lebanese cinema, its invocation of the Civil War and its meaning in present-time Lebanon. The book ends with a short epilogue critiquing Lebanese cinema's contribution to the debate on the concept of national cinema.

Endnotes

1 Willis, Sharon (1993). 'Disputed territories: masculinity and social space', in Penley, Constance and Sharon Willis (eds), *Male Trouble*, Minneapolis: University of Minnesota Press, p.266.
2 Studlar, Gaylyn and Desser, David (1988). 'Never having to say you're sorry: *Rambo*'s rewriting of the Vietnam War', *Film Quarterly* (Autumn) 42(1), p.9.
3 Studlar and Desser: 'Never having to say you're sorry', p.10.

4 Al-Ariss, Ibrahim (2006). *Interview with the author*, Beirut, April.
5 Studlar and Desser: 'Never having to say you're sorry', p.10.
6 Saab, Jocelyne (2006). *Interview with the author*, Paris, April.
7 Habchi, Samir (2005). *Interview with the author*, Beirut, April.
8 Alawiyeh, Borhan (2004). *Interview with the author*, Beirut, April.
9 Salhab, Ghassan (2004). *Interview with the author*, Beirut, April.
10 Hojeij, Bahij (2005). *Interview with the author*, Beirut, April.
11 Aractingi, Philippe (2006). *Interview with the author*, Beirut, April.
12 HadjiThomas, Joana (2006). *Interview with the author*, Beirut, April.
13 Arbid, Danielle (2006). *Interview with the author*, Paris, April.
14 Doueiri, Ziad (2004). *Interview with the author*, London, April.
15 Chamoun, Jean (2004). *Interview with the author*, Beirut, April.
16 Codsi, Jean-Claude (2004). *Interview with the author*, Beirut, April.
17 Chahal, Randa (2006). *Interview with the author*, Paris, April.
18 Kennedy-Day, Kiki (2001). 'Cinema in Lebanon, Syria, Iraq and Kuwait', in Leaman, Oliver (ed), *Companion Encyclopedia of Middle Eastern and North African Film*, London: Routledge, p.375.

PART I

CONTEXTS

Chapter One

ON LEBANESE NATIONAL IDENTITY

Lebanon is a contested concept. Historians do not seem to agree on what it means, and neither do its people. The historian Kamal Salibi rightly reflects that the Lebanese are hindered by their lack of agreement over Lebanon's past: if they do not have a common vision of their past, how can they be expected to have one of their future? He terms the situation a 'war over Lebanese history'.[1] The disagreement over what *was* is paralleled by one over what *is*: Lebanon is not only contested in terms of its origins, it is also contested in terms of its people's loyalties and primary affiliations. Kamal Salibi argues that this is a condition shared by several new states in the Arab world:

> In Europe, where nationalist thinking was already a firmly established tradition, the sense of separate nationality among the former subject peoples of the German, Austro-Hungarian and Russian empires was already in existence, and in most cases such clear and well-defined expectations were to be heeded in the formation of the new states. This was not the case with the Arab subjects of the Ottoman empire, where national consciousness, to the extent that it existed, was blurred and confounded by traditional loyalties of other kinds which were often in conflict with one another.[2]

Besides Kamal Salibi's A *House of Many Mansions*, no study so far has been able to argue that the Lebanese people have historically identified themselves as Lebanese first. However, when Salibi argues that there is 'a noticeable consensus among all but the more committed extremists today that all are Lebanese', he acknowledges that what it means to be Lebanese has been given different meanings by different groups.[3] Although it is of course difficult to operationalize what national identity refers to, it is useful to examine the different aspects of the Lebanese people's relationship with the country as this gives a more concrete overview of the issues underlying the contestation that has come to define Lebanon.

The Many Faces of Lebanon

Myths of Common Origin

Lebanese school books teach that the origin of the Lebanese people dates back to the days of the Phoenicians, an ancient merchant people who inhabited the coastal cities of present-day Lebanon and engaged in trade with the Romans and the Greeks, establishing cities further afield (like Carthage in Tunisia) and leading civilizational progress by inventing the alphabet. While the existence of the Phoenicians is not disputed historically, what is intriguing is the socio-political use of this myth of common origin in present-day Lebanon. Lebanese society is divided into those who simply regard this aspect as only one element in the historical development of Lebanon; those, like Kamal Salibi, who dismiss the Phoenician connection as a 'fictionalized history' used by the Lebanese to create national solidarity;[4] others who agree with Salibi but who contextualize their dismissal in terms of belonging to a pan-Arab nation that is at odds with perceived Phoenician non-Arabness; those who reconcile the different views by stressing the Arab origin of Phoenicians; and those who reject Lebanon's Arabness completely through emphasizing its non-Arab Phoenicianism. The myth of Phoenicia has been mostly appropriated by right-wing Christians in Lebanon whose definition of the Lebanese nation relies on the necessity of believing that they are ancestrally related.[5] In this sense, Phoenicia becomes an example of an invented tradition. Eric Hobsbawm has famously argued that the invention of tradition is a product of the exertion of power by a dominant group;[6] this argument echoes Friedrich Nietzsche's statement on tradition: 'What is tradition? A higher authority which one obeys, not because it commands what is useful to us, but because it *commands*'.[7]

As Edensor explains, 'the powerful "invent" traditions to create the illusion of primordiality and continuity, to mask the fact that nations are invariably of recent vintage, to "inculcate certain values and norms of behaviour by repetition, which automatically implies continuity with the past"'.[8] The tension over Phoenicia is an illustration of Ernest Gellner's argument that

> [i]t is nationalism which engenders nations, and not the other way round. Admittedly, nationalism uses the pre-existing, historically inherited proliferation of cultures or cultural wealth, though it uses them very selectively, and it most often transforms them radically. Dead languages can be revived, traditions invented, quite fictitious pristine purities restored. But this culturally creative, fanciful, positively inventive aspect of nationalist ardour ought not to allow anyone to conclude, erroneously, that nationalism is a contingent, artificial,

ideological invention ... The cultural shreds and patches used by nationalism are often arbitrary historical inventions ... But in no way does it follow that the principle of nationalism itself, as opposed to the avatars it happens to pick up for its incarnations, is itself in the least contingent and accidental.[9]

What is clear from the above is that understanding what Lebanese national identity means demands examining history as a process subject to revision and steeped in popular interpretation that is at odds with any 'pure' outlook on history as an objective account of 'what really happened'.

Sectarianism versus Nationalism

Jeffrey Seul argues that

religion in general tends to promote the stabilization of individual and group identity by favoring the preservation of old content (in the form of doctrine, ritual, moral frameworks, role expectations, symbols and the like), offering individuals the basis for reconstructing their identities within a stable or very slowly changing universe of shared meaning.[10]

However, in Lebanon, this very stabilizing role of religion became an element of contention amongst different religious groups. Lebanon's political system, known as confessionalism, is based on religious differences. Confessionalism is built on the relative power each sect had in Lebanon prior to the National Pact; thus, the post of the President is reserved for Maronites, Prime Minister for Sunnis, and House Speaker for Shiites. Maalouf argues that the confessional system in Lebanon started with good intentions – to guarantee political participation by all sects. As such, it is an example of how 'sometimes the treatment of "difference" involves the selective incorporation of local, regional and other differences within the nation, a process whereby difference is represented as the variety inherent in unity'.[11] However, Maalouf concedes that confessionalism 'has become a warning rather than a model'.[12]

Sectarian tension is perhaps the most known aspect of Lebanon's divisiveness. While it is misleading to assume that sectarian tension has been constant and continuous throughout Lebanon's history, it is nevertheless an important element underlying conflict in Lebanon's contemporary history. Ahmad Beydoun rightly argues that it is simplistic to view Lebanon as being based on a Muslim–Christian duality. Rather, he advocates examining the specificity and distinction of each of Lebanon's recognized 18 sects.[13] Sectarianism in Lebanon is based on religious sects forming a larger framework behind people's loyalties rather than national affiliation. This means that throughout Lebanon's modern history, Maronites for example have largely adhered to their religious community, Sunni Muslims to theirs, and the Druze have followed suit, etc. Coupled with this loyalty-based affiliation is a degree of mistrust towards the Other that has sometimes surfaced in sectarian conflict. Christians in general have sometimes expressed a perceived fear of annihilation in a predominantly Muslim area. While the Druze and the Christians share a large geographical area in the Lebanese Mountain, they engaged in armed conflict throughout Lebanon's history, with the most famous conflict between the two communities being that of 1860.[14] Although after 1860 this tension was translated into political rivalry rather than bloodshed, the Civil War reignited violence between the Christians and the Druze, which paralleled that between the Muslims and the Christians.

On the eve of the Civil War, the different religious communities were also marked by financial differences. Christians controlled most of the businesses in Lebanon, while Muslims formed the larger segment of industrial workers.[15] The Shiite community in particular 'stood outside of Lebanon's prewar political arena'.[16] Shiites were amongst Lebanon's poorest communities. Most of them lived in the South of Lebanon, an area allocated 'only 0.7 per cent of state funds for government services' in the early 1970s, despite its population being 17 per cent of that of Lebanon.[17] The Shiites were further oppressed by their own leaders, who ruled the South under a feudal system.[18]

The Civil War was a result of and a catalyst for divisions among Lebanon's different sects. However, it was also characterized by conflict among members of each religion, and even every sect, so that by the end of the war, Shiites were fighting each other (Amal versus Hizbullah), for example, as were the Maronites (Lebanese Forces versus Aoun supporters). After the Civil War ended, there were attempts by the different sects to present projects for the economic and political revival of Lebanon. However, as Bahjat Rizk argues, whenever a project was flagged by a certain sect, it would be received with disinterest by the others, because although projects would be presented on a national scale, they were inevitably evaluated from a sectarian perspective. In this sense, the 'nation' appeared 'smaller than the sect'.[19] Indeed, one cannot be a citizen of Lebanon unless one falls under one of the recognized sects that are registered in government. Civil marriage is still forbidden, secularism is still regarded with suspicion, and one simply cannot declare oneself an atheist because official records must list a religious affiliation. One cannot even register as a Buddhist or a Hindu for example because, despite Lebanon's guarantee of freedom of belief in its constitution, its legal system limits recognized religions to Islam, Christianity and Judaism, and even then does not recognize all the sects existing within those religions. Soueid argues that this narrow view of Lebanon blinds us to the country's beneath-the-surface diversity, as it harbors several ethnic and religious communities that are not officially recognized (like the Kurds).[20]

Kinship Loyalties

Sandra Mackey writes that in Lebanon 'religious identification was further subdivided by family loyalties, regional differences, economic rivalries, or simple hatred generated from past disputes and ongoing vendettas. A Lebanese was first a member of his family, then his village, then his religious group, and finally he was Lebanese'.[21] This quote points out the reliance of Lebanese society on the leadership of different families, so that different areas in Lebanon and different sects are dominated by clans under the leadership of a local *zaim* who belongs to a known family. Often certain areas and sects would see intense competition between different families, such as the Sunni Karamis (in Tripoli) and Salams and Solhs (in Beirut).[22] The continuing influence of this system is cited by Rizk as being the result of Lebanon's rapid development from a primary agrarian society to a service-based society, a development so swift that Lebanon was unable to change its original tribal, patriarchal social structure.[23]

This kinship system has been informally implemented in the Lebanese political system. Although the system is supposed to be 'democratic', parliamentary elections largely result in the nomination and victory of candidates who represent their clan.[24] And it is not uncommon for members of the same family to replace those who have died in their governmental posts. Sons, brothers and wives of deceased politicians continue their legacies by taking over their roles, thereby maintaining their families' traditional status. Even families that are relative newcomers to the political system have embraced this legacy, with the Hariri family being the most obvious example. A reason why this legacy continues today is that Lebanon possesses 'no clear sense of institutions. Because of the primacy of personal relationships, political loyalty belongs to individuals rather than organizations. As a result, bureaucracies respond only to men in power. And government most often functions to appease individuals, not necessarily to ensure the public welfare'.[25] Kinship loyalties have also been translated in the operation of the Civil War, so that the war was sometimes fought in a quasi-tribal manner based on feudal loyalties.[26]

Class Divisions

The so-called 'Golden Age' of Lebanon in the prewar era is marked by myths of peace, prosperity, and indulgence. Beirut was characterized as the Paris of the Middle East, and Lebanon as a whole was nicknamed the Switzerland of the Orient. Lebanon was a playground for the rich and famous, a hotbed for opulent lifestyles and urbane cosmopolitanism. However, as Mackey points out, the era was characterized by an acute inconsistency between the country's image and its social reality.[27] This reality was one of significant gaps between the haves and have-nots. For example, the well-educated upper classes, whether Muslim or Christian, came to adopt different values and lifestyles from those of the lower classes. And while there were plenty of empty luxury apartments in Beirut in this period, the suburbs were full of poor migrants living in shantytowns, forming a poverty belt around the city.[28] The prime role played by Beirut as the political and economic hub of Lebanon also blinded the onlooker to the relative deprivation of other areas in the country. The 'Akkar region in the north, Jabal Amil in the south, and the Bekaa Valley in the east, all largely populated by Sunni and Shiite Muslims, were forgotten zones of economic stagnation. In 1960, per capita income in Beirut was $803 compared with only $151 in the south', a gap that continued to widen.[29]

In the shantytowns, and in addition to Lebanese migrants from the South and rural areas, Lebanon was host to a myriad of migrants who existed as second-class human beings living on the margins of society: Syrian workers, Palestinian refugees, Sri Lankan maids, Indian laborers and others. The migrants existed within 'a rigidly hierarchical political and economic structure. Thus, the Lebanese and the migrants coexisted within Lebanon's borders, isolated within the boundaries of their individual communal identifications'.[30] Mackey terms the status quo of this 'Golden Age' a 'compartmentalized society'.[31] She argues that Lebanon's size contributed to the grievances felt by the different communities in this divided society, so that 'the intensity with which each group senses its own interests is magnified by the close proximity of its rivals'.[32]

East and West

Lebanon has traditionally been seen, and indeed sees itself, as a bridge between the East and the West. Its geographical location contributes to this role which endows it with a 'hybridity' unseen in any other country in the Arab world. However, this 'hybridity' is a source of contention: There is a conflict between those who view Lebanon as Arab and those who insist on Lebanon's detachment from the Arab world. Mohamad Soueid says that there is a tension between Lebanon's perceived historical authenticity as a mountain-state that acted as a refuge for those escaping from Arab military campaigns, and the view of Beirut as a hub for Arab and Islamic culture.[33] Historically speaking, there is also a tension between Christians who have affiliated themselves with Europe since the Crusades and those who insist on Lebanon's Arab identity.[34]

This tension was translated in the Lebanese National Pact that was declared when Lebanon gained independence in 1943. In order to please both sides, the Pact declared that Lebanon merely has an 'Arab character' (or 'Arab face'). Nasser's pan-Arab ideology, propagated through the Arab world since the Revolution of 1952, added to existing tension between Nasserites – largely Muslim Sunnis – and those who conceived of their identity as being separate from that of the rest of the Arab world. The Lebanese Civil War of 1958 was partly an indirect result of this schism.

Lebanon saw a redefinition of its Arabness during the Geneva Conference in 1984, which was later reproduced with the signing of the tripartite agreement between Walid Junblat, Nabih Birri and Elie Hubayqa on 28 December 1985.[35] The agreement between those three militia leaders was an attempt to resolve tensions between the Druze, Shiite and Maronite communities represented by the three leaders, respectively. The agreement's redefinition of Lebanon was as an 'Arab country as regards its belonging and identity'.[36] This belonging was limited to Lebanon's membership of the Arab League.[37] The Taef Agreement of 1989 that ended the Civil War in the early 1990s contributed to the passing of a new constitutional law in 1991, which declared that Lebanon is 'Arab in its belonging and identity' and that it is the 'final homeland for the Lebanese'.[38] Not only did this agreement illustrate a further redefinition of Lebanon's Arabness that extended it beyond the Arab League, it also made an indirect statement on its sovereignty. As Fawwaz Traboulsi explains, the 'finality of Lebanon … [meant] that it would never enter any union with any other state, namely Syria'.[39]

Foreign Intervention

The conflict in Lebanon that started in 1975 is commonly referred to as the Lebanese Civil War; however, it is a well-known fact that it was not limited to the intra-Lebanese arena. Just like Lebanon itself, the conflict involved entities beyond Lebanon. The war cannot be detached from the wider Arab-Israeli conflict. Both Israel and the Palestinians played a significant role in the war. Neighboring Arab countries have also been involved. Saudi Arabia for example has been playing the peace broker role for more than two decades. Syria on the other hand has been implicated in the military side of the conflict, deploying troops in Lebanon that only left the country in 2005, and exercising mighty political power over internal politics. The Arab League has played on and off roles in helping bridge warring factions, with various degrees of success. Among European countries, France has been playing a leading role since the days of the French mandate in the early twentieth century (and one cannot forget that Lebanon was a country brought into existence by France). Besides the involvement of other European countries, of the Soviet Union (and then Russia), and even of Latin American countries in Lebanese politics and the war, the United States continues to exercise much influence over the Middle East region as a whole.

The aim here is not to present an account of foreign intervention in Lebanon, but to examine the link between it and the concept of being Lebanese. The Lebanese state was a European creation, albeit under the guidance of the Maronites who demanded the creation of Greater Lebanon in 1920, which became the Lebanese Republic in 1926. Lebanon after the First World War was under a French mandate that resulted in the country's educational and governmental systems being modelled on the French ones. The legacy of the mandate is still visible today, with some Lebanese citizens referring to their former colonial power as 'our mother France', speaking French rather than Arabic in everyday life, and with the French educational system still being the country's most popular model. Today French affiliation can be seen alongside Iranian, American, Syrian and a multitude of other affiliations in Lebanon. Mackey puts its best: 'Lebanon has always been a battleground for someone. And each conqueror has deposited something of itself with a segment of the population, creating a people fragmented into groups possessing no common identity with the whole'.[40]

However, a prevailing myth during the Civil War, which still resonates in Lebanon today, is that of 'the war of others on our land'. This myth posits that the Lebanese war was only a civil war in overt practice, but that its causes, processes and purposes lay outside of Lebanon. The myth redefines the war as one fought between the superpowers (the Soviet Union versus the United States) over their interests in the Middle East; between Iranian fundamentalists and Western ideology; between the Palestinians and the Israelis; between pan-Arab nationalists and European and American powers; and numerous other combinations of binaries which do not include the Lebanese. This myth serves to absolve the Lebanese of all responsibility for the war and its atrocities, transforming them into mere victims of a brutal force which they were powerless to go against.

Postwar Historical Amnesia

'Claude Levi-Strauss has suggested that primitive cultures which have no past (i.e., do not conceive of or distinguish between a past and present) use myth as the primary means of dealing with cultural contradictions'.[41] In his discussion of the use of historical myths in Lebanon, Kamal Salibi bitterly argues that

> historical self deception is a luxury which only societies confident of their unity and solidarity can afford ... Divided societies, on the other

hand, cannot afford such fancilful indulgence. To gain the degree of solidarity that is needed to maintain viability, their best chance lies in getting to know and understand the full truth of their past, and to accommodate to its realities.[42]

Salibi's call for the 'truth' stems from his position as a historian, which conflicts with the Foucauldian notion of 'Truth' that this book advocates in its methodological take on the films analyzed.[43] However, Salibi's 'truth' is important to examine as it highlights the shying away from history that has accompanied the postwar period until 2005. One of the most striking aspects of the end of the war was its relegation to an untalked-about taboo. For almost 15 years, the Civil War ceased to become part of what the Lebanese publicly discussed. Effort was spent on the reconstruction of the country, but no one seemed to want to confront the very reasons behind the need for reconstruction. Perhaps the most controversial aspect of this historical amnesia is the integration of warlords into the Lebanese government and civil service. With one sweep – except for the exiled General Michel Aoun, the imprisoned Samir Geagea, and some of the figures of Hizbullah (who retained their militant positions on the basis of the group's role as a resistance force to Israeli occupation) – all other leaders who had been involved in steering the war's activities found themselves becoming MPs, ministers, or at the very least respectable politicians.[44] The same rule applied to members of the public: gone were the militiamen. Suddenly everyone in Lebanese society became a latent victim of the war. The perpetrators were nowhere to be found. The war was now firmly that of 'others on our land'.

The Cedar Revolution: The Door to the Past

As we can see, Lebanon's political landscape had lain dormant since the end of the Civil War. Elections would take place under a Syrian umbrella but very few questioned their nature. The Lebanese lira would be fixed to the American dollar to stabilize it without public expression of concern about the long-term viability of such a measure. Beirut would be rebuilt while voices of dissent would be silenced. The postwar period from the end of the Civil War till the assassination of Lebanon's ex-prime minister Rafic Hariri in February 2005 was marked by political stagnation. Lebanon remained a tool in the hands of foreign powers (Syria, Iran, United States, Saudi Arabia and others), but the Lebanese were not moved to seek an alternative, perhaps because that had been the condition of Lebanon from the day of its inception.

The assassination of Hariri on 14 February 2005 triggered a mass reaction that is unparalleled in Lebanon's history. It sparked the Cedar Revolution, with its call for national unity and for the cessation of Syrian intervention in internal Lebanese politics. Thousands of Lebanese citizens took to the streets in protest at the killing of Hariri, and to demand the withdrawal of Syrian troops from Lebanese soil. The protests led to the stepping down of the government, and to new elections in May 2005 where the March 14 coalition, led by Hariri's son Saad, won the majority of the seats. During the Cedar Revolution period, otherwise known as the Beirut Spring (February 2005–May 2005), the Lebanese flag was used by the protestors as a sign indicating their national affiliation, which to them affirmed their detachment from Syria. Ironically, it was the same flag that was used by pro-Syrian protestors who also took to the streets to emphasize their desire for the continuation of Lebanon's 'special relationship' with Syria. To the latter, Lebanon itself could not exist without Syrian patronage, and so the flag became a sign of affiliation with Syria, rather than detachment from it. The onlooker on the two biggest demonstrations by the two camps (the pro- and anti-Syrian ones) on 8 March and 14 March 2005 respectively would have been hard pressed to distinguish them on the basis of the visual presence of the Lebanese flag, or even on that of patriotic declarations or calls for finding out the 'truth' behind Hariri's assassination.

Never before had Lebanon seen such a public expression of national belonging. But the ambivalence lies in that each side's conception of Lebanon was different yet also similar. While the pro-Syrian protestors would carry signs saying 'No to foreign intervention', their definition of 'foreignness' excluded Syria, but applied to the United States. On the other hand, while the anti-Syrian protestors called for Syria to cease intervening in Lebanese politics, they did not extend this condition to other Arab states like Saudi Arabia – a major backer of Hariri and his supporters. So while the Cedar Revolution saw overt signs of national affiliation, it illuminates the way modern Lebanon is still infused with the very dilemmas, conflicts and divisions that have defined it from the start. The Civil War was a domain for the exercise of power through difference, but the Cedar Revolution's anti-war sentiment had inevitable parallels with the very demon it was supposed to be countering.

The Beirut Spring coincided with the 30th anniversary of the start of the Lebanese Civil War. The event was used by the March 14 coalition to emphasize their commitment to avoiding internal conflict in Lebanon between its different factions. Lebanese market stalls were flooded with artifacts symbolizing Lebanon's unity in diversity: intertwined signs of Islam and Christianity became de rigeur among the protestors in downtown Beirut, and journalist Gibran Tueni's speech on 14 March 2005 became a manifesto for the coalition supporters, who repeated his oath of remaining united, both Muslims and Christians.

Though the Cedar Revolution was well intended, its consequences were not as far reaching as had been hoped. A year and a half later, Lebanon would be attacked by Israel for 33 days after Hizbullah kidnapped two Israeli soldiers at the Lebanese-Israeli border. The war triggered further internal divisions in Lebanon, which saw their peak in May 2008. Ten days in May saw the worst sectarian fighting since the Civil War. The fighting had been catalyzed by anti-government protesters' calls for the government to step down, which the Lebanese government had rejected. The Beirut Spring had ended with the release of the Lebanese Forces leader Samir Geagea from an 11-year imprisonment and the return of General Michel Aoun from his exile in France. After the summer of 2006 war, Geagea had consolidated his affiliation with the March 14 coalition, while Aoun had sided with Hizbullah against the Lebanese government. The March 14 coalition – comprising the Lebanese Forces, Saad Hariri's Future Movement, the Kataeb Party and other leftist movements – backed the presence of the government, while the March 8 coalition, who came to be known as 'the opposition' – Hizbullah, Aoun's Free Patriotic Movement, the Marada, and other groups – called for the government to resign, demanded a third of the seats in the Cabinet and requested the replacement of the government with a 'national consensus' one. With no compromise on the horizon, the opposition called for a general strike on Wednesday 7 May, which ended up being a scene of riots, violence and sectarian strife that continued for 10 days. Those 10 days in May saw more than 80 people killed and 200 wounded, the takeover of most of Beirut by Hizbullah militants and their allies and street fighting between militiamen of different factions. Although the tensions were contained after foreign intervention – in the great Lebanese tradition, this time led by Qatar – they still marked a nightmarish reminder of the days of the Civil War where a person's sect could determine whether they lived or died, and of how often history repeats itself in Lebanon.

The Nation, Belonging and Exclusion

National identity is a contested notion, but so is the nation. The *International Relations Dictionary* defines the nation as:

> A social group which shares a common ideology, common institutions and customs, and a sense of homogeneity. 'Nation' is difficult to define so precisely as to differentiate the term from such other groups as religious sects, which exhibit some of the same characteristics. In the nation, however, there is also present a strong group sense of belonging associated with a particular territory considered to be peculiarly its own.[45]

Applying this definition to Lebanon, we can see that what is absent is the 'strong group sense of belonging'. Moreover, the contest over territory complicates the definition, as different people in Lebanon are divided in their imaginings of what constitutes a territory considered their own. For example, as mentioned earlier, there is tension between those who consider Lebanon to constitute a precisely defined piece of land, and those who consider it a legitimate part of Greater Syria.

Another definition of the nation is offered by Adrian Hastings. In this definition, the nation, '[f]ormed from one or more ethnicities, and normally identified by a literature of its own ... possesses or claims the right to political identity and autonomy as a people, together with the control of specific territory'.[46] What this definition adds to the previous one is the existence of a common literature. Lebanon complicates this definition in the conflict over its Arab identity, which has been reflected in its literature (while most Lebanese literature is written using the Arabic alphabet, some like the poet Said Akl have advocated the use of the Latin alphabet in writing Lebanese literature in an attempt to detach Lebanon from its Arab affiliation). The definition also highlights the claim to autonomy, which is again complicated by Lebanon's contentious relationship with Arab identity on one hand, and by Lebanon's reliance on foreign intervention since its inception on the other.

A behavioral definition of the nation is given by Hugh Seton-Watson, who says that a nation exists if 'a significant number of people in a community consider themselves to form a nation, or behave as if they formed one'.[47] This definition is interesting as it conceives of a people engaged in a will-to-nation. The problematization of this definition in the Lebanese case emerges when we consider that not all Lebanese people behave as if they have formed a nation. The Civil War is the ultimate example of this behavior.

Another key point in the theorization of nationhood is offered by Benedict Anderson. To him, the nation is 'always conceived as a deep horizontal comradeship'.[48] Hastings elaborates on this by saying that this means that people in a nation are 'held together horizontally by its shared character rather than vertically by reason of the authority of the state'.[49] Those two arguments bring to mind the often-cited – and erroneous – characterization of Lebanon as a pluralistic nation. Connor quotes the following definition of pluralism from *Webster's New International Dictionary*: 'a state or condition of society in which members of diverse ethnic, racial, religious, or social groups maintain an autonomous participation in and development of their traditional culture or special interest within the confines of a common civilization'.[50] Hastings adds that '[t]he degree of social self-consciousness required for the acceptance of such diversity within one's group is properly a characteristic of nationhood'.[51] Looking at Lebanon before, during and after the Civil War, we see that it poses a challenge to this conception of 'pluralism'. John P. Entelis published a study in 1974 in which he mapped out some of the aspects of 'pluralism' as they relate to prewar Lebanon. He argued that Lebanon is a case of pluralism where people are not culturally homogeneous but exist without conflict, because Lebanon

> is not a pluralistic society on the 'democratic' model... where pluralism is conceived as a 'dispersion of power between groups which are bound together by crosscutting loyalties, and by common values...'. This 'equilibrium' model of democratic pluralism presupposes cultural homogeneity and an integration resting on 'common values and common motivation at the individual level, and on the functional relations of common institutions at the social level', of which only the latter is present in Lebanon.
>
> Nor, on the other hand, does Lebanese pluralism resemble the 'conflict' model of plural society where 'internally autonomous and inclusive political units [are] ruled by institutionally distinct numerical minorities'. According to leading proponents of the conflict theory ... 'plural' societies – as opposed to 'pluralistic-democratic' societies – are characterized by dissensus and conflict between sub-national groups. Such a system can only be maintained, it is argued, by domination, regulation, and force; that is, a society is integrated by force, by the monopoly of power in the hands of one section of society.[52]

Entelis was only partially right, in that Lebanon does not belong to the two cited models. But he was wrong about the lack of conflict. Lebanon, before, during and after the Civil War, has been marked by conflict embedded into its very own political system. Mackey rejects the presentation of Lebanon as a pluralist society in the positive sense, arguing that 'a pluralist society is one that enjoys a basic consensus on fundamental principles and upholds a political system that prohibits any one group from dictating to the others'.[53] With a political system based on confessionalism, religious sects are ranked hierarchically. This makes it impossible for members of any given sect to imagine themselves as existing in a horizontally conceived relationship with those of other sects. Confessionalism is a consolidation of the inequality through which each sect perceives the others and itself. In this sense, the very core of Anderson's conception of horizontal comradeship is challenged.

What the above alerts us to is how the Lebanese state has come to be formed on the basis of anomalies in its sense of nationhood. In this sense, the concept of national identity in Lebanon cannot be conceived of without including the state. Grew argues that the maintenance of national identity 'may depend as much upon the existence of a state as the state relies on the loyalty identity implies'.[54] This case complicates arguments by scholars like

Connor, who say that nationalism should not be equated with state loyalty.[55] Lebanon presents a contradiction: if the Lebanese state did not exist, it would be very difficult to conceive of a nation called Lebanon.

The term 'nationalism' itself is contested. Hastings defines nationalism as

> a movement which seems to provide a state for a given 'nation' or further to advance the supposed interests of its own 'nation-state' regardless of other considerations. It arises chiefly where and when a particular ethnicity or nation feels itself threatened in regard to its own proper character, extent or importance.[56]

By contrast, Connor differentiates between the term nationalism, which he applies to loyalty to the nation, and patriotism, which he applies to that to the state.[57] Throughout the history of Lebanon, there has not been a movement that can truly be termed nationalist or patriotic, or that has been catalyzed by national identity. This absence of nationalism in Lebanon sits comfortably within Hasting's definition, whereas it challenges Connor's differentiation between nation and state.

This challenge can be linked to the difficulty of conceiving of Lebanon as a nation-state. This becomes clear when we consider Hastings' definition of the nation-state:

> a state which identifies itself in terms of one specific nation whose people are not seen simply as 'subjects' of the sovereign but as a horizontally bonded society to whom the state in a sense belongs. There is thus an identity of character between state and people.[58]

Connor also cautions against applying the term 'nation-state' to all states without discrimination, saying that most states in the world are not nation-states because rarely do the borders of a 'territorial-political unit (a state)... [coincide] with the territorial distribution of a national group'.[59] In the case of Lebanon, the absence of a national group further eliminates the possibility of application of the term nation-state.

Even when Lebanon was threatened by an outside force, it did not witness nationalism in action. The Israeli invasion of 1982 was welcomed by right-wing Christian factions, namely the al-Kataeb party, which saw the invasion as an occasion to rid the country of Palestinian *fedayeen*, whom it had perceived as a threat. Even the war of the summer of 2006 failed to generate nationalist zeal. Alter defines nationalism as

> both an ideology and a political movement which holds the nation and the sovereign nation-state to be crucial indwelling values, and

which manages to mobilize the political will of a people or a large section of a population. Nationalism is hence taken to be a largely dynamic principle capable of engendering hopes, emotions and action; it is a vehicle for activating human beings and creating political solidarity amongst them for the purposes of achieving a common goal. In accordance with this definition, nationalism exists whenever individuals feel they belong primarily to the nation, and whenever affective attachment and loyalty to that nation override all other attachments and loyalties.[60]

Unfortunately, throughout the history of Lebanon, its people's loyalties to sects, religions or political ideologies have never truly been overridden by loyalty to the nation. Alter operationalizes nationalism by listing a number of its 'structural components': 'consciousness of the uniqueness or peculiarity of a group of people, particularly with respect to their ethnic, linguistic or religious homogeneity; emphasizing of shared socio-cultural attitudes and historical memories; a sense of common mission; disrespect for and animosity toward other peoples'.[61] The arguments presented so far show that every single one of Alter's 'components' has been challenged in one way or another in the case of Lebanon. Of course, the nation should not be conceived of as static or finite. As Eugen Weber puts it, the nation should not be perceived as 'a given reality but as a work in progress'.[62] However, recurring tension in Lebanon, between its different political as well as religious groups, challenges even this optimistic imagining of the nation.

Endnotes

1 Salibi, Kamal (2005). *A House of Many Mansions: The History of Lebanon Reconsidered*, London: I.B.Tauris, p.200.
2 Salibi: *A House of Many Mansions*, p.20.
3 Salibi: *A House of Many Mansions*, p.3.
4 Salibi: *A House of Many Mansions*, p.216.
5 Connor, Walker (1994). *Ethnonationalism: The Quest for Understanding*, New Jersey: Princeton University Press.
6 Hobsbawm, Eric and Terence Ranger (eds) (1983). *The Invention of Tradition*, Cambridge: Cambridge University Press.
7 Friedrich Nietzsche, quoted in Chambers, Iain (1994). *Migrancy, Culture, Identity*, London: Routledge, p.115.
8 Edensor, Tim (2002). *National Identity, Popular Culture and Everyday Life*, Oxford: Berg, p.5.
9 Gellner, Ernest (2006). *Nations and Nationalism*, London: Blackwell (2nd edition), pp.54–5.

10 Seul, Jeffrey R. (1999). '"Ours is the way of God": religion, identity and intergroup Conflict', *Journal of Peace Research*, 36(5), p.558.
11 Edensor: *National Identity, Popular Culture and Everyday Life*, p.25.
12 Edensor: *National Identity, Popular Culture and Everyday Life*, p. 119.
13 Beydoun, Ahmad (2005). *The Adventures of Adversity: The Lebanese – Sects, Arabs, and Phoenicians*, Beirut: Dar An-Nahar (Arabic).
14 Mackey, Sandra (2006). *Lebanon: A House Divided*, New York: W.W. Norton and Company.
15 Traboulsi, Fawwaz (2007). *A History of Modern Lebanon*, London: Pluto Press.
16 Mackey: *Lebanon*, p.75.
17 Mackey: *Lebanon*, p.76.
18 Mackey: *Lebanon*.
19 Rizk, Bahjat Edmond (2006). *Lebanese Plurality in Identity and Government*, Beirut: Bahjat Edmond Rizk (Arabic), p.34.
20 Soueid, Mohamad (1986). *The Postponed Cinema: Films of the Lebanese Civil War*, Beirut: The Arab Research Organization (Arabic).
21 Mackey: *Lebanon*, p.12.
22 Mackey: *Lebanon*.
23 Rizk: *Lebanese Plurality*.
24 Traboulsi: *A History of Modern Lebanon*.
25 Mackey: *Lebanon*, p.97.
26 Mackey: *Lebanon*.
27 Ibid.
28 Traboulsi, *A History of Modern Lebanon*.
29 Mackey: *Lebanon*, p.13.
30 Mackey: *Lebanon*, p.11.
31 Mackey: *Lebanon*, p.15.
32 Mackey: *Lebanon*, p.18.
33 Soueid: *The Postponed Cinema*.
34 Mackey: *Lebanon*.
35 Beydoun: *The Adventures of Adversity*.
36 Traboulsi: *A History of Modern Lebanon*, p.226.
37 Beydoun: *The Adventures of Adversity*.
38 Traboulsi: *A History of Modern Lebanon*, p.244.
39 Ibid.
40 Mackey: *Lebanon*, p.18.
41 Studlar, Gaylyn and Desser, David (1988). 'Never having to say you're sorry: *Rambo*'s rewriting of the Vietnam War', *Film Quarterly* (Autumn) 42(1), p.10.
42 Salibi: *A House of Many Mansions*, p.217.
43 Foucault, Michel (1980). *Power/Knowledge*, London: The Harvester Press.
44 Hizbullah representatives later joined the government too, as did Aoun when he returned from exile after the Cedar Revolution. Shortly after, Geagea resumed leadership of the Lebanese Forces.
45 Plano, Jack C. and Olton, Roy (1969). *The International Relations Dictionary*, New York: Holt, Rinehart & Winston, p.119.

46 Hastings, Adrian (1997). *The Construction of Nationhood: Ethnicity, Religion and Nationalism*, Cambridge: Cambridge University Press, p.3.
47 Seton-Watson, Hugh (1977). *Nations and States: An Enquiry into the Origins of Nations and the Politics of Nationalism*, London: Westview Press, p.5.
48 Anderson, Benedict (1983). *Imagined Communities: Reflections on the Origin and Spread of Nationalism*, London: Verso, p.7.
49 Hastings: *The Construction of Nationhood*, p.25.
50 Connor: *Ethnonationalism*, p.106.
51 Hastings: *The Construction of Nationhood*, p.173.
52 Entelis, John P. (1974). *Pluralism and Party Transformation in Lebanon: Al-Kataeb 1936–1970*, Leiden: E.J. Brill, p.1.
53 Mackey: *Lebanon*, p.83.
54 Grew, Raymond (1986). 'The construction of national identity', in Boerner, Peter (ed), *Concepts of National Identity: An Interdisciplinary Dialogue*, Baden-Baden: Nomos Verlagsgesellschaft, p.35.
55 Connor: *Ethnonationalism*.
56 Hastings: *The Construction of Nationhood*, p.4.
57 Connor: *Ethnonationalism*.
58 Hastings: *The Construction of Nationhood*, p.3.
59 Connor: *Ethnonationalism*, p.96.
60 Alter, Peter (1985). *Nationalism*, London: Edward Arnold, pp.8–9.
61 Alter: *Nationalism*, p.7.
62 Weber, Eugen (1977). *Peasants into Frenchmen*, London: Chatto and Windus, p.493.

Chapter Two

A BRIEF HISTORY OF CINEMA IN LEBANON

Lebanese cinema has been occupied with depicting the Lebanese Civil War over the last 30 years. From the advent of the war in 1975 and until today – a decade and a half after its end – the war has become a central theme for Lebanese filmmakers across generations. War occupies a central role in the country's artistic representations. Poetry, paintings, music, theater and novels are other mediums through which the experience of the war has been, and still is, mediated in Lebanon. However, unlike those other mediums, cinema in Lebanon has, until recently, not enjoyed a central role in public memory. While novels are readily accessible, most Lebanese films remain hidden, made but unseen by the public because of their lack of distribution. One of the ironies of the war is that it sparked a string of films about its subject matter, yet it contributed to the destruction of the cinema industry in Lebanon. Before the war, Lebanon was slowly building a reputation as a cinema center in the Arab world, rivaled only by Egypt. This privilege would end with the war, and Lebanese cinema was transformed from an industry to a collection of films made by disparate filmmakers working independently.

The result was that most Lebanese films were not distributed widely, neither in Lebanon nor abroad. Most Lebanese films have a short life of screenings at film festivals (both in the Arab world and internationally), but are not released in cinemas or on video. Most of Beirut's universities have initiated audiovisual programs, yet there is no system in place for the funding, processing, or distribution of feature films.[1] This is not helped by the lack of financial support from the government. The war also resulted in a brain drain, where a large number of young Lebanese people left the country to study and work abroad. Randa Chahal and Ziad Doueiri are an example: Chahal had left Lebanon in 1972 to study cinema, and stayed in Paris both during and after the Civil War (although she visits Lebanon regularly). Doueiri left Lebanon in 1983, also to study cinema, but did not return to Lebanon until 13 years later when he made *West Beyrouth* (1998). The two filmmakers are not alone: a significant number of Lebanese directors live or have lived abroad until recently, like Ghassan Salhab, Jocelyne Saab, Leila Assaf and Danielle Arbid. The combination of the presence of talent outside Lebanon and the lack of resources inside Lebanon has resulted in the creation of a transnational Lebanese cinema whereby most Lebanese films made in the last 30 years are international co-productions, with the funding coming from countries like France, Belgium and Italy. With the limited distribution of Lebanese films also largely confined to Europe, the films acquired the status of urban myths in Lebanon, talked about but never encountered.

Early Cinema

The first Lebanese film was *The Adventures of Elias Mabrouk* (*Moughamarat Elias Marbouk*), directed by the Italian Jordano Pidutti in 1929. It was developed in a lab in Beirut, the first lab in Lebanon, which had been established by the same Italian in 1925. *Moughamarat Elias Mabrouk* was not screened at a cinema in Lebanon until 1932, after which it disappeared from existence. No copy of the film survives.[2] This was followed by *The Adventures of Abu Abed* (*Moughamarat Abu Abed*) in 1931. Both films were silent comedies, but the second film was the first to be made with Lebanese funding, with the funder being the man who played the lead character, Rachid Ali Shaaban.[3] Shaaban worked at a film theater in Beirut, and did not produce any more films as his budget did not extend to funding talking movies, which started appearing in Lebanon in the early 1930s.[4]

The first Lebanese film production company was established in 1933, with funding from a Lebanese woman called Herta Gargour. The company, Lumnar Film Company, signed a deal with the French Pathé Studios to train technicians from Lebanon in France.[5] In 1934 the company produced the first 'talkie'; it was titled *Amongst the Temples of Baalbak* (*Bayn Hayakel Baalbak*) and was the first Lebanese film in the Arabic language.[6] Ibrahim al-Ariss cites the earliest professional films in Lebanon as being those of Ali al-Ariss in the mid 1940s, the first of which being *The Rose Seller* (*Bayya'at al-Ward*) in 1940.[7] Ali al-Ariss had come from a theater background, where he became known as a talented set designer.[8] His films were based on the musical genre and Bedouin stories, thus following the tradition of Egyptian cinema. Al-Ariss was Lebanon's first director, although he only made one more film after *The Rose Seller*, titled *The Planet of the Desert Princess* (*Kawkab Amirat as-Sahraa'*). Copies of both films were destroyed in a fire in 1949.[9] By 1951, only eight Lebanese films were made.[10] Part of the reason why so few films were made in that early period was the Second World War, during which Lebanon was under a French mandate.[11]

In 1952 the first fully-equipped film studios were set up in Lebanon: Studio Haroun and Studio Al-Arz. Studio Haroun was equipped with film development machines fashioned from old car machinery by the studio's owner Michel Haroun, a former car electrician. Rushes were stored in large cooking pots and water was obtained from a river that ran in front of the studio.[12] But despite the lack of resources, the 1950s witnessed the first time Lebanese films set in the Lebanese countryside and using the Lebanese dialect were made. However, those films failed commercially as their target audiences – the Lebanese villagers and the Lebanese expatriates – either did not have access to film theaters (in the case of the former), or were not interested in simplistic representations of their country (in the case of the latter). Mohamad Salman diagnosed that the only way to establish a profitable cinema in Lebanon in the 1950s would be to follow the Egyptian model.[13] As a result, most of the films of the 1950s had shallow plots and were poorly executed, with the exception of George Nasr's *Whither?* (*Ila Ayn?*) which was the first Lebanese film to be shown at Cannes, in 1958.[14]

A Quasi-Egyptian Cinema

The problems of Lebanese cinema from its inception in 1929 till the beginning of the war period can be summed up as technical deficiencies as well as human ones. Lebanese cinema suffered from 'Egyptianization' – films were seen to have to follow the Egyptian model and even to have Egyptian dialogue to be successful. The Arab market was not open to Lebanese films because of heavy censorship and the dominance of Egyptian cinema.[15] Nasser's nationalizing of cinema in Egypt following the 1952 Revolution caused producers and directors to come to Lebanon to make films in the 1950s and the 1960s.[16] Soueid argues that the current problems that cinema in Lebanon faces are rooted in the 1960s. Lebanon was relatively stable at the time, both politically and economically. But Soueid laments the way resources at the time were geared towards supporting Egyptian filmmaking on Lebanese land, instead of nurturing an indigenous industry.[17] Qirdahi argues that the producers at the time were not looking ahead to the future, but were concentrating on making a quick profit.[18] There were very few serious Lebanese productions in the mid-1950s to mid-1960s period; these include the Rahbanis' *Bayya' al-Khawatem*, *Bint al-Hariss* and *Safar Barlek*, as well as Youssef Maalouf's *The Broken Wings*, an adaptation of Gibran's novel of the same title. However, the majority of films made in that period were Egyptian, Syrian or Turkish productions. The films were alienating to the Lebanese audience. First, most of them were musicals with little attention to plots. Second, the films' dialects were a mixture of Syrian, Egyptian and Lebanese, which had an unintentional farcical effect on the audience.[19]

The 1960s saw a boom in the cinema industry in Lebanon. Not only did Egyptian productions decrease under Nasser, there were also new studios being built in Lebanon, like Studio Baalbak and Studio Chammas. There was also an abundance of technicians, an increase in investment, and increased support from the Lebanese government. In 1964, the Lebanese government established the National Center for Cinema and Television, which aimed at providing financial and cultural support for cinema in Lebanon (e.g. through the establishment of a national film library). This was followed by the establishment of a number of trade unions linked with the cinema industry, like producers, distributors and actors. Between 1960 and 1965, 44 films were produced in Lebanon. In 1966, 17 films were made, 18 in 1967, and 17 in 1968. Of the latter, ten films were directed by Egyptian filmmakers.[20] Al-Kassan estimates that in the years 1963–70, 100 films were produced in Lebanon, 54 of which were in the Egyptian dialect.[21] Only one film from the 1960s gained international acclaim: *Garo* by Gary Garabatian, a drama based on the real-life story of a fugitive, considered to be an influential film that positively affected the creation of a cinema in the local Lebanese dialect.

But this boom was not to last long. Egypt did not import Lebanese films in the 1950s and 1960s, and the Arab market was generally limited. The Six Day War in 1967 contributed to the weakening of the public film sector in Egypt, but to the strengthening of the private one. Egyptian investors started pulling out from Lebanon and directing their resources to Egypt once again. With rising competition from Syrian cinema, Lebanese cinema faced a period of decline.[22] The few Lebanese films that were made did not have a distinct identity, were often poor imitations of foreign films, and cinema in general did not deal with the realities of Lebanese society at the time.[23] When a serious topic was dealt with, it was presented in a populist manner. The Palestinian resistance for example started appearing as a topic for films in that period, but it was portrayed in films based on the Western genre.[24]

In the early 1970s, however, a number of young Lebanese filmmakers returned from Europe where they had studied filmmaking to make films in Lebanon, like Jean-Claude Codsi, Borhan Alawiyeh and Maroun Baghdadi. When the Civil War began, most of those filmmakers started by making documentary films about it.[25] Ibrahim al-Ariss was quoted as saying that the Civil War generation of filmmakers like Jean Chamoun, Maroun Baghdadi and Jean-Claude Codsi 'came to resurrect Lebanese cinema'.[26] Nouri Bouzid captures the background of the new filmmakers like Borhan Alawiyeh, Maroun Baghdadi, Jocelyne Saab and Jean Chamoun by introducing them as having been born

> in the forties, they grew up on Nasserite slogans. They then tasted defeat, then experienced the May 1968 student movement in Europe, then learnt about democracy and discovered contemporary international cinema. When they returned home, they were full of hopes and

dreams. But the harsh reality hit them in the face: no resources, no market, no freedom of expression – in addition to an array of accumulated defeats.[27]

So while those filmmakers were talented and did contribute to the creation of a Lebanese cinema 'seed' in the immediate prewar period, the lack of resources in Lebanon meant that they were forced to make documentaries rather than the considerably more expensive feature films.

Cinema during the Civil War

The war impacted on Lebanese cinema mainly through the destruction of its infrastructure. In 1965, Unesco had used the National Cinema Center in Beirut, which was then part of the Ministry of Information (before briefly becoming the Bureau for Cinema, Theater, and Exhibitions at the newly founded Ministry of Culture), as the location for its Arab Cinema Liaison Center, a regional center aimed at linking cinema activities across the Arab world. However, the Liaison Center ceased operating when the Civil War began in 1975.[28]

The war also had a negative effect on production values. Lebanese films relying on the use of cameras and equipment supplied by Lebanon's two surviving studios in the early 1980s, Haroun and Baalbeck, were marred by poor sound quality as the cameras the studios supplied were not capable of capturing on-set dialogue, and the films therefore had to resort to dubbing. It was only in 1983 that the studios bought cameras allowing the recording of sound and image simultaneously.[29] In an interview for *As-Safir* newspaper, the head of the Filmmakers Union Fouad Joujou pointed out how poor production resources had forced some filmmakers to use more close-ups and mid shots in their films due to their inability to afford to hire extras.[30]

As the country came to be divided, the distribution of films in different areas became almost impossible.[31] Hamra lost its place as the center of cinema exhibition in Lebanon, with audiences from East Beirut unable to access the area after the division of Beirut. Cinemas in downtown Beirut were also destroyed. This resulted in the refurbishment or construction of new film theaters in areas east of Beirut or in East Beirut. Some theaters were converted to cinemas, like the Casino Liban theater and Al-Boustan in Beit Meri. Four cinemas were refurbished: Oscar in Jall Ed-Dib, Phoenicia and Presidence in Jounieh, and La Sagesse in Achrafieh. A number of new cinemas were constructed, like Mirage and Satellite in Bekfaya, Strada in Ajaltoun, Phantom in Ashqout, Tivoli and Printempia in Broumana, Vendome in Achrafieh, and Espace 1 and 2 in Zouk Mkael. A drive-in cinema was also constructed in

Tabarja. Those film theaters screened films to 20,000 viewers weekly. Each cinema had a capacity of around 400 seats, with tickets sold between LL 3 and 6, and each film costing between $2000 and $50,000 to exhibit. The displacement of people to Jounieh catalyzed the opening of more cinemas in the area by the owner of Presidence and Phoenicia. The cinema owners cited comedy, romance and action films to be the most popular among the audience, with the majority of films screened being Hollywood films.[32]

Cinema attendance eventually declined. A Lebanese scholar, Elie Kastoun, conducted a study in 1981/82 in the East Beirut area and found that the viewing of films on home video had increased, and that 71 per cent of the families surveyed spent more than 100 minutes per day watching videos or television. The study stated that the increase could be seen as being linked to the lack of other sources of entertainment in the war context.[33]

The human resources of cinema during the war were transferred to television.[34] The period also saw the rise of what came to be termed 'commercial films' aimed solely at the generation of profit. Between 1978 and 1982, 15 such films were made. Those films were often imitations of American films, and featured beauty queens, comedians and even famous television presenters in plots merging action sequences, melodrama and romance. The two filmmakers mostly associated with those films are Youssef Charaf ed-Din and Samir al-Ghoussaini. Both filmmakers had worked on the Egyptian productions that were filmed in Lebanon, and with the director Mohamad Salman. But they refused to include Egyptian elements in their films, insisting on acting in the Lebanese dialect, and on Lebanese productions.[35] Charaf ed-Din's first film was *The Last Passage* (1981) (*al Mamarr al-Akhir*), an adaptation of Zeffirelli's *The Champ*, and was commercially successful. He then made three films: *The Decision* (*Al-Qarar*), *The Last Night* (*Al-Layl al-Akhir*), and *The Leap of Death* (*Qafzat al-Mawt*). *The Last Night* was the only film referring to the war, through a story about displacement, but was less successful than his other films. Samir al-Ghoussaini's first film was in 1979, *The Beauty and the Giants* (*Hasna' wa 'Amaliqa*) and was a successful prototype that spurred several imitations. His other films include *The Adventurers* (*al-Moughamiroun*) and *Women in Danger* (*Nisa' fi Khatar*), which were not very successful. In 1982 he made *Women's Game* (*Lo'bat an-Nisa'*). What marks Ghoussaini's films, in his own words, is that they aim to 'merely entertain the audience'.[36] A telltale sign of the considerably low quality of those films is their abundance. Samir Nasri wrote at the end of 1982 that that year alone saw the production of 14 feature films in Lebanon, which was around half of what Egyptian cinema had produced that year. Some of those titles are *The Explosion* (Rafic Hajjar), *Women in Danger* (Samir al-Ghoussaini), *The Jump of Death* and *The Last Night* (Youssef Charaf ed-Din), *The Savages* and *A Nightingale from Lebanon* (Reda Mayssar), and *A Date with Love* (Saif ed-Din Shawkat).[37]

But the war contributed to the scarcity of film producers in Lebanon. Mohamad Soueid says that producers at the time were limited to four or five individuals with a film background. This scarcity forced directors to seek funding from businessmen who knew virtually nothing about the process of filmmaking, and whose only concern was generating profit. He cites examples of producers not knowing what the films they were producing are about, having neither read the scripts nor the films' synopses. Such producers, Soueid argues, were only concerned with whether the films' genres would appeal to a mainstream audience, which resulted in the increase in films revolving around action, sexual scenes and comedy.[38] Between 1980 and 1985, 45 films were made in Lebanon, most of which were commercial action films. The films appealed to the audience partly because of their positive portrayal of the need for law and order and of the police.[39]

This focus on commercial cinema meant that experimental cinema by comparison suffered from lack of interest of potential producers who saw it as a financial risk, which caused non-commercial filmmakers to work alone as producers and directors simultaneously.[40] Other filmmakers like Rafic Hajjar and Mohamad Salman tried to reach a compromise. In *The Explosion*, Rafic Hajjar tried to merge the use of stars (Madeleine Tabr and Abul Majid Majzoub) with a war scenario, but the result was a melodramatic take on the war. Mohamad Salman's *Man Youtfi' an-Nar* on the other hand presented a musical, comedy and melodrama with a war background. It was a failed attempt at going back to the Egyptianized Lebanese productions of the past, and was criticized as being a 'shameful attempt that copies Salman's 1950s productions'.[41] A number of other directors were unable to work in filmmaking at all, and had to resort to working in distribution, exhibition or advertising, or ended up making short documentary films.

With the spread of violence across Lebanon, filming in different areas in the country became increasingly difficult. Hasan Ni'mani and Moustapha Kassem narrated how they often had to film in the middle of shelling while working on Maroun Baghdadi's *Little Wars* (1982).[42] The combination of poor funding and the physical limitations imposed by the spread of violence also had an impact on the quality of the films made. Borhan Alawiyeh for example was only able to shoot one take of most of the scenes of *Beirut, The Encounter* (1981), resulting in an often mistake-ridden delivery of lines by the actors.

Lebanese cinema also suffered from its being tainted by the politics of the time. Maroun Baghdadi for example came from a political background, having studied political science at the Lebanese University followed by a master's degree in sociology at the Sorbonne before he studied cinema in Paris. In 1974 he worked at *Télé Liban* on news programs. Like Borhan Alawiyeh and Jean-Claude Codsi, Baghdadi was affected by the student demonstrations in France in 1968. Baghdadi moved from East Beirut to West Beirut when the war broke out, making documentaries about its various aspects in the belief that the camera is 'a weapon of struggle and means of handling the present and history'.[43] As the war progressed, Baghdadi found it difficult to secure funding to make films. He resorted to making films about the politicians of the time, from all factions, leading some to question his ideological commitments. Hassan Ni'mani, Moustapha Kassem and Elie Adabashi – who worked closely with Baghdadi – strongly refute this accusation. The three men as well as Baghdadi's widow Soraya all spoke to me about Baghdadi's strong sense of Lebaneseness, and of the great pain caused to someone as passionate about cinema as Baghdadi at having to resort to political actors to make films.[44]

This condition was not limited to Baghdadi. In 1985 the critic Mohamad Soueid published his first study of Lebanese cinema titled *Inside War, Outside Cinema: Lebanese Film 1975–1985* (Beirut: Arab Research Institute). In the study he concluded that 'there is no such thing as Lebanese cinema, the cinema itself is dying … If it had not been for the war that wave [of commercial films] would not have happened. For two years now, film production is no longer in the hands of filmmakers but in those of political parties'.[45] Politics also influenced the reading of films. Samir Nasri hinted at the mixed reception that *Ma'raka* (1985) – a film about Shiite resistance to Israeli occupation in the South – received in 1985, saying that '*Ma'raka* will suffer from readings marked by political biases and tense ideological expressions. Only in the years to come, when the grudges that tear us apart and our fear of each other die … will the Lebanese audience appreciate the beauty and importance of the film'.[46]

By the early 1990s, most of the studios in Lebanon had closed down, and the Haroun studio was rented out to television productions. The audiovisual landscape in Lebanon transformed as television rose as the primary medium in the country. Lack of funding meant that young filmmakers worked mostly with video, and for established filmmakers, European co-productions became a must.[47] The period saw the creation of films that dealt with the subject of the Civil War, all of which were funded by European countries: Leila Assaf's *Al-Sheikha* (1994), Jocelyne Saab's *Once Upon a Time, Beirut* (1994), Samir Habchi's *The Tornado*, and Jean-Claude Codsi's *A Time Has Come* (1994). Lebanon started seeing some attempts at showcasing film in the public arena. For example, between 21 and 28 June 1995, an exhibition titled *Image of the Self, Image of the Other* was held in Beirut and showcased 41 videos and films dealing with the theme of the war, but did not screen any feature films.[48]

Attention to Lebanese cinema also shyly started abroad. In 1998, the Arab World Institute in Paris hosted a season on culture in Lebanon, where a number of Lebanese films from the 1950s till the 1990s were screened. Among the films was *Beirut ya Beirut* by Maroun Baghdadi, which had been considered lost prior to that screening. The season also included screenings of commercial films like Samir al-Ghoussaini's film *The Cats of Hamra Street* (*Qutat Shari' Al-Hamra*).[49]

Cinema in the Postwar Period: History Repeats Itself

In 1966, Farid Jabre published a study titled *The Cinema Industry in Lebanon 1958–1965*, in which he diagnosed six main problems that Lebanese cinema faced at the time. The first problem is 'lack of national background', which refers to the inheritance of cinema workers in Lebanon from Egypt, as opposed to home-grown talent.[50] The second problem is that of language, whereby the Lebanese dialect is considered uncomfortable by Arab audiences who are used to the Egyptian dialect. The third problem is the lack of professional producers, and the domination of the production scene by film distributors who have little artistic, technical or even economic knowledge about film production. The fourth and fifth problems are the 'absence of governmental assistance' and 'professional formations', which caused film professionals to rely on individual efforts when making films.[51] Finally, Jabre diagnosed a 'lack of shooting sets ... which obliges directors to shoot their films most often outdoors or in private premises'.[52] As we have seen, some of those problems, like Egyptianization, were eventually resolved. But many continued to plague Lebanese cinema. In 1985, Joseph Qirdahi wrote that the main problem of Lebanese cinema was the lack of viable scripts and quality directing. He also argued that the awkwardness of acting in the Lebanese dialect was not a real problem due to the propagation of the dialect through popular songs, radio programs and theater. He also linked the rejection of Lebanese productions to the low quality of commercial Lebanese films of the 1960s and the 1970s.[53]

In 1991 the critic George Ki'di posed three questions in a two-part article in *An-Nahar* newspaper: 1. Is there a need for a local cinema industry in Lebanon? 2. How can we diagnose the problems of Lebanese cinema, from production to scripts to creativity? 3. What are the practical ways of reviving local film productions? The first respondent to those questions was the researcher and academic Emile Chahine, who agreed on the importance of establishing a local industry but pointed out that no such industry existed even before the war, whereas the second respondent, critic Mohamad Soueid, said that no such industry can exist unless it is embedded in the country's wider cultural fabric.[54] Emile Chahine summarized the problems of Lebanese cinema as being the lack of studios, the migration of talented filmmakers, censorship, lack of producers, and lack of scriptwriters.[55] The third respondent, Houssam Khayyat, emphasized the lack of scriptwriters and added the absence of funding and the role of the state, which in his opinion considered cinema a method of entertainment per se, without much awareness of cinema's greater cultural and social role.[56]

In 1997, George Ki'di revisited his report on the state of cinema in Lebanon. The new one began: 'We are continuing with no national cinema, and therefore with no memory, no image, no presence'.[57] In the report the director Borhan Alawiyeh called the filmmakers of the time 'adventurers', because they made films when no state support existed, whether financial or organizational.[58] All the filmmakers interviewed – Olga Nakkash, Elie Adabashi, Bahij Hojeij, Samir Habchi, Borhan Alawiyeh – converged in their lament of lack of funding for cinema in Lebanon, but they also highlighted the deeper problem of the lack of a cinema culture in Lebanon.

That year, filmmakers complained that in the postwar period, investors turned their attention to the construction and services industries, but not to cinema.[59] Lebanese film scholar Emile Chahine pointed out that the Ministry of Culture's promise to support cinema in Lebanon amounted to nothing.[60] He said that Lebanese cinema is built on individual efforts, an argument echoed some years later by film critics Mohamad Soueid[61] and Nadim Jarjoura,[62] and which had been identified by critic Ibrahim al-Ariss back in 1984.[63] Soueid added that the problem also lay in that existing distribution companies did not market Lebanese films, but foreign ones. He also observed that in Lebanon, where all aspects of filmmaking became the responsibility of one individual, 'a filmmaker is not expected to create a film, but to create a cinema'.[64]

Although 1998 was the year when Lebanese cinema entered a renaissance period, with *West Beyrouth* being one of the films bringing back the Lebanese audience to the cinema, and the Beirut International Film Festival seeing its second year, reports on the state of cinema in Lebanon have since oscillated between the positive and the negative. In 2000, Nadim Jarjoura wrote:

> There is no infrastructure for the existence of an industry: no studios or labs, no modern editing suites or cameras, no large-scale production companies and no state support. The state had proposed the Fund for Support of Lebanese Cinema but it has not been put into effect. University programs in audiovisual studies have started to grow, however, and a number of filmmakers have returned to Lebanon from abroad, like Ziad Doueiri and Ghassan Salhab. There is also an increase in the number of cinema clubs and organizations, and in the activities of European cultural organizations like the Centre Culturel Français and the Goethe Institute.[65]

The same year, Nadine Na'ouss wrote an optimistic assessment of the state of cinema in Lebanon, seeing the critical acclaim and viewing figures for the films *West Beyrouth* (1998), *Beirut Phantoms* (1998) and *Around the Pink House* (1998) as signs that Lebanese cinema is recovering. She also commended Future Television's broadcasting of some audiovisual studies graduates' final year projects.[66]

Five years later, Vicky Habib presented a less optimistic view, where she argued that the state of Lebanese cinema *resembled* an industry, but was actually nowhere near achieving that status. She backed up her argument with examples of the hardship faced by several Lebanese filmmakers, and the lack of state or even commercial support for Lebanese cinema, which forced the cinema to remain a matter of individual enterprise. She quoted the filmmaker Fouad Alaywan, who said that the search for funding has transformed directors into producers, diverting their attention away from the processes of writing and creating.[67]

Lebanese Cinema Today

Lebanese cinema today has made significant leaps. The cinema has been going through a renaissance period over the last decade. More Lebanese films are being made, and more are being screened in cinemas in Lebanon. The Lebanese audience is re-learning to accept watching Lebanese films. The funding remains largely European, but the films are becoming more sophisticated cinematically: scripts are getting better, and the writers are becoming more adept at molding the Lebanese dialect. An example of this is the film *Falafel* (2006). It is peppered with local expressions and succeeds in using this to create a sense of cultural intimacy with the audience. Filmmaking in the country is going from strength to strength. Films that I never thought would be seen by the public when I started the research for this book in 2003 are now being sold on DVD in Beirut. Film festivals around the world continue to screen Lebanese films, to the extent that expecting to watch a Lebanese film at the London Film Festival for example is not a fantasy any more. Lebanese cinema is still haunted by the Civil War, and with ongoing tension in Lebanon it is difficult to imagine a time in the near future where Lebanese cinema does not represent conflict. After all, cinema is a product of the social environment. But Lebanese cinema has also extended its subject matter to confront social taboos. Randa Chahal's film *The Civilized* (1998) addresses racism. *When Maryam Spoke Out* (2002) addresses the pressure put on women to procreate in Lebanese society. *In the Battlefields* (2004) makes us face class divisions. *Bosta* (2005) refers to the issue of homosexuality.

However, it would be grossly misleading to allow this sunny view of Lebanese cinema to become the dominant one. Cinema in Lebanon is still not an industry, though it has the seeds of one, as we can see above. Lebanese cinema remains a collection of films made by disparate filmmakers. And it suffers from many of the same problems it has faced since its inception. Due to a myriad of obstacles, the process of development of film projects often moves at a snail's pace. Scripts often never see the light until years after they had been written. Philippe Aractingi for example drafted the script of *Bosta* in 1989, but was not able to realize it as a film until 2005. Borhan Alawiyeh worked on his biopic of Gibran Khalil Gibran for more than a decade and it is still not finished. Through researching books, newspaper articles and interviews with filmmakers and critics, the list below assesses the main issues facing Lebanese cinema today.

The Role of the Government

The role of the government in supporting cinema has oscillated between complete absence, empty promises and tokenism. On 23 May 1984, the Cabinet passed on to Parliament a law proposing the addition of LL 10 in tax on every home video for distribution. The law also proposed that any importers or distributors of videos should register their details with the tax office, and the details of the rights owners with the Ministry of Trade. Fines would be imposed on anyone not complying with the law. The Cabinet declared that the law was needed because of the increase in the piracy of videos since the beginning of the war, and the potential of raising 10 million Lebanese liras annually through the new law (based on the estimated sale of 1 million videos per year).[68] However, the law was never implemented.

A cinema section exists at the Ministry of Culture, but it is limited to making promotional touristic videos. The one time the Ministry organized an event on cinema – in 1995, celebrating the centenary of cinema – it ignored mentioning the achievements of Lebanese cinema pioneers like Assia Dagher and Marie Queeny, who played seminal roles in the development of cinema in Egypt in the early twentieth century.[69] In 1998, the National Cinema Center at the Ministry of Culture was expanded into one also dealing with theaters and exhibitions, drawing criticism from Mohamad Soueid who saw this expansion as an indication of the government's lack of appreciation of the distinction between the three fields.[70]

That year, the Ministry of Culture announced that it would launch the long-awaited Cinema Support Fund, which would allow filmmakers to obtain public funding. The announced plan indicated that the Ministry would fund 25 per cent of the budgets of up to seven feature films per year, with a limit of $200,000 of state funds per film, in addition to funding up to ten short films with $50,000 each.[71] However, in practice, the Ministry's financial assistance to filmmakers has been nominal, mainly aimed at guaranteeing a mention of the Ministry in the film credits. The director Elie Khalifeh criticized the Ministry of Culture's (theoretical) blank offer of 5 million Lebanese liras to individual film projects, without taking the projects' budgets into consideration, or the films' length or quality, in its attempt at 'helping everyone'.[72]

In 2002 the Ministry of Culture established the Cinematheque, a division of the (now re-named) National Cinema Center devoted to establishing a library of Lebanese films, restoring film prints, and archiving film-related documents. The Cinematheque started with 15 films, and the Minister of Culture at the time, Ghassan Salameh, hoped to have 1000 films archived by the end of 2002. He also announced that the Ministry of Culture had for the first time set aside funds in its budget for Lebanese cinema.[73] However, the filmmakers I interviewed have some sorry tales to tell about their experiences with the Ministry of Culture. Assad Fouladkar said about *When Maryam Spoke Out* (2002):

> I was invited to a festival in India and I had only one copy of the film. I asked the Lebanese government to pay the price of a copy so I could create another one; they only paid for it three years later. Someone from the government said to me, 'if we had known the film was going to be like this, we would have approached it differently'.[74]

Danielle Arbid had a similar experience with *In the Battlefields*:

> I did not get any government support apart from US$15,000 which I received four years after applying. I told the Minister of Culture to cancel this funding, or spend the money on something else, because they think they own you if they give you this money. The money is not enough to support cinema.[75]

Both Fouladkar and Arbid lamented the extreme bureaucracy that filmmakers in Lebanon are subjected to, where even paying a bill is a long, complicated process. As Fouladkar commented, 'if Einstein had been born in Lebanon, he would never have realized his potential; he would have remained still, trying to go through red tape'.[76]

Mohamad Soueid highlights another problem with the government: the contradiction in the official classification of the Cinema Union as a workers union but the denial to Union members of services such as pensions, health benefits, transportation cost grants, education funding, maternity leave, and overtime pay, which are available through the Ministry of Labor to members of other workers unions. Soueid says that the Cinema Union tried to ask for it to be reclassified as a professional union, and to impose a minimum wage requirement for film technicians, but for 30 years almost all its proposals have been unsuccessful.[77]

The only method in which the Lebanese government has succeeded in supporting cinema is through providing military equipment to films that need them. During the 'Liberation War' that started on 14 March 1989, the only film that was made was *The Scream* (*As-Sarkha*) by Youssef Charaf Ed-Din, about a man who avenges the death of his wife, which utilized a great deal of live ammunition, including bullets, bombs and missiles. This was done with the wide participation of soldiers and helicopters of the Lebanese army.[78] Ziad Doueiri also relied on the army when making *West Beyrouth*: 'The army gave me a couple of helicopters, tanks, jeeps. They helped me out. We ended up not using the helicopter shots, although the pilots took a lot of risks to get me the shots I wanted'.[79] A similar experience is recounted by Samir Habchi about *The Tornado*:

> I would not have been able to make the film without the government. The Russians were helping me with the processing in Russia, but they did not pay for anything outside. I had just finished university and had limited means and I borrowed money for the production. The extras in the film were government workers, the army cut off some roads to allow the filming and helped with the explosions, the police helped too. All this was for free. At the time the Minister of Interior and the head of the army Emile Lahoud agreed to help because they believed it was a film for peace.[80]

Censorship

Like all cinemas in the Arab world, Lebanese cinema is subject to government censorship. Censorship of cinema in Lebanon is handled by the Sûreté Generale (General Security) – a military department within the Ministry of Interior. Lebanese law allows the censorship of 'political and religious materials, which could harm the national security of the country'.[81] The basis for censorship laws is a directive issued on 27 November 1947, which in itself is based on laws from the 1920s prohibiting publications and broadcasts that go against public mores, threaten Lebanon's relationship with friendly countries, and cause sectarian divisions.[82] However, censorship in Lebanon is not consistent. In 1979, when questioned about the screening of pornographic films in cinemas in Lebanon, the then Minister of Economy admitted that sometimes certain films 'slipped through the net of censorship', although he did not elaborate on how or why that was happening.[83]

The inconsistency continued after the war. In 1992, the government censored parts of the film *The Tornado* by Samir Habchi because they were deemed unacceptable. One scene was of the sky raining blood, and another depicted a massacre in a church – both judged to be profane. But what is baffling is the change in stance towards the film by the censors. Habchi said that the film's script had been approved by the censors, but then banned:

> When the film was banned, the Lebanese President interfered to let it be screened because he said it was a film advocating peace. Even the

General Security had facilitated sending the rushes to Russia for processing, so I was shocked when they later banned the film. They deemed certain segments in the film offensive to certain sides. The film was screened uncut only abroad, in France. In Lebanon, the audience only saw the censored version. There was a festival for Arab and Iranian cinema in New York and I did not want to screen the cut version there, so the Lebanese censors allowed it to be screened in its entirety there.[84]

When *West Beyrouth* was made, the General Security told Ziad Doueiri that his film would have to be approved by a Muslim sheikh and a Christian priest before it could be distributed in the country. Following their approval, the film was released uncut.[85] But in 1999 the government went as far as cutting 47 minutes of Randa Chahal's *The Civilized* – just over half of the film – blaming its decision on the film's 'vulgar language and slurs against both Christians and Muslims'.[86] This censorship was coupled with the denouncing of the film's director in some Beirut mosques and the receiving of death threats by her and her crew.[87] The film has only been seen in Lebanon once (at the Beirut Film Festival in 1999), though it has gained awards abroad, winning the Unesco Award at the Venice Film Festival in 1999 and the Nestor Almendros Award at the Human Rights Watch Film Festival the following year.

Randa Chahal commented on the case by saying that

> the General Security asked me to remove 47 minutes of a 90-minute film, which is practically just over half of it. What they want cut varies between one word in an individual sentence, whole sentences in a scene, parts of scenes, and whole characters![88]

Al-Hayat listed the content of some of the scenes that the General Security objected to: 'one of the Egyptian female characters touches her girlfriend's dress in the area over her genitals (although this was filmed in long shot); a man sings Christian hymns sarcastically; militiamen exchanging insults; a boy saying the sentence "Moustapha, let's kidnap this French doctor and sell him" (in reference to a man from *Médecins Sans Frontières*); a man swearing at a woman; a man kicking a coffin; and a sniper shooting a priest dead'.[89] The press release issued by the General Security stated that the bureau 'emphasizes that the feelings of the audience in its different ages, its morals and its traditions, especially those of the Lebanese society and the current laws, are more important than the desires, insults and complexes that the film revolves around'.[90] Mohamad Soueid commented in An-Nahar on the irony of the General Security's censorship of the scenes and phrases in the film, and its simultaneous decision to publish their full details in its press release; he also extended the irony to the applause that Randa Chahal received when she declined a joint prize for the film with the Israeli director Amos Gitai, by the same people who later joined the moral crusade against her film.[91]

In the Battlefields and Bosta also had flirtations with the censors. Danielle Arbid says of In the Battlefields:

> the censors wanted to remove the sex in the car and on the stairs, and a sentence where a girl says she doesn't care about God and refuses to go to church. I refused, and told the censors that the film is not theirs, but mine. Is the Lebanese society incapable of watching sex when they can see worse on television and on the internet? This is an insult to the audience! So in the end they gave it an 18 rating.[92]

Philippe Aractingi says that the censors gave Bosta a 15 rating because of some swearing:

> I was too tired to fight against that. Then Fondation Liban Cinema talked to the Minister of Culture and persuaded him to ask the censors to give it a lower rating. The censors objected to some specific swear words nevertheless. So the film was allowed to be screened as it was. The viewing figures became higher as a result.[93]

Funding

Censorship however is not the main problem faced by Lebanese cinema. The major problem identified by filmmakers is funding, both in terms of the absence of government funding and the increasing difficulty of obtaining European money.[94] Ziad Doueiri for example stressed that there can be no industry without government support.[95] Ghassan Salhab explains that local 'television stations do not want to co-produce films. Private funding is problematic. There is money in Lebanon, but it is not directed towards cinema'.[96] This problem is also because of the scarcity of Lebanese producers. Only a handful of Lebanese films made during the last three decades are locally funded. *Lebanon in Spite of Everything* (1982), for example, was funded by a Christian church organization, The Uskofiyaa Organization for Media.[97] *Ma'raka* (1985) was funded by 'well-to-do Shiite people who donated money to the South Support Fund', as the film was regarded as a social project benefiting the people of the South, 'but many things did not cost anything: we did not pay extras, or to use people's houses'.[98] *When Maryam Spoke Out* was produced by its director Assad Fouladkar, with funding from the Lebanese American University where he teaches filmmaking.

Bosta was marketed as a '100% Lebanese Film' based on its being a locally produced film. Although the film relied on a French seed fund, it is not a French co-production. *Bosta*'s funding process deserves attention as it marks the first time such a method has been used in Lebanese cinema. Its director Philippe Aractingi describes the process as follows:

> I thought there should be a purely commercial enterprise to create a mass cinema in Lebanon. You need independent films, but you also need entertaining films. I thought that we have money in Lebanon, but what we don't have is the rhetoric that would convince funders to support films. I had to come up with a language that business people would understand. I needed a document to show potential funders. I got advice from a business bank: I had to put my author and director egos aside and sell my film to them as a product. That involved understanding the market.
>
> So I began researching the market. This was a departure from the way I was used to thinking about making films. It took us six months to come up with a business plan that shows what the Lebanese market looks like: 150,000 viewers for *SL Film*, 76,000 for *West Beyrouth*, 11,000 for *Around the Pink House*, 4000 viewers for *Beirut Phantoms*; *Bosta* has had 140,000 viewers so far [April 2006]. We were realistic about our expectations. We estimated getting 75,000 viewers based on LBC's support. We wrote about all this, and the investors were approached for four months without success. I approached 140 investors, and found 26 funders who I sold 10,000 US dollar certificates-of-participation to. With the French grant, I got around 980,000 US dollars, which is a lot of money.
>
> As a director I wanted my vision to reach the audience, and as a producer I wanted the Lebanese audience to come to the cinema. I find selling boring, but I've become a producer in spite of myself.[99]

Despite *Bosta*'s relatively large budget compared to other Lebanese films, its ambitions went beyond its funding capacities. While the scenario required shooting on location in Lebanese villages as far as the Bekaa Valley and the South, shooting the film took only 55 days. Bshara Atalla, one of the film's actors and a professional dancer, commented that 'we used to finish one dance per day, or in a day and a half at best. We did not have much time and it was exhausting'.[100] Considering that the film is reliant on several dance tableaux, Atallah's statement is revealing of the difficulty of working under such budgetary constraints.

When Maryam Spoke Out remains the Lebanese feature film with the smallest budget to have emerged in the last 30 years (in relative terms);

however, the tight budget was a source of frustration for Assad Fouladkar. He explains:

> The biggest problem when making the film was that the people working on it did not take the project seriously. Shooting on video, with a small crew, on a low budget, surrounded by my students – to the actors it looked like a university project, not a set. We finished shooting in 15 days. There was little money; I barely paid the actors anything. So I could not ask people to give me more of their time. I did not try to have different takes of scenes for example. I shot only the exact scenes I wanted. Some people thought the film *might* be shown on television, but it was not looked at as a film to be screened in cinemas. I had little money to be able to negotiate. I had to work with whoever I could afford to work with financially, as opposed to who I would have liked to work with.[101]

The rest of the Lebanese films are all co-productions. *Beirut, The Encounter* was produced with Tunisian and Belgian money. The funding of *In the Battlefields* was mainly French with some Belgian, German and Lebanese money. *Little Wars* was supported by an American technical team facilitated by Francis Ford Coppola.[102] *The Civilized* was funded by French production companies including Arte and Studio Canal +. *West Beyrouth* was funded by Belgian, Norwegian and French money (including funding from France's Ministry of Culture). *The Belt of Fire* was produced by Lebanese producers Marwan Tarraf and Wassim Hojeij, with funding from the Agence de Francophonie and the French Foreign Ministry.[103] *The Tornado* is a Russian co-production. Its director Samir Habchi is also its producer; he describes the impact the difficulty of obtaining local funding had on the process of making the film:

> The film was a Russian co-production with a Russian technical team. All the cash paid in Lebanon, I had borrowed. I used to film during the day and look for funding at night, maybe 5000 or 2000 US dollars at a time to pay for fuel. For one of the scenes, we put a real car in the middle of a road and blew it up because there was no other way of filming this scene. In a country with an established cinema industry, this would not happen.[104]

Jocelyne Saab encountered a similar experience when working on *A Suspended Life* – a French co-production – saying how she had to borrow money from her assistants to survive on during the time of shooting the film, and how the crew had to stay at her place to cut down costs.[105] So even foreign funding is often barely enough to cover a film's expenses.

A snapshot of the budgets of some Lebanese films gives an indication of the extreme low cost of those films, compared to European cinema (all figures have been obtained from the filmmakers themselves):

Film Title	Budget	Year of Production
Beirut, The Encounter	3–4 million French francs	1981
Ma'raka	LL 400,000	1985
Letter from a Time of Exile	700,000 French francs	1988
The Tornado	$600,000	1992
A Time Has Come	$450,000	1993
The Civilized	2,400,000 French francs	1998
Beirut Phantoms	$420,000	1998
Around the Pink House	just under $1,000,000	1998
In the Shadows of the City	$450,000	2000
When Maryam Spoke Out	$15,000	2001
The Belt of Fire	$350,000	2003
Kite	1,000,000 euros	2003
In the Battlefields	1,000,000 euros	2004
Bosta	$1,100,000	2005
A Perfect Day	400,000 euros	2005

The reliance on foreign funding does present its problems. Danielle Arbid insists that she is not affected negatively by relying on French funding: 'Over here, you have to apply for public funds to make films. They don't care what you say about Lebanon in the films. France is the only country that funds non-French films. That's why people come here to get funding. It's an oasis for getting funding'.[106] But other filmmakers have felt restricted by foreign funding. Back in 1989, Rosen wrote an article about Lebanese filmmakers exiled in Europe:

> the geographical displacement of the Arab filmmaker is not only a mirror of existing dislocations within the society. The cinema itself becomes uprooted. Attentions, if not allegiances, are suddenly divided. The international production implies international distribution, international audiences, international thinking as well. Jocelyne Saab comments, 'I don't have any more complexes about the openness [of Lebanon] to East and West; as filmmakers, we are the synthesis of these two poles, and if that translates itself into the image, it's

fantastic. But it's dangerous: when I get financing of five million francs from France, I run the risk of having to change my scenario'.

Not always, but frequently enough, changes are made. The Western viewer becomes a major factor in the filmic equation. In the worst instances, the director-as-guide is suddenly conducting an audience of tourists through his or her culture.[107]

Philippe Aractingi spoke of the difficulty of trying to counter this pressure when making *Bosta*:

> I decided to write something that presents a different image of Lebanon from the one we're used to. The French refused it and told me it's far from the reality of Lebanese society. It was humiliating. Cinema du Sud refused to fund it because it is not a 'serious' film. When you go to festivals showing films from the South, you will see that they have the same language. But I have my own language. Rotterdam invited me to talk about this film because they were very curious about the film's success. Normally they are interested in art house films. I felt I needed to go beyond the themes normally addressed in Southern films.[108]

French funding often comes with restrictions on the use of language. Randa Chahal says about public French funding:

> the French used to say, to get funding, you have to have 50 per cent of the dialogue in French. Now they say it should be 70 per cent. Why should they fund a film in Arabic? The situation is becoming more difficult. My film *Kite* had less funding than *The Civilized* because it is in Arabic.[109]

Jocelyne Saab says that the dialogue in her films *A Suspended Life* (1984) and *Once Upon a Time, Beirut* (1994) is part-French, part-Arabic partly 'because it's an obligation from the National Fund for Cinema [in France] who funded the film: we can give you a lot of money if all the language is in French'.[110] However, both of Saab's films (as well as Chahal's *The Civilized*) get around this issue by presenting either French characters, or Lebanese characters who come from a French-speaking background. A similar situation could be seen in a number of films by Maroun Baghdadi. While *The Veiled Man* is completely in French and is marketed as a French film, *Outside Life* and *Land of Honey and Incense* merge French and Arabic. In both films, Baghdadi succeeds in manipulating the use of the French language by the Lebanese characters, especially the militiamen, by giving them strong Lebanese accents which signifies their unease at being forced to use the language in their dealings with the Frenchmen they encounter or kidnap, and by peppering their use of French with Lebanese slang.

Jean-Claude Codsi presents another problem with foreign funding. He explains that the European audience is more used to watching experimental and art house films, especially when it comes to what is characterized as 'world cinema'. He says that when considering proposals from Lebanon, for example, European producers therefore tend to prefer projects for films that would appeal to this European audience. But this means that the films that are produced are not always well received in Lebanon, where the audience is not used to this particular cinema language. Films that might appeal to the mass audience in Lebanon, therefore, are marginalized.[111] But even art house films encounter problems when they rely on European funding. As Ghassan Salhab explains, 'our co-productions are not really "co". We go to the French funders having secured 20,000 dollars in local funding, which is nothing. So those funders feel they can dictate what we do'.[112] Bahij Hojeij agrees:

> European funders have their own presumptions about what constitutes a Lebanese film. Sometimes Lebanon is fashionable as a topic and sometimes not. That's why it's important to have a local industry. This needs support from the government, maybe to give 25 per cent or 30 per cent of the budget. This would help get foreign producers because you can show that you are bringing something. Then you have a stronger position and more control over the film. We are now approaching them with nothing, so they have more control over the scripts and the technical side.[113]

Exhibition

If filmmakers manage to get enough money to make a film, their next hurdle is exhibition and distribution. In 1991, Mohamad Soueid calculated that 15 years since the beginning of the war, the number of film theaters in Lebanon decreased by 85 per cent, from 180 to only 27.[114] The number has increased since then with the rise of the multiplex cinema; however, only a handful of screens are available for local films, with the majority of screens reserved for Hollywood, French and Egyptian films. Cinema attendance in Lebanon has also decreased significantly since the start of the Civil War in 1975. Philippe Aractingi illustrates: 'Last year [2005], 2 million people attended the cinema in Lebanon. In the 1970s, attendance was 3.5 million'.[115] A number of Lebanese films have never had a local cinematic release, or have a limited or delayed one (examples are *Beirut, The Encounter, A Suspended*

Life, Martyrs (1988), *The Civilized, Terra Incognita* (2002) and *The Belt of Fire* (2003)).

In an interview with Mohamad Soueid in 1998, the owner of Lebanon's largest film production and distribution company, Sabbah, declared that his company did not support Lebanese films because 'almost all commercial Lebanese films to date have been failed attempts, and the company is not interested in distributing art house films because they do not attract large audiences'.[116] The success of *West Beyrouth* sparked a change in attitude, and since 1998 Sabbah has started releasing some Lebanese films on DVD (*In the Battlefields, When Maryam Spoke Out*). In 1999, Cinema Empire launched a special screening space called Screen 6, which was initially devoted to European cinema, but was later also open to showing Lebanese films.[117] Arab Film Distribution, a Lebanese-owned, Seattle-based film distribution company, has also started distributing some films in the United States and worldwide through its online video sales service (*A Time Has Come, The Tornado, A Suspended Life, In the Shadows of the City* (2000)).

But often the filmmakers themselves have to perform the role of distributor (Jean Chamoun, Samir Habchi, Philip Aractingi and many others). They also have to contend with empty promises and even abuse. Jocelyne Saab says:

> HSBC wanted to release a box set of my films, but then said no because of the politics in the films. I said to them, but this is the reality. I am waiting for someone in Lebanon to regard my films as heritage, just like I gathered the heritage of others (in *Once Upon a Time, Beirut*). Maybe I'll be dead by the time this happens. Last year [2005], someone called Kamal Hakim wanted to show my films in Lebanon so I gave him copies of all my films on video to screen for free. The films were to be screened for political awareness [as part of the 30th anniversary of the Civil War commemoration event]. If I hadn't done that, your generation would not have seen them. People don't see that we live out of our films.[118]

Mohamad Soueid also pointed out the problems with promoting Lebanese films in Lebanon: 'Cinema owners may advertise on their billboards only. A television station may offer to promote a film but may take its rights'.[119] The success of *Bosta* – the Lebanese film with the highest ever attendance – can be partly attributed to its advertising campaign on the Lebanese television station LBC. But films are often promoted through nothing but word of mouth. *In the Shadows of the City* and *When Maryam Spoke Out* are examples, the first running for 11 weeks at Empire, and the second for four months at the same cinema.

The problem with local exhibition is that the managers of film theaters seem to regard Lebanese films as if they are one category, without attention to their generic differences, and the success or failure of any one film has a trickle down effect. As Soueid explains, 'West Beyrouth encouraged people to watch Lebanese films. But if a film fails, it will discourage people from watching more Lebanese films. Because Bosta was successful, it encouraged A Perfect Day [2005] and Zozo [2006]'.[120] Ibrahim Al-Ariss agrees: 'After the success of In the Battlefields and When Maryam Spoke Out ... distributors were encouraged to show more Lebanese films'.[121] There is also the problem of piracy. If a film is released on video, it is likely that the video shops in Lebanon would start making their own pirated copies of it and selling them instead (this is something I have witnessed first hand). And of course, DVD copies of films shot illegally as they are being screened in cinemas are created and distributed even outside Lebanon. For example, Ziad Doueiri says that 'there were pirated copies [of West Beyrouth] in Lebanon before the film was released there', and pirated DVD copies of Bosta are on sale in Jordan.[122]

Lebanese films have more success abroad. Most Lebanese films have been shown on television across the globe (though mainly in Europe, Canada and Australia), and virtually all of them have been exhibited at international film festivals (many winning prestigious awards). Examples include The Belt of Fire (Fipresci award), West Beyrouth (shown at the Directors' Week at Cannes) and The Civilized. However, as Samir Habchi explains, 'in Europe, it is very difficult to screen a film in cinemas that was not co-produced there'.[123] Lebanese films also face problems in the Arab market, where they are often subjected to censorship. Sometimes this censorship severely affects the films' artistic integrity and vision. For example, while When Maryam Spoke Out was not

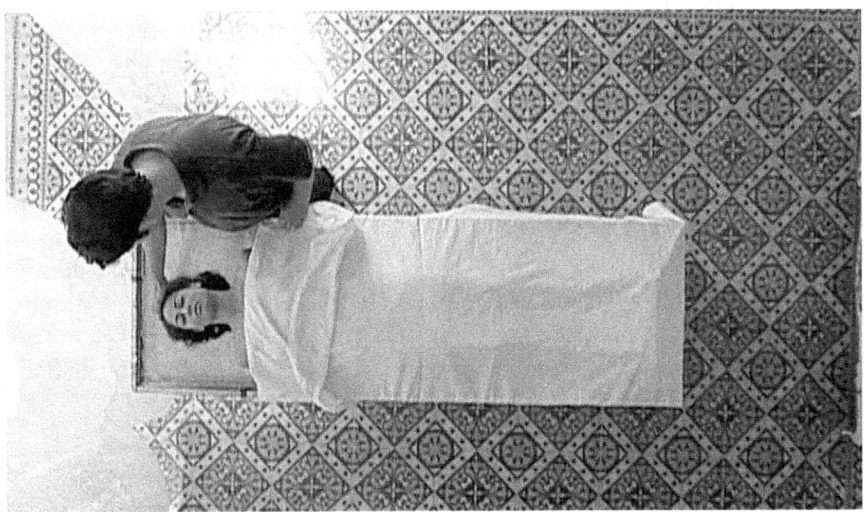

When Maryam Spoke Out

censored in Lebanon, when it was broadcast on Dubai TV, scenes depicting the washing of Maryam's (dead, as we later find out) body, which form the essence of the film's visual field and narrative, were cut.[124] Speaking about *The Tornado*, Samir Habchi acknowledges that due to its avant-garde style and subject matter, 'this kind of film would not be shown in Arab countries'.[125] While Borhan Alawiyeh says, 'You can get over the funding problem of cinema if there is freedom of expression in the Arab world. You have 250 million potential viewers in the region. Their diversity is positive. But the filmmakers don't have the freedom to reach out to this audience'.[126]

Other Problems

Lebanese cinema suffers from a number of problems going beyond funding, exhibition and distribution. There are very few set designers working in Lebanese cinema. This shortage has been historically linked to the reliance of Lebanese films on Lebanon's attractive natural resources – and later on the war's natural, dramatically devastated landscapes – which has resulted in limited attention to the creation of sets.[127] There is also a shortage of screenwriters. As Ziad Doueiri explains, 'there are no schools that teach screenwriting in Lebanon. It's a complex field of study; there are methods that you learn. It's about hard work and technique. In Lebanon, they don't teach it well. I see short films that lack a good structure. But the screenplay is how a film starts. You have to have a solid story'.[128] Doueiri also says that 'there is a shortage of male performers between the ages of 20 and 50. It's because Lebanese males are so expected to raise money that they don't work in cinema. It's more acceptable that women make arts. It's a mentality problem'.[129]

There is also an absence of cinema culture and appreciation for the arts in Lebanon on a wide scale. Mohamad Soueid says that part of the problem lies in the readership of film criticism:

> how much are people reading? If a film is critiqued, are people accessing this criticism? People are interested in gossip and got used to expecting it from magazines. So cinema critics do not have readers. In Lebanon, newspapers used to have a serious take on culture. With television, the situation is changing ... There is a space for cinema in people's lives in Lebanon, but it's reduced to entertainment. People don't remember film titles.[130]

Samir Habchi on the other hand links the problem to a more general one in Lebanon:

Cinema is a social phenomenon that is linked with other phenomena. It cannot evolve in a country that is not evolved. If the cultural, social and economic infrastructure is not developed, the cinema won't either. Cinema in Lebanon is relatively undeveloped, like the country. But the country is developing. I am optimistic though and am not worried about cinema in Lebanon, it will find itself eventually. We cannot have a country in this day and age without a cinema. Just like there is no people without poetry, now there cannot be a people without cinema.[131]

Solutions

It is disheartening to see that the problems facing Lebanese cinema have been largely unchanged since the 1970s. What has mostly improved since then is that the technical infrastructure is more solid, which lessens the need to rent equipment from abroad. But there are a number of solutions that could help establish a cinema industry in Lebanon. Two of the respondents to Ki'di's questions in his article on Lebanese cinema in 1991 offered solutions to those problems, which are still relevant today. Khayat suggested the screening of Lebanese films in schools and film clubs.[132] Soueid went further by listing a number of other suggestions:

1. The resurrection of the National Cinema Center to support the creation of a cinema infrastructure in the country as opposed to giving limited financial help which is barely enough to cover the cost of few 16mm film reels.
2. The taxation of cinema tickets where the revenue generated is used to support local productions.
3. Allowing a tax relief on the screening of Lebanese films in local film theaters.
4. Requiring television stations to part-fund local film productions in return for exclusive broadcasting rights of such films.
5. Imposing a tax on television adverts to generate funds for film production.
6. The re-organization of the Filmmakers Union to guarantee the rights of filmmakers (currently the Union is part of the Ministry of Labor and Social Services).[133]

The filmmakers interviewed for this book also came up with a similar list of practical solutions. Ziad Doueiri says, 'filmmaking is an effective way to stimulate the economy. Hollywood is the third largest exporter in the USA. You can take 2.5 per cent of the revenue of each ticket sold at the box office and put it in a treasury box and create a national cinema fund, as they do in France. France also forces its television stations to invest in local films. It's beneficial, profitable, creates an industry. You need people with a vision'.[134] Samir Habchi echoes this sentiment:

> We need state support. This needs awareness on behalf of society and officials, as officials are from this society too. In France, there would not be a cinema without state support. Unless you are talking about the United States, where a film can fund itself from the local market. Over here, say I pay 500,000 dollars on a film. If 150,000 people watch it, it won't be enough to pay back the costs. It might make a profit if 500,000 people watch it, but that's a large chunk of the Lebanese population and it's impossible. That's why people over here rely on French funding.[135]

Danielle Arbid adds:

> I don't think we can have an industry with a population of 4 million. But we still need more money that is allocated with respect, without humiliating the director. The people responsible for cinema at the Ministry of Culture in the past knew nothing about cinema. Now the committee has become better. We need to improve the infrastructure.[136]

There is also a lack of communication among Lebanese filmmakers. The scarcity of resources has meant that filmmakers are reluctant to cooperate or share expertise. Assad Fouladkar says, 'There is no cinema industry; there are directors all following their own individual paths, and we have our own methods. But this is out of necessity, it's a question of existence'.[137]

This problem can be resolved through the creation of local film organizations. The Fondation Liban Cinema was recently established with the aim of helping Lebanese filmmakers obtain local funding. However, the foundation's main role today is lobbying. For example, it has helped Philippe Aractingi liaise with the Lebanese censors when they wanted to cut part of his film *Bosta*, and it has represented Lebanon at the Cannes Film Festival. In recent years, other active local film and arts organizations (Beirut DC,[138] Ashkal Alwan[139] and Né à Beyrouth[140]) have started appearing on the Lebanese scene. Those organizations are important not only for the opportunities for production and exhibition they provide local Lebanese filmmakers, but also, in the case of Ashkal Alwan and Beirut DC, in starting an effort at archiving artistic work. This archiving effort is still at an embryonic stage, but its importance cannot be overstated in the context of the absence of any serious, official, i.e. state effort to this purpose.

The founder of Beirut DC, documentarist Eliane Raheb, has been quoted as saying that 'in the absence of a film industry structure in Lebanon, short films have performed the invaluable task of chronicling life in Lebanon after the war. They provide the material for a potential cinema'.[141] Short films are popular among students and graduates of audiovisual programs at Lebanese universities. Samir Habchi observes:

> Universities in Lebanon are forming the basis for the creation of a cinema in Lebanon. When I went to Russia in 1980, nobody in Lebanon had heard of learning directing. Directing was limited to Télé Liban [Lebanon's only – state-funded – television station at the time]. When I came back in 1992, I found that there were five universities here teaching directing. Now if you say to anyone that you're studying directing, they will know what you're talking about.[142]

Most of the filmmakers I interviewed said they believed that the future generation of filmmakers in Lebanon has talent, judging by the outputs of audiovisual graduates. However, they also stressed that a lot of those talented individuals end up working in television or advertising because of the lack of an infrastructure that would support them working in cinema.

Most of the short films made by such young people are shot on digital video. But digital video is slowly becoming more popular amongst established filmmakers. *The Belt of Fire* was shot digitally (on digi-beta). Bahjij Hojeij comments:

> digital is the future for us here because it's difficult to get funding. In Lebanon there is no production, there is no law to force broadcasters to work with you, no cinema support fund. But there are whole cinemas elevated by digital technology, like in Argentina ... Digital also gives you freedom to interact with actors; you can improvise more and work ideas through.[143]

But even digital cinema is limited in the possibilities it offers filmmakers with few resources. *When Maryam Spoke Out* is the first Lebanese feature film to be shot on digital video. As mentioned above, the unfamiliarity of the medium created problems as the cast was not used to working with a small camera and a minimal crew. The film's small budget contradicted the fluidity that digital technology usually affords the filmmaker. Fouladkar says:

> If you have the time, you can experiment with digital technology. But I did not have that luxury. I did not shoot the film the way I wanted to. But this technology is creating directors where it would

not have been possible otherwise, and will soon create its own film language.[144]

Ibrahim al-Ariss believes the moment has already arrived:

> Now, with digital technology, making films has become cheap. And Lebanese cinema does not need stars. Lebanese cinema, especially youth films and short films, has created a school for the Arab world. Young directors in Egypt are being inspired by young Lebanese filmmakers, so the trend is being reversed. Lebanese films are being screened at festivals all over the world, and are teaching the rest of the Arab world how cinema can be made with little money and no stars, and that is different from the traditional Egyptian model. From Baghdadi till Arbid, Lebanese cinema has become a school for contemporary Arab cinema.[145]

Researching this Book

In light of the above overview, I feel it is important for me to reveal the process of researching this book, as it is symptomatic of the malaise associated with Lebanese cinema.

The process of researching this book began in 2003 with an attempt to identify and collect all Lebanese feature films made since the start of the Civil War in 1975. My first destination was the National Cinema Center at the Ministry of Culture. I arrived at the Center to discover that it is a number of offices and storage spaces with no databases whatsoever. I had tried to assemble a list of Lebanese films based on my own memory and on internet searches. I hoped the Center would be able to provide me with some more. They did, but their lack of databases meant that the workers there were sometimes unable to find films by title, asking me to supply them with names of actors present in the films for example. The Center was able to provide me with limited documentation on Lebanese cinema, and material from an event in 1996 organized by the Ministry of Culture to mark the 100th anniversary of the birth of cinema. But other material I was promised, namely an out-of-print book on Lebanese cinema, I could not get because its writer, an employee at the Center, changed his mind at the last minute.

I visited a number of video stores in Beirut to try to collect some films that the National Cinema Center could not supply. I managed to get some, which were bad quality copies on VHS. A local contact pointed me in the direction of a cultural club in Beirut which held some films. I managed to borrow some on video to view from there, but when I returned to the place a couple of years later to gather more information, I found out that the rickety cupboard that the videos had been stored in was no longer there, as the club had stopped organizing film events. When I inquired about the whereabouts of the cupboard's contents, I was told they were divided among a number of people who I could not track down despite various attempts.

I needed to view films that I knew did not have any kind of distribution, and realized that the only way of obtaining those was by contacting the filmmakers themselves. Beirut DC and Ashkal Alwan were able to provide me with several useful phone numbers, and I mobilized my father, friends and contacts in Beirut to collect more details. The search for films and filmmakers often involved going through a long chain of people, where one person would direct me to another and another, which sometimes ended up being a vicious circle. I needed to contact the filmmakers not only because I wanted to view their films. I also realized that they are my only recourse to information on filmmaking, as there is so little published information on Lebanese cinema.

I visited the libraries of the American University of Beirut and the Lebanese American University, but found that the material they held on Lebanese cinema was mostly from the 1960s. Library searches in the UK also came up with very few resources. I visited the Arab World Institute in Paris where I managed to photocopy some written material and buy some rare books, and I also found two books, one in Arabic (Mohamad Soueid's *The Postponed Cinema*) and one in French (*Le Cinema Libanais* by Hady Zaccack), in bookshops in Beirut, after a meticulous search. I was advised to visit the Arab Information Center at the offices of *As-Safir* newspaper, which I was told held an archive on Lebanese cinema. I managed to buy the archive for a significant sum of money after a process of negotiation. I was told the archive contained articles by different Lebanese newspapers. It did indeed, but then the Center told me that they had a separate file on Lebanese directors, which would cost extra. After buying both, and upon viewing the CD-ROM they were stored on, I realized that the archive did not contain articles from the early 1970s, or ones from the present. The response at the Center, when I went back to complain, was 'but this is an archive! It is about the past'. The staff eventually agreed to supply me with this extra material 'at no extra charge'.

And so four years went by, four years of searching, discovery and many closed doors. Sometimes a newspaper article would make me aware of a film I had missed, and the process of tracking down would start again. Other times a filmmaker would mention a film they had made which I had never heard of, and my filmography would grow (thanks to Leila Assaf for alerting me to the presence of her film *Martyrs* – a film never shown or heard of in Lebanon due to political sensitivities). At times I would receive misleading information. I was told that *Ma'raka* did not exist. I was only able to see it when I mentioned this by chance to Hassan Ni'mani, who happened to have a copy. Hassan Ni'mani himself had heard a rumor that *The Veiled Man* by Maroun Baghdadi was being sold at Virgin Megastores in Beirut but could not find it there. I was only able to find it when I saw it by chance on the French cinema shelf. On the other hand, I was never able to view Baghdadi's *Beirut ya Beirut*, despite using several methods to try to track the film down. The National Cinema Center denied having the film, but when Hassan Ni'mani showed me Hady Zaccack's documentary *Lebanese War Cinema*, I saw a scene where Hady puts the reel of the film on a projector at the Center! I tracked down Maroun Baghdadi's widow in France, who insisted that the Center has the film. But the Center continued to deny having it.

In a way, the process of researching this book has mirrored that of making films in Lebanon. The lack of archives and databases. The absence of an infrastructure. The need to rely on individual effort. The feeble assistance of the government. The dependence on European money (I would not have been able to write this book without two grants from the Arts and Humanities Research Council in the UK, in addition to paying for many of the materials myself). I know there are a number of films that I missed, and for that I apologize. But this book is a labor of love, just like Lebanese films are. Its limitations parallel theirs. And its hopes do too.

Endnotes

1 Westmoreland, Mark (2002). 'Cinematic dreaming: on phantom poetics and the longing for a Lebanese national cinema', *Text, Practice, Performance*, issue IV: pp.33–50.
2 Soueid, Mohamad (1990a). 'Sixty years since the establishment of cinema in Lebanon', Part 1. *Al-Hayat*, August 28 (Arabic).
3 Qirdahi, Joseph (1985). 'Lebanese cinema has been searching for an identity for six decades', *As-Sayyad*, November 27 (Arabic).
4 Soueid, Mohamad (1990b). 'Sixty years since the establishment of cinema in Lebanon', Part 2. *Al-Hayat*, August 30 (Arabic).
5 Ibid.
6 Qirdahi: 'Lebanese cinema'.
7 Al-Ariss, Ibrahim (1984). 'Reflections on Lebanese cinema and its history', *Al-Anwar*, March 5 (Arabic).
8 Soueid, Mohamad (1990d). 'Sixty years since the establishment of cinema in Lebanon', Part 5. *Al-Hayat*, September 2 (Arabic).
9 Soueid, Mohamad (1990e). 'Sixty years since the establishment of cinema in Lebanon', Part 6. *Al-Hayat*, September 4 (Arabic).
10 Qirdahi: 'Lebanese cinema'.

11 Bacha, Abido (1995). *Lebanese Cinema 1929–1995*, Beirut: Lebanese Ministry of Culture (Arabic).
12 Qirdahi: 'Lebanese cinema'.
13 Al-Ariss: 'Reflections on Lebanese cinema'.
14 Qirdahi: 'Lebanese cinema'.
15 'Lebanese cinema between the past and the present: a mysterious future?', *Al-Amal* (1982) December 10 (Arabic).
16 Al-Ariss: 'Reflections on Lebanese cinema'.
17 Hamza, Radwan (1997). 'Al-Kifah al-Arabi opens the Lebanese cinema file', *Al-Kifah A-Arabi*, April 29 (Arabic).
18 Qirdahi: 'Lebanese cinema'.
19 Ibid.
20 Al-Kassan, Jean (1982). 'Lebanese cinema from a critical historical perspective', *Al-Anwar*, April 22 (Arabic).
21 Ibid.
22 Ibid.
23 Qirdahi: 'Lebanese cinema'.
24 Al-Kassan: 'Lebanese cinema'.
25 Ibid.
26 Khalaf, Ghazi (1994). 'Documentary Cinema: a true human testimony to the harshness of war', *Ad-Deyar*, October 18 (Arabic).
27 Bouzid, Nouri (1995). 'New realism in Arab cinema: defeat conscious cinema', *Alif: Journal of Comparative Poetics*, number 15, Arab Cinematics, pp.246–7.
28 Soueid, Mohamad (1998). 'Lebanese cinema: the migrant image', *An-Nahar Culture Supplement*, October 3 (Arabic).
29 Soueid, Mohamad (1983a). 'At the start of the new round of film productions: on which edge does production stand?', *As-Safir*, June 20 (Arabic).
30 Soueid, Mohamad (1982). 'The condition of filmmakers according to the head of their union', *As-Safir*, October 18 (Arabic).
31 Soueid, Mohamad (2000). 'The cinema industry in Lebanon', *Al-Hiwar*, April 15 (Arabic).
32 Farah, Joseph (1979). 'Thirteen new film theaters in the Eastern area', *Al-Anwar*, September 3 (Arabic).
33 Moufarrej, Nada (1985). 'Home video: people's best companion', *Al-Anwar*, March 24 (Arabic).
34 Soueid, Mohamad (2006). *Interview with the author*, Beirut, April.
35 'Lebanese Cinema', *Al-Amal*.
36 Ibid.
37 Nasri, Samir (1982). 'The Lebanese filmmakers' excuse is that they are passionate', *An-Nahar*, December 30 (Arabic).
38 Soueid, Mohamad (1983b). 'Stories from cinematic production in Lebanon', *As-Safir*, September 12 (Arabic).
39 Soueid: 'The cinema industry in Lebanon'.
40 'Lebanese Cinema', *Al-Amal*.
41 Moufarrej: 'Home video'.
42 Conversation with the author in 2006.

43 Wazen, Abdo (1995). 'War as subject for cinema', translated by Ferial J. Ghazoul, *Alif: Journal of Comparative Poetics*, 15, p.231.
44 Conversations with the author in Beirut and Paris, April 2006.
45 Quoted in Nasri, Samir (1985b). 'Soueid, Birjaoui, Qaboos: A matter of enlightenment and critical knowledge', *An-Nahar*, December 3 (Arabic).
46 Nasri, Samir (1985a). '*Ma'raka* in South Beirut, Nabatieh and South Lebanon', *An-Nahar*, November 18 (Arabic).
47 Soueid: 'The cinema industry in Lebanon'.
48 Ki'di, George (1995a). 'Graduates write the image and we are in light and darkness', *An-Nahar*, June 26 (Arabic).
49 Al-Ariss, Ibrahim (1998). 'A panoramic representation of the history of Lebanese cinema at l'Institut du Monde Arabe', *Al-Hayat*, October 9 (Arabic).
50 Jabre, Farid (1966). 'The industry in Lebanon 1958–1965', in Sadoul, George (ed), *The Cinema on the Arab Countries*, Beirut: Interarab Centre of Cinema and Television, p.177.
51 Ibid.
52 Jabre: 'The industry in Lebanon', p.178.
53 Qirdahi: 'Lebanese cinema'.
54 Ki'di, George (1991a). 'The file: Emile Chahine, Mohamad Soueid', *An-Nahar*, October 21 (Arabic).
55 Ibid.
56 Ki'di, George (1991b). 'The file: Houssam Khayat, Khaled Itani', *An-Nahar*, October 28 (Arabic).
57 Ki'di, George (1997a). 'An-Nahar opens the file of the disappeared Lebanese cinema and its possible horizons 1', *An-Nahar*, January 20 (Arabic).
58 Ibid.
59 Hamza: 'Al-Kifah al-Arabi'.
60 Ibid.
61 Soueid: 'The cinema industry in Lebanon'.
62 Jarjoura, Nadim (2000). 'The Lebanese cinema file', *Al-Itihad*, June 29 (Arabic).
63 Al-Ariss: 'Reflections on Lebanese cinema'.
64 Hamza: 'Al-Kifah al-Arabi'.
65 Jarjoura: 'The Lebanese cinema file'.
66 Na'ouss, Nadine (2000). 'Lebanese cinema is fine despite war, poverty, and governmental neglect', *Al-Hayat*, January 14 (Arabic).
67 Habib, Vicky (2005). 'Where is Lebanese cinema after the last few years' achievements of its ambitious innovators?', *Al-Hayat*, November 18 (Arabic).
68 'Proposed law to impose taxes on home videos', *Al-Ahrar* (1984), April 14 (Arabic).
69 Ki'di, George (1995b). 'The centenary of cinema reaches Lebanon too', *An-Nahar*, August 14 (Arabic).
70 Soueid: 'Lebanese cinema'.
71 Ibid.
72 Ki'di, George (1997b). 'An-Nahar opens the file of the disappeared Lebanese cinema and its possible horizons 2', *An-Nahar*, January 21 (Arabic).

73 Hajjar, Ghassan (2002). 'The Cinematheque is national cinema's home in Lebanon', *An-Nahar*, February 19 (Arabic).
74 Fouladkar, Assad (2006). *Interview with the author*, Beirut, April.
75 Arbid, Danielle (2006). *Interview with the author*, Paris, April.
76 Hamza: 'Al-Kifah al-Arabi'.
77 Soueid: 'Lebanese cinema'.
78 Soueid, Mohamad (1989). 'Lebanese expat cinema: war, exile and the French Revolution', *Al-Hayat*, December 6 (Arabic).
79 Doueiri, Ziad (2004). *Interview with the author*, London, April.
80 Habchi, Samir (2005). *Interview with the author*, Beirut, April.
81 Wettig, Hannah (2004). 'Lebanese authorities ban "The Da Vinci Code"', *The Daily Star* (Thursday September 16) [Online]. Available: http://www.dailystar.com.lb/article.asp?edition_ID=1&article_ID=8424&categ_id=2
82 Soueid: 'Lebanese cinema'.
83 Abu Mrad, Ilham (1979). 'Why the new film theaters?', *As-Safir*, January 28 (Arabic).
84 Habchi: *Interview with the author*.
85 Doueiri: *Interview with the author*.
86 Hoang, Mai (2004). 'Lebanese filmmaker: Randa Chahal Sabbag', *World Press Review*, 51:3 (March) [Online]. Available: http://www.worldpress.org/Mideast/1803.cfm
87 Riding, Alan (2000). 'A filmmaker without honor or outlets in her own land', *The New York Times* (Wednesday June 14) [Online]. Available: http://www.library.cornell.edu/colldev/mideast/chahal.htm
88 'The Lebanese General Security bans *The Civilized* and distributes a proof of insults... and scenes', *Al-Hayat* (1999) October 21 (Arabic).
89 'The Lebanese General Security', *Al-Hayat*.
90 Quoted in 'The Lebanese General Security', *Al-Hayat*.
91 Soueid, Mohamad (1999). 'Lebanese cinema in the hands of the censors', *An-Nahar*, October 30 (Arabic).
92 Arbid: *Interview with the author*.
93 Aractingi, Philippe (2006). *Interview with the author*, Beirut, April.
94 Saab, Jocelyne (2006). *Interview with the author*, Paris, April.
95 Doueiri: *Interview with the author*.
96 Salhab, Ghassan (2004). *Interview with the author*, Beirut, April.
97 Soueid, Mohamad (1986). *The Postponed Cinema: Films of the Lebanese Civil War*, Beirut: The Arab Research Organization (Arabic).
98 Assaf, Roger (2006). *Interview with the author*, Beirut, April.
99 Aractingi: *Interview with the author*.
100 Atallah, Bshara (2006). *Interview with the author*, Beirut, April.
101 Fouladkar: *Interview with the author*.
102 Soueid: 'Lebanese cinema'.
103 Hojeij, Bahij (2005). *Interview with the author*, Beirut, April.
104 Habchi: *Interview with the author*.
105 Saab: *Interview with the author*.
106 Arbid: *Interview with the author*.

107 Rosen, Miriam (1989). 'The uprooted cinema: Arab filmmakers abroad', *Middle East Report*, Number 159 (July/August), Popular Culture, pp.34–7.
108 Aractingi: *Interview with the author*.
109 Chahal, Randa (2006). *Interview with the author*, Paris, April.
110 Saab: *Interview with the author*.
111 Codsi, Jean Claude (2004). *Interview with the author*, Beirut, April.
112 Salhab: *Interview with the author*.
113 Hojeij: *Interview with the author*.
114 Soueid, Mohamad (1991). 'Beirut's film theaters on the eve of the war', *Al-Hayat*, August 2 (Arabic).
115 Aractingi: *Interview with the author*.
116 Soueid: 'Lebanese cinema'.
117 'The opening of Screen 6 at Cinema Empire: exclusive to European cinema', *An-Nahar* (1999), May 5 (Arabic).
118 Saab: *Interview with the author*.
119 Soueid: *Interview with the author*.
120 Ibid.
121 Al-Ariss, Ibrahim (2006). *Interview with the author*, Beirut, April.
122 Doueiri: *Interview with the author*.
123 Habchi: *Interview with the author*.
124 Fouladkar: *Interview with the author*.
125 Habchi: *Interview with the author*.
126 Alawiyeh, Borhan (2004). *Interview with the author*, Beirut, April.
127 Soueid, Mohamad (1990c). 'Sixty years since the establishment of cinema in Lebanon', Part 3. *Al-Hayat*, August 31 (Arabic).
128 Doueiri: *Interview with the author*.
129 Ibid.
130 Soueid: *Interview with the author*.
131 Habchi: *Interview with the author*.
132 Ki'di: 'The file: Houssam Khayat, Khaled Itani'.
133 Ki'di: 'The file: Emile Chahine, Mohamad Soueid'.
134 Doueiri: *Interview with the author*.
135 Habchi: *Interview with the author*.
136 Arbid: *Interview with the author*.
137 Fouladkar: *Interview with the author*.
138 Beirut DC (2007). 'About us', *Beirut DC Official Website*. Available: http://www.beirutdc.org/template.php?menu=1&temp=1&table=submenu&id=1&EF=About
139 Ashkal Alwan (2007). 'What we o', *Ashkal Alwan Official Website*. Available: http://www.ashkalalwan.org/
140 Né à Beyrouth (2007). *Official Website*. Available: http://www.neabeyrouth.org/index_english.html
141 Quoted in Westmoreland, 'Cinematic dreaming', p.47.
142 Habchi: *Interview with the author*.
143 Hojeij: *Interview with the author*.
144 Fouladkar: *Interview with the author*.
145 Al-Ariss: *Interview with the author*.

PART II

REPRESENTATIONS

Chapter Three

IMAGINING BEIRUT

Introduction: Beirut Before, During and After the Civil War

The city is a site of changing networks of power.[1] Power relations are not only inscribed in spatiality, they are also 'spatially inscribed into cultural texts' like cinema.[2] As Mark Shiel argues, 'the fortunes of cinema and the city have been inextricably linked'.[3] Perhaps nowhere does this statement ring true more than in the case of Beirut in Lebanese cinema. Lebanese cinema is a product of the landscape. The Civil War left its mark on the physical appearance of the city, and on the cinematic imagination of Beirut. The representation of Beirut in prewar and wartime Lebanese cinema closely follows the city's own war patterns.

Before the Civil War, Beirut was a cultural and economic center in the Middle East. Its strategic location made it a link between the East and the West.[4] It was also a host to mixed communities. Beirut's center was its lifeline: 'when one arrived in Beirut one arrived in the center, when one left Beirut one left from the center'.[5] The center of Beirut was its meeting space and the hub of its activity, harboring 'the parliament, municipal headquarters, financial and banking institutions, religious edifices, transportation terminals, traditional souks, shopping malls and theaters'.[6] During this period, Beirut featured in Lebanese cinema as the playground of the rich and famous, the setting for commercial action films and romantic comedies. In both sets of films, Beirut was a place of freedom and fantasy, the meeting place of lovers and the crossroad of the high powered.

The Civil War destroyed almost all of Beirut's center. The markets were gone, the banks were abandoned, and most of the landscape was transformed into a vast collection of rubble. The city center was deserted, its inhabitants reduced to warring militias who transformed its heart into what became known as the Green Line dividing the Eastern and Western sections of the city. The spheres of destruction went beyond the center, and the whole of Beirut came to be scarred by the war. The scars were both physical and social as both the city's buildings and people shared the suffering. The city that was a prime destination for the rich and famous of the Middle East became a ghost city, haunted by warring factions. 'Beirut' was no more; it was now either 'East' or 'West' Beirut – the East being the predominantly Christian side, the West the predominantly Muslim one. With the war, the image of Beirut began to change. The sight of buildings eaten up by bombs, abandoned shops and empty streets transformed Beirut in wartime Lebanese cinema from a lived place into an imagined urban nightmare. This image of Beirut has become iconic, shared not only by Lebanese films but also by Western cinematic representations of the city. If there is an everlasting image of Beirut in cinema, it is that of the broken city. Beirut, in such images, is both a military and a symbolic battleground.[7]

After the war, a major project of reconstruction began in Lebanon. Its focus was, unsurprisingly, the center of Beirut, as the city was reunified. But reconstruction was not done through mere restoration. Although a selected number of streets in downtown Beirut were restored to their prewar glory, most of the center was simply cleared to make way for the erection of new buildings: 'The clearing of downtown created a collective homesickness for Beirutis even if they resided in Beirut. All manners of nostalgia and sentimentalized recollection were unleashed'.[8] Beirutis wanted the city restored to its old self. Parents would tell their children about the lost souks in anticipation of their revival. But the new face of the city was different from its old one. More than 15 years after the end of the war, most of Beirut's city center remains empty, with the rebuilding project progressing significantly slower than anticipated. The emptiness of the center mirrored the emptiness felt by the Lebanese people following the end of the war. With no national reconciliation taking place after the end of the war, the war was swept under the carpet and forgotten about. The Lebanese chose not to confront their demons. The war became an untalked about myth. This forgetfulness manifested itself in people's relationship with the city. Many buildings suffering from bomb holes remained in the city, but they were simply ignored by the people: the 'physical marks of the war in Lebanon are still visible, habitable, coped with and normalized in the inattentiveness of daily life to their persistence'.[9] It is as if the people, as they walked through the streets of Beirut, chose to look straight ahead but not above at the collapsing buildings surrounding them. Had they raised their heads, they would have seen the traces of the war staring them in the face. Lebanese cinema has reacted to this indifference. While reconstruction was taking place, Lebanese cinema remained stubbornly focused on the devastated image of Beirut, whether by representing it graphically or by invoking it symbolically. This can be seen as a challenge to the postwar amnesia in Lebanese society. When the Civil War ended, the Lebanese people seemed collectively to want to leave it behind; it was too guilt-inducing as it did not have clear victims when all factions were involved in its execution. Cinema is one of the few arenas in Lebanon where the ugly reality of the war is confronted.

The Obsession with Beirut

Perhaps the best way to start an analysis of the representation of Beirut in Lebanese cinema is by discussing the film *Once Upon a Time, Beirut*. The film is almost entirely composed of a collage of clips from British, American, Egyptian, Lebanese, French and other films and newsreels that Jocelyne Saab selected from an original 350 films about Beirut that she searched for and obtained.[10] Those clips are intercut with the representation of two Lebanese girls – Leila and Yasmine, who have just returned to Beirut from abroad – as they view, comment on, and sometimes 'participate' in the clips through simulated film texture. Over 104 minutes, the girls jump across time, from 1914 to the 1950s and the 1960s, back to the early twentieth century and again to the 1970s and the 1980s. This is done through the editing of clips of films from those eras, with each section preceded by a silent-movie-style title card. The film uses those clips to narrate the story of Beirut's past. The clips do not progress chronologically, but are woven together more or less thematically, although they are interspersed with a critical political subtext that emerges throughout. Saab uses the merger of factual newsreel footage and fiction, and Western and Arabic representations, to comment on the many media constructions of the Beiruti (and Lebanese) identity. Her deliberate composition of a fractured sense of time, where history is not reconstructed chronologically, but almost haphazardly, acts as a hint at the complex identity of Beirut and the intersection of representations across time and space.

The story revolves around two main themes. The first is the representation of Beirut as a fantasy and a commodity that is subjected to foreign possession and manipulation, and the positioning of Beirut as a playground for foreign activities. The second is the relationship between Beirut as a city and history, from colonialism to present-day conflict. The first theme constructs a romanticized image of Beirut, but also sees the city as a victim: Beirut seems unaware of the attempts at its possession. For example, the film presents clips showing foreign spies roaming the city, unnoticed by its local inhabitants who mistake them for tourists, and thus rejoice in their presence. In this sense, the supposed Golden Age of the prewar era becomes sharply tragic. The second theme constructs a harsher image of Beirut as the film refers to issues like the Civil War, pan-Arabism, the Arab-Israeli conflict, and sectarian divisions in Lebanon. Beirut becomes the symbolic stage 'upon which national identities are played out'.[11] As Edensor argues, 'by conceiving of symbolic sites as stages, we can explore where identity is dramatized, broadcast, shared and reproduced, how these spaces are shaped to permit particular performances, and how contesting performances orient around both spectacular and everyday sites'.[12] But Beirut in Lebanese cinema is not a mere background space. It is another character with its own story to tell. It is 'immersed in narrative', its stories linked with those of its inhabitants.[13] It is witness to their connections and divisions, their past and their present, and therefore plays an important role in countering attempts at recovering from the war by mere forgetfulness. In other words, Beirut is a psycho-geographic landscape. Lebanese cinema is almost obsessed with being in and returning to Beirut, a city that is a site of memory and lived experience. As Hirsch and Spitzer comment:

> In reconnecting with both the *positive* and the *negative* in the past at the site, journeys of return require a renegotiation of the conflicting memories that constitute the returners' ideas of 'home'. Once they make the journey back to the places they had left, their recognition of change generates corrective anecdotes and narratives. 'Let me tell you *how it was* …' … At each moment of their journeys, the past-*positive* is also overlaid by the past-*negative*. Nostalgic memory clashes with *negative* and *traumatic* memory, and produces *ambivalence*.[14]

The Disfigured City

The Civil War redefined people's relationship with Beirut, and resulted in the 'redrawing of Lebanon's social geography'.[15] The country in general, and Beirut in particular, came to be largely divided along religious lines, with communities from most of Lebanon's sects moving closer together to create homogenous clusters. The change in place therefore reflected the change in people.[16] With the city being the center of militia fighting during the war, Beirut was transformed from a 'playground' into a 'battleground'.[17] Lebanese cinema reflected this change in territorial identity by foregrounding the representation of a wounded Beirut. Most films depicting Beirut are shot on location; the destroyed center of Beirut became 'a natural backdrop that filmmakers were keen to exploit before the area is rebuilt'.[18] By seeking out those areas of Beirut that highlight the material impact of war, Lebanese cinema excavates what Boyer calls the '*disfigured city*': 'the invisible city', or the 'abandoned segments' surrounding the figured city.[19] He says: 'the disfigured city remains unimaginable and forgotten and therefore invisible and excluded'.[20] Dominant discourse on Beirut after the war focused on it as a figured city, a city being resurrected. This discourse (propagated through the media and by those politicians and business people involved in rebuilding the city center) seemed to forget those segments of the city that were not considered worth preserving and consequently demolished, or that were ignored completely by the restoration project. The media in particular spent lengthy amounts of time foregrounding the 'new and improved' Beirut, but they shied away from representing those abandoned areas of the city. While Boyer uses the term 'disfigured' symbolically to refer to the idea of lack of representation and imagination, in the case of Beirut, 'disfigured' can also be applied in the literal sense. Not only is wartime Beirut ignored in the Lebanese public imagination, the war-torn *body* of Beirut is disfigured and scarred.

Lebanese cinema uses different methods of highlighting this disfigurement, from lingering shots of physical destruction to shots of graffiti and other physical marks of war (examples include *Little Wars*, *In the Shadows of the City* and *West Beyrouth*). It is as if Lebanese filmmakers are compelled to dwell on the image of broken Beirut, even if the city is not the overt focus of their films. *In the Battlefields* for example is set during the war and narrates the stories of a 12-year-old Lebanese girl, Lina, whose family is torn apart, and of the family's teenage maid Siham. The film follows Siham as she explores her identity and sexuality, and dreams of a future away from the harsh conditions inflicted on her by Lina's cruel aunt. But the film ends not with the long shot of Siham finally running away to start a new life (which would have made a logical conclusion to a film centered on her story), but with a sequence – that immediately follows Siham's – of destroyed buildings in Beirut. While the director Danielle Arbid insists that she did not want Beirut to be a 'character' in the film,[21] the shots of Beirut at the end function to symbolize the scars left on Lina and Siham by linking the interior drama with an exterior one.[22] We see mid shots of buildings on the verge of collapse and close-ups of others full of bullet holes intercut with wide shots of the city as a whole. The body of Beirut comes to mirror the bodies of its inhabitants. But this is not a causal relationship whereby 'nature' is mirrored in 'artifice': 'Rather, there is a two-way linkage which could be defined as an interface ... a model of the relation between bodies and cities which sees them not as megalithic total entities, distinct identities, but as assemblages or collections of parts ... defining and establishing each other'.[23]

Perhaps the best illustration of this mutuality between bodies and cities is found in Maroun Baghdadi's film *Little Wars*. Abdo Wazen argues that in *Little Wars*, 'Baghdadi tries to lay the scandal of the War bare by attributing it to the whimsicality of fate. The war is portrayed as a curse descending on the city, transforming it into a crazy battleground'.[24] The film revolves around the story of four young Lebanese men and women, who are caught up in the war and who try to cope with it in different ways. One of them, Nabil, realizes that the only way of survival in the city is through death.[25] Posters of martyrs were a

Little Wars

familiar feature of Beirut during the war. It was almost impossible to walk through the city while avoiding the gaze of the martyrs on the walls. One of the most haunting scenes in *Little Wars* is one where Nabil decides to create martyr posters of himself and to declare himself dead. The film presents a right-to-left pan of a street in Beirut full of posters of martyrs. The shot of the poster-filled street is cut to reveal Nabil in a room, empty but for the tens of black-and-white posters bearing his image on the walls. It is in this way that Nabil's body is shown as merging with that of Beirut to form one entity, scarred by the war but unable to escape from it.

The city and its people shared a destiny during the war. Both lost their points of reference. The war changed the dynamics of interaction in Lebanese society, introducing new parameters of good and evil. It also forced Beirut to lose its prominent landmarks, its identity points. The Lebanese could no longer use the landmarks to orient themselves spatially, just like they could no longer rely on older forms of knowledge to orient themselves morally.[26] The Burj Square – also known as Martyrs' Square – in downtown Beirut was the most significant of such lost landmarks. The hub of interaction in the city, and its main transport link, the Square became the heart of the Green Line. Its gleaming statue that had been erected to glorify Lebanon's independence martyrs was now punctured with bullet holes. The image of the 'new' Burj Square with its perforated statue became a symbol of the war, reproduced in the press, on television, and in cinema. Lebanese films like *To you wherever you are*, *Once Upon a Time, Beirut* and *Around the Pink*

Little Wars

House are examples of how the Square is used to comment on the destruction of the war. The first two films – set in the postwar present – contain nostalgic sequences using archival footage set in the prewar Square, a reminder of the loss created by the war. *Around the Pink House*, a film about the effects of reconstruction in downtown Beirut, shows us a still image of the Square in its opening credits. The photograph bounces up and down on the screen, in and out of sight. The first time we see the photograph, it is a postcard-like image of the prewar Square with its leafy palm trees. However, each time it disappears and reappears, more (computer-generated) bullet holes cover it, until the original photograph is barely visible.

The Fragmentation of the City

Roland Barthes[27] has argued that 'individuals "speak" the city by moving through it, enunciating a private language of place and practice'.[28] Patterns of life in the city therefore can be seen as constructing difference as a 'profoundly spatial reality'.[29] The war changed the spatial patterns of life in Beirut as the city ceased to belong to all its inhabitants. A number of Lebanese films depict the fragmentation of Beirut at the start of and during the Civil War. The fragmentation of the city in those films is a symptom of the fragmentation of Lebanese society: during the war, 'Beirut ... became ... a microcosm of Lebanon's fragmented political culture'.[30] Films like *West Beyrouth* and *In the*

To you wherever you are

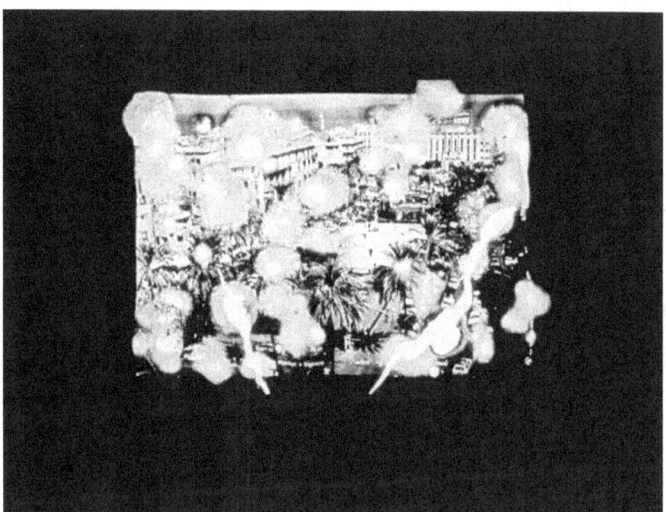

Around the Pink House

Battlefields deal with the breakdown of Beirut from a whole city into exclusive, homogeneous sectarian zones. *West Beyrouth* starts with the idyllic existence of a Muslim middle-class family (the Noueiris) living in Beirut. The only thing upsetting the harmony of this existence is the harmless clowning around of the teenage son Tarek at school.

This equilibrium is disturbed by the incident which catalyzed the Civil War in Lebanon: On 13 April 1975, a bus carrying Palestinian passengers was attacked by right-wing Christian militants, killing 31 people and wounding another 30. The Noueiris are shown to be bewildered by the incident, not understanding its causes or its implications. Oblivious to the social and political cracks forming around them, they attempt to continue their life as usual. The father (Riad) talks of a planned family holiday in France, and the mother (Hala) insists on taking Tarek to school despite his assertion that school was now closed. Riad's misunderstanding of the situation leads him to distance himself as a Lebanese from the incident, saying it is 'between Palestinians and Israelis, nothing to do with us'. This statement echoes a sentiment that was prevalent in Lebanon during the war, where the war was referred to 'the war of others on our land'. *West Beyrouth* works to dispel this myth, forcing Riad to accept that the event of 13 April is not a mere 'incident', but a massacre.

But Riad and his family's realization of what is going on does not happen immediately. The family try to cling on to normality as much as they can, resisting the tearing apart of their city, and constantly engaging with trying to recapture prewar spatial patterns when they had access to all parts of the city, now that the city has been divided into two. Hala, a lawyer, insists on going to work although the Palace of Justice is on the then-still-unnamed 'other' side of the city, while Tarek and his best friend Omar try to come up with ingenious ways of crossing the border, even if it means being held up by a militia. As the family drive through Beirut in their car, they are surrounded by military jeeps. A militiaman with a kaffiyah around his neck (to signify his Muslim affiliation) stops the car and asks for Riad's identity card (in Lebanon, before the introduction of new identity cards after the war, ID cards stated the bearer's sectarian affiliation). The militiaman tells Riad that the Christians are 'not letting anyone *in*'. This statement is significant as it points out the division of the city into two zones. If there is an 'in', then there must be an 'out':

> Riad: *But we're from here.*
> Militant: *Only Christians can cross.*
> Riad: *But we're from Beirut.*
> Militant: *Beirut is no more, it's East and West.*
> (Hala wonders which one they are in)
> Riad: *West, I guess.*

The conversation between Riad and the militiaman illuminates changing notions of place. The notion 'here' became contested. Beirut during the war, and as reflected in the film, was both close and distant to its inhabitants. It was still their city, but it also became a city of Others. As the war progressed, the gap between 'us' and 'them' widened. The contest over place was not only *between* militants and civilians, but also *among* militants and civilians, where each side claimed its own segment of the city that was dissociated from the Other. Beirut became the focal point of conflict, the 'platform for the expression of conflicting sovereignty claims'.[31] The division of Beirut into a Muslim side and a Christian side transformed the city into 'an assortment of cloistered zones representing reawakened religious identities and communities: a series of enclosed territories founded upon the logic of exclusion and separation'.[32] In war-torn Beirut, each group claimed the city as their own.[33]

While *West Beyrouth* – set at the outbreak of the war in 1975 – represents the transition to this stage of exclusion, *In the Battlefields* is set in 1983 and depicts Beirut as it is settled in its division, focusing completely on life on the Eastern side. East Beirut in the film is shown as having a distinct life from that of West Beirut. Like Berlin in *Wings of Desire* (Wim Wenders, 1987), in Beirut, the only thing East and West shared was the sky. As Maha Yahya argues, the Green Line became 'the stoneless "Berlin Wall" of Beirut'.[34] *In the Battlefields* focuses on the life of a middle-class family living in the then Christian East Beirut. The film does not focus on the representation of the war, but on the internal turmoil felt by the family members, especially the 12-year-old daughter Lina. The war is present in the film but not in the foreground. Instead, the breakdown of the family, with a gambling father and a tyrant aunt, mirrors the breakdown of Lebanese society at large during the war. But since the film focuses on life in East Beirut, and does not represent the other side of the city, it mirrors the experience of people living on the East side during the war who had very little contact with those from West Beirut. The film highlights the ambivalence of this experience, and is an example of how each community during the war saw its territory as an unpolluted utopia.[35] The people in charge of East Beirut in the film (the militias) do not feel the need to leave their space. They express their satisfaction with the way their community survives on its own, and their preparedness to do whatever it takes to maintain this community's sovereignty. The fact that they perceive themselves as Lebanese highlights the re-definition of nationalism from being an inclusive sentiment, to one based on religion and ethnicity. Ethnic nationalism is by definition exclusive and fragmentary.[36] Beirut in *In the Battlefields* is a place of multiple exclusions, its inhabitants kept apart by the fear of the Other.[37] This fear is voiced in one scene where the family and their neighbors have to stay in an underground shelter to escape from the shelling of their side of the city by Muslim militants. One of the neighbors says how he heard that the Other side (Muslims) have recruited '2-meter tall' Somalis to attack the Christian side. The film references the myths of the monstrous Other that circulated in Beirut during the war, where different warring factions would attribute to the 'enemy' superhuman qualities that justified their own 'resistance' and presented the war as a necessity for self-preservation.[38]

In the Battlefields, like *West Beyrouth*, illustrates the 'retribalization' of Lebanon in general and Beirut in particular, 'the reinforcement of kinship, confessional, and communal loyalties' that predate the nation.[39] Both films portray how the fragmentation of the city created multiple boundaries between different ethnic and religious groups.[40] Khalaf argues that '[b]orders are usually more porous and malleable ... On the other hand, boundaries conjure up images of confinement and exclusion'.[41] Beirut in the films was transformed from a whole into several 'medieval cities' separated from one another by invisible walls.[42] Those invisible walls were supplemented by visible markers of demarcation. Yahya says that '[p]articular fragments of territory become representative of different groups of citizens, as various physical structures give visible articulation to new identities'.[43] Each warring side had its own such structures: from its choice of graffiti to its selection of martyrs' posters. Beirut was no longer controlled by its people collectively, but by different militias, their control of the space enforcing their psychological control over the population. The militias set about expelling 'outsiders', resulting in the homogenization of their areas.[44] Beirut became a city contested, 'located on the fault line between cultures'.[45] This contest manifested itself in the way 'each militia imposed its own vision of the city'.[46] Neighborhoods came to imply not only proximity but also group cohesion and attachment to the territory and separation from the Other.[47] However, viewing *West Beyrouth* and *In the Battlefields*

In the Battlefields

together, one cannot help but draw similarities between the lives of people on both sides. Perhaps the most salient link is the separation between militias and civilians, where each community seems to be oppressed by its supposed 'protectors'. In *West Beyrouth*, terrifying Muslim militiamen interrupt Tarek and Omar's forays into the city. In *In the Battlefields*, Christian militiamen enter the shelter where the families are huddled to carelessly inform them that they have taken over the roof of the building to launch missiles from, making the building an almost definite target for counter-bombing.

Exile from the City

One of the recurring themes in Lebanese cinema is that of exile. Films like *Zozo, Beirut, The Encounter, Little Wars, The Explosion* (1982), *A Country above Wounds* (1983) and others present characters either leaving the country or contemplating such a move. A doctor in *Lebanon in Spite of Everything* is torn between leaving and staying. Soraya in *Little Wars* and Ghoussoun in *A Country above Wounds* are also caught between the desire to leave and the necessity of staying. Zeina in *Beirut, The Encounter* and Zozo in *Zozo* actually leave. Soueid says that the link between such films is their presentation of characters facing the choice between exile or death.[48] *Zozo* is one of two films depicting the experience of being in exile. Its second half is dedicated to recording the hardship and discrimination faced by the ten-year-old boy Zozo after he is forced to move to Sweden following the death of his parents in the war.

Letter from a Time of Exile (1988) depicts the experiences of four Lebanese men in France and Belgium during the Lebanese Civil War. The men are introduced through a voice-over by the film's director Borhan Alawiyeh, who explains that the characters represent people he knows.[49] The first man we meet is Abdallah, standing in front of a metro map in Paris. The voice-over informs us: 'I met him in Paris. He was 17 when the war started. Weapons are the only thing he knows. Since the age of 19, he has become an ex-fighter. He got disgusted and wanted to start a new life in Paris, the way others who had fled before did'. Abdallah represents the alienation of the Lebanese exile in a strange city. We see him smoking silently on the metro platform. As Parisians walk by a violin player in the metro station, Abdallah stands motionless in a corner. The voice-over tells us, 'he didn't want to kill or to return'. Abdallah is always represented as being detached from his surroundings. He is silent but Alawiyeh's commentary gives him a voice that hints at his inability to detach himself from the war. As Abdallah sits on a bench in the metro station, the voice-over comments on the 'battles of the metro': 'The metro: it's incredible. You don't know where people come from, like devils. With the

Letter from a Time of Exile

metro, incredible battles can happen. Corpses can be thrown into the metro tunnels – imagine the smells! In Beirut, there's no metro. Good. In Beirut, we had to bury the dead, there was no metro'.

The voice-over goes on to describe how the metro could have been used in the war, and concludes that 'with the presence of the metro, I hope battles won't start in Paris'. Abdallah represents exile as the only way out of being part of the war machine. But it is also the producer of an 'ethics of indifference ... a capacity to be unseen, to be unexceptional, to be impersonal in a social field where "differences remain unassimilated" and strangeness a matter of fact'.[50]

Another inhabitant of the Paris metro is Karim. Having looked for a job for six months before finding work as a translator, Karim is the 'king of the metro'. Unlike Abdallah, Karim is a dreamer. The voice-over tells us: 'The metro is like magic, an illusion, a big illusion, a factory of illusions. In the city, it's like veins for blood drops, and we are blood drops. It's like a dark room, it develops pictures, reveals colors and brings out dreams. It merges people into one body, it cancels sandbags and green lines. If Beirut had a metro, things wouldn't have happened the way they did. The metro blends people together, there's us and them in the same space. If Beirut is reconstructed, the first thing they have to do is to build a metro'. Karim therefore represents another aspect of the city, the city 'as a primary site for the production of community'.[51] His vision presents a dream of Beirut as a national space.

In Brussels, the man we meet is Rizq'allah. In sharp contrast to the silence of Abdallah and the dreaminess of Karim, Rizq'allah talks directly to the camera loudly. Wearing a black suit and sitting behind the desk in his office, he represents the migrant who tries to make the best out of where he is, even through dishonesty. Rizq'allah explains that he wants his brother to join him in Brussels:

> People are killing for a visa to Europe; Belgium is a good and developed country. Yesterday I spent an hour on the phone to him. He exhausted me! Philosophizing! He has five children, three boys and two girls. Here you get *allocations familiale, sécurité sociale, vacances* for the children for free. Here you are scared to flush the toilet after 10pm as it makes a noise. Don't give me patriotism. Your country is what hosts you. Who cares about his education? He says if he leaves Lebanon ... his children will forget Arabic. Isn't it better than dying? Arabic will be forgotten anyway. And here is better than Germany where they [immigrants] are in tents.

Rizq'allah goes on to state all the good things about Brussels:

> Fuck this, why were we born in Lebanon? The people here are sweet, they believe anything and don't know how to lie. See all those Lebanese restaurants? They're crap, but the people in Brussels think they're great. Here they speak two languages. We told them, we all speak the same language, and what did we gain?

The final man we meet is Nessim. The voice-over informs us that Nessim's father died three months before: 'he never thought the days would turn and he'll be buried in Strasbourg'. Nessim's father had tried his best to adjust to life in France. We are told that he used to say, 'Strasbourg is like us, with all the wars that took place in it'. Nassim sits smoking a pipe near a fireplace. He contemplates the fates of his father and himself: 'All his father's ancestors did not leave Marj'eyoun [in the South of Lebanon]! His grandfather had gone to Beirut to get an education. He was the last to be buried there, but his father will be the first one to be buried in Strasbourg'. The last shot of Nessim is of him at his father's grave: 'Marj'eyoun is very far'.

The different, even contrasting, experiences of the four characters de-essentialize the experience of exile. However, they all point out the way exile means that identity is 'nationally deterritorialized'.[52] Abdallah does not belong. Karim tries his best but sees Beirut in Paris. Rizq'allah remains an outsider. And Nessim contemplates his fate with nostalgia to the Lebanese land. In this sense, all four characters are engaged in projecting a nationalist memory. As Hodgkin and Radstone argue, '[n]ationalist memory describes a geography of belonging, an identity forged in a specified landscape, inseparable from it'.[53] Exile emphasizes the inability to detach oneself from the homeland.

Displacement

Paralleling exile is the experience of displacement. During the Civil War, many people had to abandon their homes and move to different areas in the city or the country. Displacement affected all communities in Lebanon, in a way unifying the inhabitants of the country through fear.[54] Displacement was a collective destiny. However, it was also a marker of difference. Beirut was the main destination of those displaced from the South of Lebanon. Those people were not always welcome in the city, not because they necessarily faced discrimination, but because they very often arrived with little to their name, and had to live on the margin, in the shanty towns surrounding Beirut. The shanty towns were an example of how war can change the dynamics of public and private space, introducing new barriers between places.[55] War also resulted in the loss of distinction between public and private space. With militias taking over people's homes, spaces in private homes became 'part of the logistics of combat'.[56] At the same time, displacement meant that public space was 'domesticated', as people sought shelter in schools and public buildings.[57] Displacement also occurred in reverse, with people sometimes fleeing Beirut to set up home in rural areas. This resulted in cities being ruralized and rural and suburban areas being urbanized.[58]

In Lebanese cinema, the displaced are shown feeling that they do not belong to where they have sought shelter. The films highlight their marginalization and their frustration. *In the Shadows of the City* for example depicts the hardship faced by a family from the South as they become refugees in Beirut. The father is forced to take his 12-year-old son out of school and to find him a job. The father himself only survives by performing the menial job of collecting and selling scrap metal from the rubble of bombed buildings. Another father from the South in *A Suspended Life* is hit by depression as he is forced to work as a builder in Beirut. He is shown lamenting the irony of him building other people's houses while having no house of his own. Even those who were not poor still suffered from the label of displacement. In *Lebanon in Spite of Everything* (1982), two friends of the mother of a displaced family arrive at the house where the family is seeking shelter, and observe that the house is dusty. One of them comments, 'poor them, they are displaced. There are no more servants. Philippe should get a Sri Lankan maid'. Khalaf argues that the displaced suffered because of dislodgement, the 'stigma of being outcasts', and the 'urge to reassemble a damaged identity and a broken history'.[59] The displaced in those films are all shown longing to return home. As Hayden says, 'in times of anxiety and fluctuation, place-bound identities often become more rather than less important – homeland, neighborhood, and hearth seem more precious when groups are forced to leave them behind'.[60]

The displaced in Lebanese cinema are located in Beirut, but they are both inside and outside the city. Beirut in the films, 'even as it presses people up close, enacts and re-enacts what Simmel elsewhere calls the "merciless separation of space"'.[61] The space of Beirut does not seem to belong to those people. Perhaps the best illustration of this issue is found in the film *Beirut, The Encounter*. The film uses visual and aural clues to comment on the inhospitability of Beirut towards the displaced. The first shot of Beirut we see shows a pile of rubbish on a street corner as the sound of buzzing flies is heard. The camera then goes inside a building where two brothers from the South are sheltering. The apartment they are in is bare except for mattresses on the floor, a broom placed against a wall, and prayer beads hanging from a radiator. We see one of the men, Haydar, going out to the balcony. The camera shows his point of view as he stares at destroyed buildings in the city. A loud noise is heard. The camera goes down to the street to show us a truck removing rubble. The scene lingers and the noise intensifies, creating a feeling of discomfort that mirrors that felt by Haydar. Haydar goes back inside, and argues with his brother Moustapha who wants them to join the militia controlling their area because 'we are obliged'. Haydar refuses, saying that they had left the village in the South because 'we did not want to be involved with militias'. Haydar and Moustapha are thus established as placeless: outsiders in the South, and outsiders in Beirut.

Khalaf argues that displacement also made people 'homeless in their own homes ... outcasts in their own communities'.[62] *Beirut, The Encounter* illustrates this point through the character Zeina, Haydar's Christian friend who lives in Achrafieh in East Beirut. Haydar and Zeina arrange to meet at a café in the area they used to frequent as university students. Zeina arrives at the café, and is told by the owner that 'things are not how they used to be'. Oblivious to his remark, Zeina sits down and orders her usual drink. Behind her, a group of militiamen gathers. The men play an arcade game, and exchange obscene remarks. Zeina eventually leaves the café, disgusted by their words and behavior. A similar example is found in *The Belt of Fire*, when a man, Shafik, arrives home one day to find that the concierge had installed his cousin's widow and son in Shafik's apartment 'because they have

Beirut, The Encounter

nowhere else to go'. This appropriation of space shows how urban areas of conflict are not passive.[63] Instead, space is active in producing and destroying social ties.[64]

Sarkis wrote about wartime Beirut: 'Destruction, like violence, homogenizes its victims. The rubble of West Beirut cannot be distinguished from the rubble of East Beirut'.[65] While this comment is valid in the sense that all those who were displaced as a result of the destruction of their homes shared a common destiny (as did Beirut), it is nevertheless complicated by the undeniable visual differences between East and West Beirut at the height of the war. It is West Beirut that bore most of the symptoms of destruction. *Beirut, The Encounter* is the only film referencing this point. It presents a sharp contrast between the chaos of West Beirut and the leafy streets of Achrafieh. A scene of a traffic jam that Haydar is caught up in shows cars honking loudly, people shouting, close-ups of cars stacked bumper to bumper on a narrow road. An armed man tries to sell a militia magazine to taxi passengers. The scene cuts to Zeina walking in the quiet streets of Achrafieh. Another such contrast is shown through juxtaposing Haydar's bare apartment with Zeina's lavishly furnished one. The contrasts become an illustration of how 'cities collect differences together and spread people apart'.[66] However, it would be grossly misleading to assume that the film aims at constructing essential differences between East and West Beirut. The film's highlighting of difference is paralleled by Haydar and Zeina's endeavors to meet in Beirut. They fail to meet physically, and resort to recording lengthy monologues on cassette tape to communicate with each other. Though this attempt also fails, they remain an example of the Lebanese people's resistance to the logic of segregation imposed by the war.[67]

In Search of Postwar Beirut

There is still no consensus in Lebanon on the exact date the war ended. Some say it ended in 1990, while others say it was 1992. But there is a sentiment, shared by a number of filmmakers like Ghassan Salhab, Khalil Joreige and Joana HadjiThomas, that the war has never ended. Those filmmakers only started making feature films after the war. Their films are set in the present, but feature the war both implicitly and explicitly. The explicit focus on war, such as in Salhab's film *Beirut Phantoms*, is understandable when perceived from the director's point of view, that the war needs to be discussed in the public arena and confronted before Lebanese society can truly claim to move on.[68] However, it is the implicit focus on the war in postwar cinema that is of interest here, the way war features in the background, in the actions of the characters, and in the city they inhabit. *A Perfect Day* and *Around the Pink House* represent this through a shared concern with the 'difficulty of living in the present in Beirut' that is the result of postwar amnesia.[69]

A Perfect Day is set in a present-time Beirut haunted by the war: 'a dystopian present defined by a sense of historical past'.[70] The postwar anomie felt by the young people in the film is sublimated through their attachment to material things: cigarettes, cars, alcohol, and mobile phones. According to Joreige, the characters represent postwar addiction that is filling an otherwise unfillable void.[71] Khalaf sees such actions as being the result of how '[v]ictims of collective suffering ... rage with bitterness and long to make up for lost time and opportunity'.[72] The film portrays Beirut as a living nightmare: a bleak place often shot in the dark. While Beirut had become claustrophobic during the war as people's movement within the city was restricted, in *A Perfect Day* the claustrophobia is maintained, albeit differently. The film has several mid shots of traffic jams in Beirut, where cars seem to be closing in on each other, and where almost every driver is inundated with street vendors selling newspapers and cigarettes. The crowded streets of Beirut are also framed by seemingly endless advertising billboards. The martyrs' posters of the war have disappeared from the walls, but they are now replaced with those of pop stars. We often see the main character, Malik, roaming around the city in his car, eyes barely open after many sleepless nights. Malik never manages to escape the watchful eye of the pop stars who peer at him from every wall, bridge and billboard. The pop stars are notable for their surgically enhanced appearance:

fake hair, fake lips, fake breasts, fake noses ... they seem to mirror the fakeness of Beirut after the war. Its reconstruction was seen by many as cosmetic, empty and inauthentic.

The reconstruction of Lebanon after the war saw its greatest scale in downtown Beirut. The focus on the city center emerged from its perception as the missing national center that will bring the different factions in the country back together as one. As Bollens argues, 'the management of war-torn cities holds the key to sustainable coexistence of warring ethnic groups subsequent to cessation of overt hostilities'.[73] However, the process of reconstruction was contested. On one hand, it was seen as a chance for Beirut to become a modern economic center; on the other hand, reconstruction provided hope of restoration of the city center into its prewar self. The result of this contest is that the little that has been rebuilt in the city center of Beirut has elements of both visions. It is traditional and modern at the same time. But what was not anticipated by the Lebanese people who welcomed the reconstruction was their own exclusion from this space. The new downtown Beirut, with its exclusive apartments, designer shops and expensive restaurants, is beyond the means of most Lebanese. The only thing they can afford is to walk through the city in wonder, strangers in their own land. The last shot in *Around the Pink House* 'reveals the new Beirut, a giant construction site, from which the poor are being excluded'.[74]

Borhan Alawiyeh's film *To you wherever you are* (2001) also comments on this exclusion. In the film, one of the old inhabitants of Beirut, Ahmad Beydoun, says:

> The restoration that has taken place, despite the good appearances, has excluded 'you'; you have no past here. When you think of the past, it contradicts the current buildings. They now have no age, no depth, no relation to you. The youth excludes you. We the old become tourists, like in Rome or Larnaca.

Therefore it is not just the economic factor that is sidelining the Beirutis, it is also the erased connection with the past. The focus on the rebuilding of downtown Beirut, and the preservation of parts of it as memorial sites, is a comment on the struggle over the meaning of the city itself.[75] As Khalaf argues, '[w]hat we are witnessing at the moment is a multilayered negotiation or competition for the representation and ultimate control of Beirut's spatial and collective identity'.[76] This is expressed in HadjiThomas and Joreige's film *Around the Pink House*. *Around the Pink House* stresses the importance of place against 'deterritorialization'.[77] The film tells the story of an old, colonial-style pink house in Beirut that was selected for demolition with the aim of constructing a modern shopping center in its place, triggering a conflict between those in favor of modernism and those in favor of tradition. The film focuses on the inability of the state to produce space:

> The city does not function in the film as a choreographed spectacle celebrating the scientific, cultural, intellectual, political and economic grandeur of the ... nation-state. Rather, the film's representation of the city registers the traces of power, the decaying colonial infrastructure and the increased role of capital in the production of space. Multiple historical layers come together in the space of the city.[78]

The film begins with a still image of prewar Burj Square. The camera zooms out to reveal the image as a picture carried by a man standing in the middle of a traffic jam in downtown Beirut, signaling the transformation of the landscape from an idyllic to a congested one. A news bulletin is heard from one of the cars' radios, stating how reconstruction in downtown Beirut has stopped the traffic and how 'the sound of construction has replaced the sound of bombs'. *Around the Pink House* proceeds to offer further comments on the city's changing character. We hear a man in the traffic jam saying 'it's no longer a city, it's an amusement park'. Unlike most Lebanese films, the film is not set in a recognizable area in Beirut. Joana HadjiThomas says: 'We built the city in *Around the Pink House* in a place that did not exist. It's a fictional city. There is a link between this theme and the rebuilding that was taking place in Beirut at the time'.[79] Selected areas in downtown Beirut were chosen for preservation and restoration in the aim of retaining 'Beirut's memory', while most of downtown has been cleared in preparation for the building of modern buildings. In *Around the Pink House*, the businessman who wants to demolish the house to build a shopping center in its place wants to retain the house's façade so the shopping center can be built around it, because 'the façade is our memory'. 'Beirut's memory' is therefore selectively reduced to token links with the past, forcefully severing the identity of the new city from its old one.

It is this forceful severing of the relationship with the past that links Joreige and HadjiThomas' films. HadjiThomas says:

> our films talk about the present and how we can live in it. This present is linked to the past and to memory. But how come we are not able to live in the present? Maybe we are severing our relationship with the past in a too artificial a way. It's like being on a treadmill, you run and you run and you are not progressing. When we wrote *A Perfect Day*, we felt that we are dead in this city and are not having much influence on the society around us or on the city itself.

Around the Pink House

Maybe the relationship with the past is what is preventing us from moving on.[80]

The reconstruction of Beirut is a symptom of the postwar amnesia experienced in Lebanon and that Lebanese cinema tries to counter. By insisting on linking present-day Beirut with the war past, the films perform an important role in the process of national recovery. Lebanese cinema – during and after the war – does not offer a romantic vision of Beirut, and seems incapable of ignoring the city as a witness to what has been. Whether by highlighting Beirut as a disfigured city, by re-presenting the social divisions of the war, or by commenting on the need for postwar reflection, the films use Beirut as a trigger of memory. As Dolores Hayden argues:

> Places trigger memories for insiders, who have shared a common past, and at the same time places often can represent shared pasts to outsiders who might be interested in knowing about them in the present. Places also permit people who have lived in them to re-experience their pasts while simultaneously experiencing the place in the present. They may stimulate individual memory while mirroring current circumstances.[81]

Beirut emerges as a city contested between dominant discourse and the resistant voice of cinema. The stubborn image of war-torn Beirut stands as a reminder of the cruelty of war, and of its remaining legacy. Like Freud's Rome, where he attempted 'to imagine the city… as different times co-existing in a single space', Beirut is a reminder of the past, a comment on the future, and an illustration of the present.[82] Beirut is a representation of the complexity of what it means to be Lebanese. As Hodgkin and Radstone argue, '[i]dentity is often located in a specific physical landscape, and through the changes in that landscape, the memory of times when it was different, changes in the self may be perceived and registered'.[83] Beirut's representation in Lebanese cinema is a necessary image fighting against the sanitizing of the war and the induced forgetfulness of its monstrosity.

Endnotes

1 Mahoney, Elisabeth (1997). '"The people in parentheses": space under pressure in the postmodern city', in Clarke, David B. (ed), *The Cinematic City*, London: Routledge, pp.168–85.
2 Shiel, Mark (2001). 'Cinema and the city in history and theory', in Shiel, Mark and Tony Fitzmaurice (eds), *Cinema and the City: Film and Urban Societies in a Global Context*, Oxford: Blackwell, p.5.
3 Shiel: 'Cinema and the city', p.1.
4 Gavin, Angus and Maluf, Ramez (1996). *Beirut Reborn: The Restoration and Development of the Central District*, London: Academy.
5 Yahya, Maha (1993). 'Reconstituting space: the aberration of the urban in Beirut', in Khalaf, Samir and Philip S. Khoury (eds), *Recovering Beirut: Urban Design and Post-War Reconstruction*, Leiden: E.J. Brill, p.132.
6 Khalaf, Samir (2002). *Civil and Uncivil Violence in Lebanon: A History of the Internationalization of Communal Conflict*, New York: Columbia University Press, p.246.
7 Bollens, Scott A. (2000). *On Narrow Ground: Urban Policy and Ethnic Conflict in Jerusalem and Belfast*, Albany: State University of New York Press.
8 Sarkis, Hashim (2005). 'A vital void: reconstructions of Downtown Beirut', in Vale, Lawrene J. and Thomas J. Campanella (eds), *The Resilient City: How Modern Cities Recover from Disaster*, Oxford: Oxford University Press, p.286.
9 Sarkis, Hashim (1993). 'Territorial claims: architecture and post-war attitudes toward the built environment', in Khalaf, Samir and Philip S. Khoury (eds), *Recovering Beirut: Urban Design and Post-War Reconstruction*, Leiden: E.J. Brill, p.119.
10 Saab, Jocelyne (2006). *Interview with the author*, Paris, April.
11 Edensor, Tim (2002). *National Identity, Popular Culture and Everyday Life*, Oxford: Berg, p.69.
12 Ibid.
13 McArthur, Colin (1997). 'Chinese boxes and Russian dolls: tracking the elusive cinematic city', in Clarke, David B. (ed), *The Cinematic City*, London: Routledge, p.20.
14 Hirsch, Marianne and Spitzer, Leo (2003). '"We would never have come without you": generations of nostalgia', in Hodgkin, Katharine and Susannah Radstone (eds), *Contested Pasts: The Politics of Memory*, London: Routledge, p.84, emphasis in original.

15 Khalaf, Samir (1993). *Beirut Reclaimed: Reflections on Urban Design and the Restoration of Civility*, Beirut: Dar An-Nahar, p.18.
16 Khalaf: *Beirut Reclaimed*.
17 Khalaf: *Beirut Reclaimed*, p.107.
18 George Nasr, quoted in 'Lebanese cinema in its new season', *An-Nida'* (1983) August 9 (Arabic).
19 Boyer, M. Christine (1995). 'The great frame-up: fantastic appearances in contemporary spatial politics', in Liggett, Helen and David C. Perry (eds), *Spatial Practices*, London: Sage, p.82.
20 Ibid.
21 Jaafar, Ali (2004). 'Domestic battlefields: Danielle Arbid on *Maarek Hob*', *Bidoun*, issue 2 (Fall: We Are Old) [Online]. Available: http://www.bidoun.com/issues/issue_2/02_all.html#article
22 Arbid, Danielle (2006). *Interview with the author*, Paris, April.
23 Grosz, Elizabeth (1998). 'Bodies-cities', in Pile, Steve and Heidi Nast (eds), *Places Through the Body*, London: Routledge, p.47.
24 Wazen, Abdo (1995). 'War as subject for Cinema', translated by Ferial J. Ghazoul. *Alif: Journal of Comparative Poetics*, 15, p.232.
25 Hamam, Iman (2005). 'Shooting for real', *Al-Ahram Weekly* [Online]. Available: http://weekly.ahram.org.eg/2005/740/cu5.htm
26 Rykwert, Joseph (2000). *The Seduction of Place: The City in the Twenty-First Century*, London: Weidenfeld & Nicolson.
27 Barthes, Roland (1997). 'Semiology and the urban', in Leach, Neil (ed), *Rethinking Architecture: A Reader in Cultural Theory*, London: Routledge, pp. 166–72.
28 Tonkiss, Fran (2003). 'The ethics of indifference: community and solitude in the city', *International Journal of Cultural Studies*, 6(3), p.304.
29 Tonkiss: 'The ethics of indifference', p.300.
30 Khalaf: *Beirut Reclaimed*, p.74.
31 Bollens: *On Narrow Ground*, p.3.
32 Yahya: 'Reconstituting space', p.128.
33 Bollens: *On Narrow Ground*.
34 Yahya: 'Reconstituting space', p.132.
35 Khalaf: *Civil and Uncivil Violence*.
36 Bollens: *On Narrow Ground*.
37 Khalaf: *Civil and Uncivil Violence*.
38 As detailed in chapter four.
39 Khalaf: *Civil and Uncivil Violence*, pp.262–3.
40 Yahya: 'Reconstituting space'.
41 Khalaf: *Beirut Reclaimed*, p.138.
42 Yahya: 'Reconstituting space', p.134.
43 Yahya: 'Reconstituting space', p.128.
44 Yahya: 'Reconstituting space'.
45 Bollens: *On Narrow Ground*, p.5.
46 Yahya: 'Reconstituting space', p.133.

47 Herbert, David T. and Thomas, Colin J. (1997). *Cities in Space, City as Place*, London: David Fulton Publishers.
48 Soueid, Mohamad (1989). 'Lebanese expat cinema: war, exile and the French Revolution', *Al-Hayat*, December 6 (Arabic).
49 Alawiyeh, Borhan (2004). *Interview with the author*, Beirut, April.
50 Tonkiss: 'The ethics of indifference', p.299, quoting Young, I. M., 1990, p.241.
51 Tonkiss: 'The ethics of indifference', p.298.
52 Edensor: *National Identity*, p.28.
53 Hodgkin, Katharine and Radstone, Susannah (2003b). 'Patterning the national past', in Hodgkin, Katharine and Susannah Radstone (eds), *Contested Pasts: The Politics of Memory*, London: Routledge, p.169.
54 Khalaf: *Civil and Uncivil Violence*.
55 Hayden, Dolores (1999). 'Landscapes of loss and remembrance: the case of Little Tokyo in Los Angeles', in Winter, Jay and Emmanuel Sivan (eds), *War and Remembrance in the Twentieth Century*, Cambridge: Cambridge University Press, pp.142–60.
56 Khalaf, *Civil and Uncivil Violence*, p.249.
57 Ibid.
58 Khalaf: *Civil and Uncivil Violence*.
59 Khalaf: *Beirut Reclaimed*, p.96.
60 Hayden, 'Landscapes of loss and remembrance', p.144.
61 Tonkiss: 'The ethics of indifference', p.300.
62 Khalaf: *Civil and Uncivil Violence*, p.241.
63 Bollens; *On Narrow Ground*.
64 Tonkiss: 'The ethics of indifference'.
65 Sarkis: 'Territorial claims', p.119.
66 Tonkiss: 'The ethics of indifference', p.303.
67 Khalaf: *Beirut Reclaimed*.
68 Salhab, Ghassan (2004). *Interview with the author*, Beirut, April.
69 Joreige, Khalil (2005). Introduction to the screening of *A Perfect Day*, London Film Festival, November.
70 Easthope, Antony (1997). 'Cinecities in the sixties', in Clarke, David B. (ed), *The Cinematic City*, London: Routledge, p.133.
71 Joreige: Introduction to the screening of *A Perfect Day*.
72 Khalaf: *Civil and Uncivil Violence*, p.260.
73 Bollens: *On Narrow Ground*, p.4.
74 Walsh, David (2000). 'War and peace', *World Socialist Web Site* [Online]. Available: http://www.wsws.org/articles/2000/may2000/sff3-m26.shtml
75 Hodgkin, Katharine and Radstone, Susannah (2003a). 'Introduction: contested pasts', in Hodgkin, Katharine and Susannah Radstone (eds), *Contested Pasts: The Politics of Memory*, London: Routledge, pp.1–21.
76 Khalaf: *Civil and Uncivil Violence*, p.309.
77 Shiel: 'Cinema and the city'.
78 Narkunas, J. Paul (2001). 'Streetwalking in the cinema of the city: capital flows through Saigon', in Shiel, Mark and Fitzmaurice, Tony (eds), *Cinema and the City: Film and Urban Societies in a Global Context*, Oxford: Blackwell, p.154.

79 HadjiThomas, Joana (2006). *Interview with the author*. Beirut, April.
80 Ibid.
81 Hayden, 'Landscapes of loss and remembrance', p.144.
82 Hodgkin and Radstone, 'Introduction: contested pasts', p.11.
83 Hodgkin and Radstone, 'Introduction: contested pasts', p.12.

Chapter Four

SOCIAL AND RELIGIOUS BREAKDOWN

The Contest over Identity

The conflict in Lebanon is an example of how 'nationalism is primarily not so much a "discourse of origin" as "a discourse of identity" ... constituted in a relationship of otherness'.[1] This relationship of Otherness is not about 'how to build identity, but how to preserve it'.[2] The Civil War was an articulation of clashes of identities perceived to be under threat. At the same time, the uncertainty of the war itself acted as a catalyst, increasing awareness of the need to belong. As Bauman argues, '[o]ne thinks of identity whenever one is not sure of where one belongs ... "Identity" is a name given to the escape sought from that uncertainty'.[3] This attachment to 'identity' meant that each group in Lebanon viewed its involvement in the war as a prerequisite for survival, so that the conflict rested 'on the causal mechanism of group insecurity, or fear of extinction'.[4] As conflict is concerned with 'mobilization, organization and collective action', identity became one element in this mobilization.[5] The link between violence and identity has led Amin Maalouf to label the latter '[i]dentities that kill'.[6] He says that identity is a '"false friend". It starts by reflecting a perfectly permissible aspiration, then before we know where we are it has become an instrument of war'.[7] Violence was packaged as a method for the protection of the Self and the family:[8]

> Because individual identity is partially dependent upon the integrity of the in-group's identity, threats to the in-group are experienced as threats to the individual identity ... Conversely, threats to the identity of individual group members often will be perceived as threats to the group as a whole.[9]

Stein argues that identities tend to strengthen during crises, where enemy images become self-reinforcing and self-fulfilling.[10] But the uniqueness of civil war is that it presents a challenge to simple binaries of good and evil. An invading enemy or a tyrant ruler is easy to vilify, but when war breaks out between members of a society, it becomes difficult to identify heroes. The Lebanese Civil War was a case of mutual Othering by Lebanon's many factions. Each side was at once victim and victimizer. With each warring side assuming the existence of a different Lebanon, the presence of the Other was regarded as an intrusion into the claimed national space and was controlled by attempting to confine the Other to the periphery or to the outside of the national body.[11]

The Civil War is therefore an example of the constitution of identity in terms of difference in an attempt at self-definition and differentiation. This process is an illustration of Stuart Hall's argument that 'identities are constructed through, not outside, difference'.[12] Hall goes on to say:

> Throughout their careers, identities can function as points of identification and attachment only *because* of their capacity to exclude, to leave out, to render 'outside', abjected. Every identity has at its 'margin', an excess, something more. The unity, the internal homogeneity, which the term identity treats as foundational is not a natural, but a constructed form of closure, every identity naming as its necessary, even if silenced and unspoken other, that which it 'lacks'.[13]

In what follows, this chapter maps out the different representations of such processes of exclusion in Lebanese cinema through a discussion of the cinema's depiction of social and religious breakdown – the two main ways in which the war impacted on Lebanese society. The chapter starts with a discussion of social breakdown by addressing the representation of the political economy of the war and the way conflict excluded 'ordinary' people. This discussion is then expanded to address the impact of the war on everyday life. The chapter then moves on to a discussion of religious breakdown, analyzing the ways in which Lebanese cinema has dealt with the topic of sectarianism. The chapter ends with a critique of those two tropes, and the way Lebanese cinema has been both silent and vocal in its representation of those issues.

Social Breakdown

The absence of social contract

Lebanese cinema illustrates how the Lebanese Civil War was a product of the absence of a social contract that binds the citizens of Lebanon.[14] A consequence of this was a change in the political economic system in Lebanon. The militias did not only control the political arena and the space of Beirut, but also economic activities. Militias took over the state's revenue-generating functions, like the ports of Beirut and Jounieh. They set up checkpoints at the intersections of their different 'cantons' which served as 'customs posts' imposing 'tolls on passengers, vehicles and merchandise'.[15] Those activities were supplemented by looting, theft and house robberies. The money generated by the militias was partly reinvested in their military operations, through the buying of arms for instance, and partly kept by the militia leaders who accumulated vast personal wealth.[16] The militias also imposed their own rules on people in the neighborhoods they controlled.

A number of Lebanese films allude to the presence of this new economic 'system' in Beirut. A marginal example is found in *A Country above Wounds*, where a quick shot shows a young cigarette seller promoting his cigarettes on the streets as being 'foreign' and 'freshly smuggled'. A similar example is presented in *A Time Has Come*, where we hear people discussing the case of a kidnapped man who managed to be freed after bribing his kidnappers with his Rolex watch. *Land of Honey and Incense* refers to the existence of a militiaman nicknamed 'Abu Ali, the Benzene', who controls all the petrol stations in Beirut. *Outside Life* shows militiamen clapping as a stolen BMW is unveiled after they change its color from pistachio green to red to disguise it. *Beirut, The Encounter* presents different examples of this issue too, from the taxi driver informing his passengers of a place selling stolen carpets ('It's a real bargain. I can take you there if you want') to the militiaman stealing food aid boxes as they are being distributed to people.

In *Lebanon in Spite of Everything*, the father, Philippe, is conned by a business partner, Mounir, who promises him to release goods imported by Philippe's trading company from the port, after the goods were confiscated by militias. Mounir informs Philippe that this task is no longer possible; when Philippe replies that only the day before Mounir had said it was possible, Mounir replies, 'Yesterday. Today, they changed the snipers'. Mounir cons Philippe into handing over $50,000 to get the merchandize out of the port, but later sends him a message that the merchandize had been 'stolen'. *The Explosion* presents the character of the war profiteer Jamil, a tradesman who moves from selling food into selling guns at the outbreak of the war in 1975. Jamil acquires an army of bodyguards, and arranges to arrest a journalist, Samir, after the latter publishes an article titled 'Hashish is the Petrol of the Bekaa' that describes the endless fields of marijuana in the Bekaa valley – a hint at another of Jamil's trade activities.

Characters merging aspects of both Jamil and Mounir are found in *In the Shadows of the City*. The characters are used to point out the continuation of war profiteering even after the end of the war. Abu Samir is introduced as a worker at Beirut Port, who we first see turning a blind eye when a wooden box carried by a crane slips and falls to the ground, and turns out to be filled with weapons, just before the war starts. When the war breaks out, Abu Samir transforms from a weapons smuggler into a Muslim militia leader. His nemesis, known as 'The Hyena', becomes the leader of a rival Christian militia. When the war ends, we see Abu Samir in a lavish car, having traded his military fatigues for a sharp suit. The car roams the streets of downtown Beirut, allowing Abu Samir to survey the different buildings in the area and to issue instructions on whether they should be restored or destroyed to make way for a new road. His car passes by that of The Hyena, who is also dressed in a sharp suit. Both men order their cars to slow down. They lower their car windows, and exchange a knowing salute.

War profiteers are also seen in *The Belt of Fire*. The film revolves around a university professor, Shafik, who returns to war-torn Beirut from abroad. Walking down the street the morning after a night of heavy shelling, Shafik runs into an old man selling Arabic coffee from two jugs. Shafik stops the seller and buys a cup of coffee, but when he attempts to start a conversation with the seller, the latter tells him that he is in a hurry. He says that he is 'going to where the fighters are, as they were fighting all night and must need coffee. The people who had fled their homes last night and are walking back to their homes, like you, would also need coffee'. Upon arriving at his old apartment, Shafik is greeted by the new concierge, Abdo, a bearded, middle-aged man. Abdo is a quiet man. We never hear him raise his voice. And yet he manages to turn the war machine to his advantage, using his militia connections to drain the residents of the building where he works and lives of their money.

Abdo's methods are sly; when meeting Shafik for the first time, he presents himself as a man in need, but is ready to change his story and his approach in the most subtle of ways until he succeeds in his mission. His ability to adapt is what allows him to survive the war, but he is no victim. He is an illustration of how for many Lebanese, survival during the war was only possible through the misfortune of others. The first time Abdo meets Shafik, we get a hint into his intrusive character as he knocks on Shafik's door and proceeds to sit in Shafik's armchair, uninvited. He presents himself as both a victim and a friend, telling Shafik that he paid 1500 liras on his daughter's medical treatment but that no one helped him out with any money, and that 'they' – a vague reference to militias – have occupied the empty apartments in the building, let them out to refugees and pocketed the money. He tells Shafik how everyone in the building is transforming their balconies into extra rooms as there is 'no government'. Abdo goes through Shafik's possessions as he volunteers his stories, his greedy, inquisitive eyes surveying Shafik's living room, assessing what could be his. Abdo translates Shafik's prior absence from Lebanon into practical inexperience with the war game. By the end of the film, Abdo transforms from a profiteer into a potential active participant in physical violence. He buys a Kalashnikov with the excuse that it is needed for

The Belt of Fire

the protection of the building, and seals the building's entrance with sandbags and a new iron gate. When Shafik arrives home one day and discovers that he cannot enter the building due to this gate, he is unable to protest as he is greeted by Abdo who informs him that he now owes him 2000 liras of the cost of this new 'protection mechanism'.

War in everyday life

Edensor argues that little attention has been paid to the way the nation 'is represented and experienced through everyday life'.[17] Lebanese films show daily activities affected by war that are united by their focus on victimization: a mother does not pay attention to her son as she is engrossed in watching the news in *Zozo*. People cannot get access to loved ones due to the breakdown of telephone lines in *Lebanon in Spite of Everything* and *A Country above Wounds*. Others cannot cross the city without being stopped and harassed by militias at checkpoints in *In the Battlefields*, *The Civilized* and *Beirut Phantoms*.

Films also show the physical violence of the war. We see people huddled in shelters in *The Shelter*, *Zozo*, *In the Battlefields*, and *The Belt of Fire*, others dying or running away after their houses are hit by bombs in *The Explosion* and *Zozo*, kidnapped in *In the Shadows of the City*, and killed by snipers in *The Shelter* and *The Civilized*. The figure of the sniper represents the militiamen's control over space in Beirut. In *The Civilized*, *The Shelter*, and *A Suspended Life*, we gaze at Beirut through the viewfinder of the sniper's rifle. *The Shelter* goes further by representing an attempt by civilians to kill the sniper sabotaging their neighborhood, only for a new one to replace him the day after they succeed in their mission.

Zozo

No aspect of everyday life is shown to have escaped the curse of the Civil War. In *The Belt of Fire*, Shafik is shown meeting other professors who inform him of the case of a student who planted a bomb at the university because he failed his exams. Later, a lesson by Shafik is interrupted by noises coming from the windows, as students in the courtyard celebrate the establishment of a new political 'party' (militias were often referred to as 'parties' during the war, blurring the lines between politics and terrorism). A male student in the class objects to the university's detachment from the events 'outside' and says they should 'learn in the trenches instead, where we can perform our national duty'. Shafik evicts the student, but he returns to the classroom and declares a general strike. One by one, the students exit the room, leaving Shafik alone, staring at the empty desks.

Beirut Phantoms offers a symbolic representation of everydayness: two sequences show images of couples posing for the camera on the Corniche (sea front) in Beirut. The non-diegetic sound of bullets is heard every time the camera cuts between the images; this use of sound transforms the war into a punctuation of everyday life. Leila Fawaz observes:

> Around the central figures in these films are others representing victims of all the problems generated by war, from the inconveniences, such as cuts in the supply of electricity and water, to major disruptions or life-threatening situations like dislocation, exile, kidnapping, shooting, car bombs, snipers, and heavy shelling, to self-destructive behavior, depression, despair, and violence against others. One character in *Time Has Come* kills himself; another in *Once Upon a Time, Beirut* tries to get killed; others are fighters, snipers, and car-bomb makers, and they take part in a violence that sooner or later ends in their own death.[18]

But what is more interesting is the representation of the absurdity of living during the war, where life becomes almost surreal as violence is normalized. A *Country above Wounds* and *A Suspended Life* both portray children play acting scenes from the war. In *A Country above Wounds*, we see children playing in a courtyard with planks of wood that they pretend are guns. In *A Suspended Life*, a sequence represents children pretending to be at a funeral procession. Young boys stand in a line, carrying a coffin made of cardboard boxes on which they have written 'the South is in danger, save the South'. One of the children pretends to be blind, carrying a stick and reciting verses from the Quran. This absurdity is also found in *The Civilized*, where a Muslim militiaman, Hussein, comments that because the World Cup was on, 'everybody is watching football, no time to fight'. The war even found a way into local discourse. Characters in *Lebanon in Spite of Everything* greet each other not by asking after each others' health, but by inquiring about injured relatives and the safety of parents.

Billig constructs the term 'banal nationalism'[19] to emphasize the point that 'besides ... overt displays and self-conscious cultural assertions, national identity is grounded in the everyday, in the mundane details of social interaction, habits, routines and practical knowledge'.[20] Lebanese cinema complicates this concept in its representation of everydayness. The war changed people's routines and dynamics of social interaction, but eventually the war itself was absorbed into a constructed system of normality. As Samir Habchi says:

> people got used to the war; shelling became like rain. When there was shelling, people would shelter, and when it stopped, they would go out. I remember walking around with a friend of mine when I was younger: There would be shelling and we'd be talking about our love lives. We were used to the shelling, as if it had nothing to do with us.[21]

It is through cinema's representation of the absurd normality of the war that Billig's concept is challenged. Cinema shows that the small details of everyday life do not speak of a sense of 'cultural intimacy', but of divisions.[22] In this sense, the 'mundane details of social interaction, habits, routines and practical knowledge' are not the grounding of national identity, but of national breakdown.

Religion and Sectarianism

The contest over national identity in Lebanon has often constructed the Civil War in sectarian terms. However, the war was not based on religious differences. It was not a war fought by people to prove that their religion is right, or to convert others to their faith. Rather, it was a war where religion was mobilized for political and economic purposes by competing factions in a country where the link between religion and politics is seen as a condition of their mutual existence. As McAllister argues, '[i]n most societies, religion is a variable, not a constant, factor and its strength varies between different social classes and sub-groups within the population ... however, where religious affiliation is synonymous with political outlook, religious affiliation is almost universal', as most people in this context not only feel the need to adhere to, but also declare their religious affiliation as a means of exercising political power.[23] The danger of this is articulated by Berger: "When the socially defined reality has come to be identified with the ultimate reality of the universe, then its denial takes on the quality of evil as well as madness'.[24]

The war highlighted sectarian differences as catalysts of terror. From the early days of the war in the 1970s, Lebanon came to witness several incidents of 'killing according to ID cards', where individuals would be stopped at checkpoints and killed if their ID cards revealed them to be from the 'other side': Lebanese identity cards in the 1980s and before listed the sectarian affiliations of their holders. In Lebanon, it was therefore impossible to declare oneself an atheist, agnostic, or even merely secular. Religion is pre-determined for Lebanon's people, not only reflecting their family background, but also their social positioning. Jobs are often allocated on the basis of sectarian affiliation. The non-existence of civil marriage means that no two people from different sects can marry without one of them converting to the other's sect. Civil marriage continues as a non-fact in Lebanon today, seen as a threat to religious institutions by all sides involved.

The war was both a result of and a cause for sectarian divisions. The prewar divisions were consolidated with the progression of national conflict. Each side declared itself right, announced its paranoia about the threat from 'Others' to its existence, and in doing so justified its actions against them. Lebanese cinema does not reflect the full spectrum of sectarian divisions in the country; however, it remains one of the few public arenas in which the issues of sectarianism and social fragmentation have been addressed. Lebanon in the films emerges as a place ceasing to belong to all its inhabitants, imagined differently by different people who are all nevertheless 'citizens'. Whether in films made during or after the war, wartime Lebanon is depicted as a space where morality is at risk, where sacredness is threatened by profanity, and where religion is a marker of Otherness.

The defense of religion

Lebanese cinema seems to construct a separation between religion itself and its politicization. This separation can be seen as defending religion vis-à-vis its mobilization during the war. *The Explosion* revolves around a Muslim man, Akram, and a Christian woman, Nada, who want to get married despite the rejection of their union by those around them. Nada is shown attending mass despite her intention to marry a Muslim man. This representation serves to comfort the audience that her marrying outside her religion does not mean that she has abandoned her beliefs, and also to present Christianity as a *religion* in the pure sense (i.e. non-politicized) as a non-contributor to sectarian divisions during the war. *In the Battlefields* presents a quick reference to religion through the character of a priest who is summoned by a pregnant mother, Thérèse, to try to talk her husband Fouad out of his gambling addiction. Fouad – a negative presence in the film – is shown defying the priest by refusing to swear on the life of his daughter and the Virgin Mary that he would stop gambling. This positive representation of the Church is also found in *Lebanon in Spite of Everything*, where we see a church wedding stopped as large trucks carrying militiamen pass through a village. The militiamen descend from the trucks and approach the church, as the bell-ringer continues to ring the church bell. Seeing the militia, the priest signals to the bell-ringer to keep going. The church bell rings louder and louder in a message of defiance as the militiamen approach the church. Another positive comment on religion in the film is presented through informing the audience that the character Rif'at, a refugee from the South, is staying with nuns at a convent. *Al-Sheikha* is similar in representing a convent in the North of Lebanon as a safe haven where the nuns embrace the presence of a street child, al-Sheikha, after she is rescued by a kind man. *A Time Has Come* also detaches the Christian militias from Christianity in its opening sequence. The sequence, set at night, starts with the image of Christian militiamen dancing in a jeep, after which the jeep crashes into the wall of a church. The priest protests against the militia's 'invasion' of the church, screaming 'what are you doing? Isn't this God's house?' The men ignore him and proceed to ring the church bells aggressively. They light candles inside the church, giving the scene a striking visual contradiction between the serenity of the inside of the church, and the black clothes of the militiamen. We find out that the militiamen are there to conduct the wedding of their 'chief', René.

The film later presents a strong condemning statement on the role of religious institutions in inciting hatred towards the Other, but externalizes this condemnation through articulating this message via a foreign character. In a flashback to his childhood, a Catholic character in the film, Kamil, remembers the religious teaching he had at school. A scene shows a classroom full of young boys with a French priest dressed in white standing at the blackboard. The priest draws a chain of light bulbs, linked together by an electric wire. He then draws some loose light bulbs of varying proximity to the chain. The priest proclaims 'only the light bulbs connected to the wire can light up. Only those are the Christians. Some bulbs are a bit far: the Orthodox and the Protestants. But only the Catholics bulbs, the ones actually connected to the wire, can light up'. With religious certainty merged with political mobilization, the priest's statement becomes an example of the way '[r]eligion provides an ideal blueprint for the development of an informal political organization. It mobilizes many of the most powerful emotions which are associated with the basic problems of human existence and gives legitimacy and stability to political arrangements by representing these as parts of the system of the universe'.[25] Kamil, as an adult, ridicules this Catholic teaching: 'Only Catholics go to Heaven! Thank God I escaped! On my way to Heaven, I see my friend Michel who is Orthodox. Sadly, he won't make it'.

The film also tries to detach this 'foreign' fundamentalist Christian teaching from 'true' Christianity. It presents a Lebanese priest who responds to Kamil's mocking statement by saying, 'light should be directed at everyone, no matter who they are'. It also presents an opportunity for redemption to the Christian militiamen through the character René, except that this redemption is only possible through death. At the end of the film, we find out that René, the groom in the film's opening sequence, shot himself outside the church. In a flashback, we see René's bride Raya telling him that she cannot marry him if he remains a militiaman. He replies by saying that he became one to defend Lebanon, not to kill Muslims or innocent people. But he soon discovers his men assassinating a group of Muslim civilians, and shoots himself in the head in protest. The film also presents characters who pronounce antisectarian expressions. An old theater actor, Ni'man, laments the breakdown of his theater company to Kamil: 'They separated into sects. All the theater people left and are not coming back'. He shows Kamil a picture of two peasants fighting in quicksand: 'the more they fight, they more they sink. Who would have thought the educated and the intellectuals would end up like this?' The film's positive representation of religion serves to locate it outside the war.

The representation of sectarianism

Seul writes about the role of religion in conflict that '[t]he commitment of the group's members to one another becomes an expression – and in times of crisis, perhaps even the litmus test – of their commitment to God'.[26] On one hand, Lebanese cinema is affected by sectarianism. It is telling that the first film about the Civil War, *The Shelter* (1980), was released in two different versions, which were shown in East and West Beirut respectively.[27] On the other hand, it is surprising that Lebanese cinema is generally not concerned with an overt representation of sectarian divisions. Only nine films – *In the Battlefields, The Civilized, In the Shadows of the City, The Explosion, Beirut, The Encounter, Martyrs, A Time Has Come, West Beyrouth* and *Bosta* – refer to the issue of sectarianism in Lebanon. As we saw above, In the Battlefields and A Time Has Come balance references to sectarianism with the defense of religion. The Civilized, Beirut, The Encounter and Martyrs all present stories of Christian women in love with Muslim men. Those characters in the films are shown having conversations about the necessity of their transcendence of this division (although in neither film does the couple manage to get together (the woman is killed in The Civilized; she leaves the country in Beirut, The Encounter; and performs a suicide operation in Martyrs)). Bosta carries the same storyline into present-day Lebanon, showing a Christian woman and a Muslim man struggling with their past, but eventually overcoming it. However, this recurring storyline is not the main one in those films, with the exception of Beirut, The Encounter which revolves almost entirely around the attempts by the man and the woman to meet in Beirut at the outbreak of the war.

The only two films commenting overtly on sectarianism are The Explosion and West Beyrouth. Referring to the Christian Nada's intention to marry a Muslim man (Akram), Nada's friend in The Explosion quotes her the popular Lebanese saying 'illi byekhod min gher millto, bimout bi illto' (the one who marries outside his people, dies from his faults). Nada's brother Fadi opposes her marriage because he does not want her 'to repeat the mistake of our parents'. We find out that their parents were a Muslim/Christian couple who were killed by the mother's brother who disapproved of their marriage.

West Beyrouth represents the moment – at the outbreak of the Civil War – where people were forced to adhere to their religious group. The film's two main characters, the teenage boys Tarek and Omar, are introduced as non-practicing, even non-believing, Muslims. In a scene where Omar tells Tarek about Omar's sexy aunt Leila, Tarek is asked to swear that he will keep the matter a secret:

> Omar: Swear!
> Tarek: I swear to God.
> Omar: No! Swear!

Omar and Tarek soon find themselves fighting their characterization as Muslims which would establish an Otherness that is new to them. Omar tells Tarek that his father 'wants us to start praying at the mosque on Fridays, and to fast in Ramadan, and wake up at the crack of dawn to pray'. He says that his mother has bought a veil, and that his father said that 'cinema is *haram*, theater is *haram*, and Western music is the work of the devil'. Tarek responds by saying he has never read a word of the Quran. Tarek is warned by a shop owner, Hassan, to respond by saying he is Lebanese whenever anyone asks what his religion is. The boys soon realize that the war has a sectarian basis, and Omar reacts with a degree of apprehension to the joining of their group by Tarek's new neighbor, the Christian girl May. The first thing that Omar notices when he meets May is a golden cross on a chain around her neck. When Tarek and Omar decide they need to cross to East Beirut to develop a Super 8 film, Omar nominates May to complete the task 'as she is a Christian'. Omar's jealousy of Tarek's new preoccupation with May leads him to refer to her sarcastically as 'the Virgin Mary'. Tarek's other neighbor, Azouri, is similar in his reaction to May when he first sees her. A close-up of May's necklace precedes Azouri's calling Tarek 'a traitor' for being with May, and his subsequent chanting of an obscenity-filled take on 'In the name of the father'. Azouri's reaction is an illustration of 'living in a society where one's cultural origins are regarded as a stigma'.[28]

The films seem to buffer their representations of sectarianism by constructing them within a 'safe' context. In *The Explosion*, Nada and Akram are shown to be defiant to those opposing them. They conduct a poll about civil marriage at the university they teach at and show that the majority of students support the idea. Nada tries to convince her friend of the errors of her judgment, saying 'if we all refuse to marry those from other religions, how can we claim to be free?' Akram refuses to run away and instead confronts an assassin hired by Fadi. Ultimately, Nada and Akram succeed in getting married, and the film ends on a positive note. *West Beyrouth* on the other hand filters the rise of sectarianism through the representation of children. Doueiri comments

The Explosion

that the presentation of religious tension through children is deliberate: 'When you take a child or a teenager and make them say a political statement, it goes down better with the audience. So when Omar in the film is saying those things about Christianity, you accept it because he is a teenager. You can afford to be more risky. I could have taken the same words and put them in an adult's mouth, but it would not have gone down well'.[29] Although those films are more daring in their criticism of sectarianism, they barely scratch the surface of sectarian divisions, reducing the tension between sects in Lebanon to one simply constructed as being between Muslims and Christians.

Cleansing the Self

Stuart Hall argues against the essentializing of identity. He says that the 'concept of identity does *not* signal that stable core of the self, unfolding from beginning to end through all the vicissitudes of history without change',[30] and adds that

> identities are never unified and, in late modern times, increasingly fragmented and fractured; never singular but multiply constructed across different, often intersecting and antagonistic, discourses, practices and positions. They are subject to a radical historicization, and are constantly in the process of change and transformation.[31]

The Civil War challenges this argument as it was a process whereby identity was essentialized and fixed, and where violence was presented as a strategy of social control.[32]

During the war, militias engaged in what they termed 'cleansing', which refers to the killing of those belonging to other sects in their or Others' territories. This had an impact on the social and psychological structures of those areas. Fawwaz Traboulsi gives a good account of this process:

> When the militias finally 'cleansed' their territories and came to control 'their own people' and run their affairs, pressure on the individual to define himself/herself in terms of a unique social and cultural sectarian identity reached its climax. Militia power not only practiced ethnic, sectarian and political 'cleansing' of territories but also committed what Juan Goytisolo has aptly called 'memoricide', the eradication of all memories of coexistence and common interests between Lebanese. Instead, they imposed their discourse of 'protection' on their own 'people': the 'other' wants to kill you, but we are here to save your lives.
>
> Paradoxically, however, when the sectarian system achieved its paramount goal – self-rule of each community on its own territory –

the contradictions inherent in the system exploded in the most violent forms. War shifted from inter-sectarian fighting to a bitter struggle for power and control inside each community. The notion of a unique political and military representation of the community, undertaken for a brief period under Bashir Jumayil, became the dream of each and every militia leader.[33]

The term 'cleansing' is only used once in Lebanese cinema, in Maroun Baghdadi's *Little Wars*, where it is pronounced by a militiaman whose affiliation is not declared. However, other films represent this issue obliquely through references to clashes between warring militants, visual representations of snipers (*The Shelter*, *A Suspended Life*, *The Civilized*), and scenes of people being killed by militiamen. *The Shelter* for example presents a scene where a man and a woman are shot at by a militiaman. As the woman tries to support her injured partner, they are stopped by militiamen who throw him to the ground. The woman falls on top of him. A militiaman drags the woman by her long hair. Another shoots her partner in the head, then proceeds to kill her as well. A similar scene is found in *The Tornado*: A close-up of a bloodied man at a checkpoint shows him with his hands on his head, being kicked by a militiaman. The militiaman orders him to lower his head, then shoots him dead when he does not. *In the Battlefields* represents the fixing of the identity of Muslims as Other by Christians in a scene set in a shelter, where a man comments that the sound of bombs heard indicates that 'they are being launched from our side' and another man responds, 'they deserve it, the bastards'.

The profanity of the war

The only two films that go beyond the Muslim/Christian binary are *The Civilized* and *The Tornado*. Both films present the war as a profanity (and consequently both have been censored for this representation, as mentioned in chapter two). The difference between those films and *A Time Has Come* is that they do not feel the need to balance this representation with a defense of religion. *The Civilized* juxtaposes the sacred and the profane in a scene where the Muslim call for prayer is heard as a boy hangs a sign advertising a brothel on a gate in 1980s Beirut. The film continues its statement by representing the religious motivation behind the war, and how it became warped so that violence was directed at oneself, blurring the boundaries defining the Other. This is shown in a sequence where a Christian funeral at a graveyard is watched by two Christian militiamen. Raymond, one of the militiamen, is high on drugs. His fellow militiaman asks him if Yvonne, an elderly woman who visits the graveyard daily, arouses him sexually. The conversation is cut to a scene of a priest reciting verses from the bible at the funeral. The priest's speech gets faster and faster, trying to finish the prayer as the shelling starts. He and the mourners eventually abandon the graveyard, running for their lives. Raymond approaches and kicks the coffin into the open grave. Another scene depicts a sniper surveying a priest trying to cross the road. The sniper shoots the priest dead, then turns around to a picture of Jesus on the wall and starts praying: 'He tried to pass behind my back! Now he's gone to earth. This I learned from you. You have to forgive me after all this time I spent for you. I killed and robbed for you. Now you're abandoning me? "Thou shall not kill"? But you are killing me every day!'

The profanity of the war is constructed at the very start of *The Tornado*. The opening sequence merges the sound of monks' chants with traffic jam noises and the sound of a *minjairah* (a traditional flute-like musical instrument usually played at weddings). The superimposed sounds are heard over shots of a dark, cloudy sky. Shots of the sky are used repeatedly in the film, inserted after scenes of violence. Towards the end of the film, a fantasy sequence starts with a panning shot of the inside of a church. All the benches have dead bodies scattered over them, and more bodies lie on the floor. An elderly man, Ibrahim, lies wounded. We realize that the scene is the aftermath of a massacre. The prayer chant *kiryalayson* is suddenly heard, non-diegetically. The camera turns to the door of the church, where a white light can be seen, enveloping a Christ-like figure whose outline is only visible. The figure slowly enters the church, and we notice that he is wearing flowing robes. Ibrahim stares at the figure in awe, and removes his hat in respect. Our and Ibrahim's expectation of an apparition of holiness is thwarted however as soon as the 'Christ' figure turns around at the altar to face the camera and the church door. The figure is revealed as an armed militiaman who promptly shoots Ibrahim.

The scene cuts to that of a long funeral procession where several coffins are covered with the Lebanese flag, shown through a high-angle shot. Women dance as they carry the Lebanese flag, white handkerchiefs and photos of martyrs (including a photo of Ibrahim). This is intercut with close-ups of a rifle being loaded with bullets and a militiaman aiming a gun. The militiaman shoots at the funeral procession, and people start dropping to the ground, dead. A woman, zombie-like, slowly gets up from the ground and starts dancing as she carries a rifle above her head. The film's main character, Akram, snatches a gun from the hand of a corpse. He climbs a hill overlooking Beirut, and shoots at the sky. The sky rains blood. If the sky can be seen as the symbol of God, then the shots of the sky can be read as invocations of blame, where God is alluded to as either supervising the violence on earth, or as being absent – and in either case, guilty.

The Tornado

Conclusion: The Spectacle of Victimization versus Multiple Exclusions

Lebanese cinema is problematic in its representation of social and religious breakdown. The cinema has largely shied away from representing the fear of the Other overtly, and from confronting the complexity of sectarianism. Instead, the cinema generally chooses to represent people in a state of fear, being victimized (the only exception is *The Civilized* – a detailed discussion follows in chapter six). Boltanski writes that the 'spectacle of suffering' serves to locate the spectator as an observer who does not share the suffering of those observed.[34] If we are to argue that the intended spectator of Lebanese cinema is an outsider, then the spectacle of suffering can be seen as exoticizing the Civil War. This sustains an image of Lebanon that revolves around the issue of the Civil War and victimization. But if the intended spectator is Lebanese, or at least someone who can be seen as sharing the suffering of those on the screen, the situation is equally problematic. The dwelling on victimization, destruction and helplessness may serve to generate sympathy for the Lebanese people who are negatively affected by the war; however, its persistence almost normalizes suffering, thereby also essentializing the experience of being Lebanese as one defined by victimization. As Borhan Alawiyeh argues, 'no one talks about the war in a way that resembles that of the others. Everyone talks about their own experiences only, and only as victims. It's like there are 3 million wars in Lebanon, not 3 million people. No one considers that they could have been responsible'.[35] Beirut becomes a melodramatic character in a spectacle of violence. Gazing at the broken city becomes gratuitous, and almost pornographic, turning the war into a parody of itself:

> The worst is that it all becomes a parody of violence, a parody of the war itself, pornography becoming the ultimate form of the abjection of war which is unable to be simply war, to be simply about killing, and instead turns itself into a grotesque infantile reality-show, in a desperate simulacrum of power.[36]

What this representation (or the lack of it) misses is an important aspect of the relationship between identity and conflict. As Smith argues, 'it is not society or ethnicity that determines war, but conflict itself which determines the sense and shape of ethnicity. War may not create the original cultural differences, but it sharpens and politicizes them'.[37] The focus on victimization lessens the impact of the films' representation of the politicization of difference by the war.

But at the same time, Lebanese cinema succeeds in its complication of the issue of marginality. As Ferguson argues:

> When we say marginal, we must always ask, marginal to what? But this question is difficult to answer. The place from which power is exercised is often a hidden place. When we try to pin it down, the center always seems to be somewhere else. Yet we know that this phantom center, elusive as it is, exerts a real, undeniable power over the whole social framework of our culture, and over the ways that we think about it. Audre Lorde calls this center the mythical norm.[38]

This is what prompts Michael Morgan and Susan Leggett to refer to notions of mainstream and marginal in the plural tense. They say this use is 'to highlight the notion that what is dominant is neither necessarily monolithic nor static, hence, the contours of the "margins" need not be fixed'.[39] Poonam Pillai elaborates by arguing against regarding the center as 'dominant and defining'.[40] She critiques Derrida's notions of presence and absence, whereby the first defines the second, and theories based on binaries because 'they do not adequately account for the interconnectedness and complexity among different histories, identities and social formations'.[41] Lebanese cinema confirms this by denying the existence of a knowable center in Lebanon. The Lebanese people in the cinema all live on the margins of Others. The films show how the Civil War contributed to a revelation of the deep fractures in Lebanese society – fractures that dehumanize the Other while glorifying the Self.

In this sense, the social, religious and political dynamics of the Civil War echo Giorgio Agamben's concept of 'Homo Sacer'. Agamben introduces this concept as a condition of sovereignty, which he says is based on the idea of exclusion: 'the hidden foundation on which the entire political system rested'.[42] He starts by asking, 'What is the relation between politics and life, if life presents itself as what is included by means of an exclusion?'[43] This paradox of inclusion/exclusion is found in sovereignty because the sovereign is both inside and outside the judicial system: 'the sovereign, having the legal power to suspend the validity of the law, legally places himself outside the law'.[44] Sovereignty is defined as the ability to decide on the state of exception, the state that determines who is included and who is not.[45] However, exclusion in this case is not interpreted as being essentially 'outside' and forgotten about; on the contrary, as Deleuze and Guattari argue, '[s]overeignty only rules over what it is capable of interiorizing'.[46] Agamben cites Maurice Blanchot to illustrate this point, saying that it is a case of society's attempt to 'confine the outside'.[47]

While the Lebanese Civil War was not one waged by a reigning power over Others, Agamben's ideas on sovereignty are useful as they illustrate the multiple relationships between the war's major actors, who all behaved in the manner ascribed to Agamben's sovereign. As seen in the discussion of the films above, different actors in the war assigned themselves a role outside of the law while claiming the right to impose their version of order on Others. They attempted to dominate the Other by relegating them to an outside space that is nevertheless controlled by the 'sovereign'. The war saw a gradual homogenization of areas under sectarian terms, seen in the representations of 'cleansing' and of the attempts by militias to gain control over Lebanon as a whole.

Agamben writes that the result of this process is the reduction of the Other to Homo Sacer – the 'sacred man' who comes to simply represent bare life. By existing as bare life, Homo Sacer can be killed: Homo Sacer is a 'life that does not deserve to live'.[48] Lebanese cinema shows how the warring factions all viewed one another as Homo Sacer, thereby legitimizing the elimination of the Other whose life is deemed without value. Agamben says that the ultimate representation of Homo Sacer is the inmate of the concentration camp. The concentration camp is a space resulting from the attempt at controlling an excluded Other who exists outside the local imagination and whose life is considered worthless. As Agamben writes, 'When our age tried to grant the unlocalizable a permanent and visible localization, the result was the concentration camp. The camp ... is the absolute space of exception'.[49] But Agamben recognizes that different societies have different levels of applying this formula of exclusion. He argues:

It is as if every valorization and every 'politicization' of life ... necessarily implies a new decision concerning the threshold beyond which life ceases to be politically relevant, becomes only 'sacred life', and can as such be eliminated without punishment. Every society sets this limit; every society – even the most modern – decides who its 'sacred men' will be.[50]

This statement highlights Homo Sacer's relevance to the representation of the Civil War in Lebanese cinema. While the concentration camp remains the most extreme implementation of the exercise of 'bare life', the spaces to which Lebanon's different groups were relegated by Others during the war are a manifestation of the warring factions' definitions of who their 'sacred men' were. Thus, the parallel between the concentration camp and the case of Lebanon is most visible in spatial terms: Agamben describes the concentration camp as a state of exception transformed into 'a permanent spatial arrangement, which as such nevertheless remains outside the normal order'.[51] Therefore, as Agamben says:

if the essence of the camp consists in the materialization of the state of exception and in the subsequent creation of a space in which bare life and the juridical rule enter into a threshold of indistinction, then we must admit that we find ourselves virtually in the presence of a camp every time such a structure is created, independent of the kinds of crime that are committed there and whatever the denomination and specific topography.[52]

Endnotes

1 Hodgkin, Katharine and Radstone, Susannah (2003b). 'Patterning the national past', in Hodgkin, Katharine and Susannah Radstone (eds), *Contested Pasts: The Politics of Memory*, London: Routledge, p.169.
2 Bauman, Zygmunt (1996). 'From pilgrim to tourist – or a Short History of Identity', in Hall, Stuart and Paul du Gay (eds), *Questions of Cultural Identity*, London: Sage, p.19.
3 Bauman: 'From pilgrim to tourist', p.23.
4 Crighton, Elizabeth and Iver, Martha Abele Mac (1991). 'The evolution of protracted ethnic conflict: group dominance and political underdevelopment in Northern Ireland and Lebanon', *Comparative Politics*, 23(2), p.138.
5 Oberschall, Anthony (1978). 'Theories of social conflict', *American Review of Sociology*, 4, p.305.
6 Maalouf, Amin (2000). *On Identity*, London: The Harvill Press, p.26.
7 Maalouf: *On Identity*, p.28.

8 Maalouf: *On Identity*.
9 Seul, Jeffrey R. (1999). '"Ours is the way of God": religion, identity and intergroup conflict', *Journal of Peace Research*, 36(5), p.557.
10 Stein, Janet Gross (1996). 'Image, identity and conflict resolution', in Crocker, Chester, Fen Hampson and Pamela Aall (eds), *Managing Global Chaos*, Washington DC: USIP Press, pp.93–111.
11 Ardener, Shirley (1993). 'Ground rules and social maps for women: an introduction', in Ardener, Shirley (ed), *Women and Space: Ground Rules and Social Maps*, Oxford: Berg, pp.1–30.
12 Hall, Stuart (1996). 'Introduction: who needs "identity"?', in Hall, Stuart and Paul du Gay (eds), *Questions of Cultural Identity*, London: Sage, p.4.
13 Hall: 'Introduction', p.5.
14 Murshed, S. Mansoob (2002). 'Conflict, civil war and underdevelopment: an introduction', *Journal of Peace Research*, 39(4): pp.387–93.
15 Traboulsi, Fawwaz (2006). *A History of Modern Lebanon*, London: Pluto Press, p.235.
16 Traboulsi: *A History of Modern Lebanon*.
17 Edensor, Tim (2002). *National Identity, Popular Culture and Everyday Life*, Oxford: Berg, p.1.
18 Fawaz, Leila (1997). 'Once Upon a Time, Beirut; A Suspended Life; The Tornado; Time Has Come', *The American Historical Review*, 102(1), p.253.
19 Billig, Michael (1995). *Banal Nationalism*, London: Sage.
20 Edensor: *National Identity*, p.17.
21 Habchi, Samir (2005). *Interview with the author*, Beirut, April.
22 Herzfeld, Michael (2004). *Cultural Intimacy: Social Poetics in the Nation-State*, New York: Routledge.
23 McAllister, Ian (2002). 'The devil, miracles and the afterlife: the political sociology of religion in Northern Ireland', *British Journal of Sociology*, 33(3), p.332.
24 Berger, Peter L. (1967). *The Sacred Canopy*, New York: Anchor, p.39.
25 Cohen, Abner (1969). *Custom and Politics in Urban Africa*, Berkeley: University of California Press, p.210.
26 Seul: 'Ours is the way of God', p.559.
27 Khalaf, Ghazi (1994). 'Documentary cinema: a true human testimony to the harshness of war', *Ad-Deyar*, October 18 (Arabic). Unfortunately, I only managed to view one version of the film, bought from a video shop in 'West' Beirut.
28 Baubock, Rainer (1996). 'Social and cultural integration in a civil society', in Baubock, Rainer, Agnes Heller and Aristide R. Zolberg (eds), *The Challenge of Diversity: Integration and Pluralism in Societies of Immigration*, Aldershot: Avebury, p.109.
29 Doueiri, Ziad (2004). *Interview with the author*, London, April.
30 Hall: 'Introduction', p.3.
31 Hall: 'Introduction', p.4.
32 Ball-Rokeach, S.J. (1980). 'Normative and deviant violence from a normative perspective', *Social Problems*, 28(1), pp.45–62.
33 Traboulsi, *A History of Modern Lebanon*, p.233.

34 Boltanski, Luke (1999). *Distant Suffering: Morality, Media and Politics*, Cambridge: Cambridge University Press, p.3.
35 Alawiyeh, Borhan (2004). *Interview with the author*, Beirut, April.
36 Baudrillard, Jean (2006). 'War Porn', *Journal of Visual Culture*, 5(1), p.86.
37 Smith, Anthony (1986). *The Ethnic Origins of Nations*, Oxford: Blackwell, p. 39.
38 Ferguson, Russell (1990). 'Introduction: invisible center', in Ferguson, Russell, Martha Gever, Trinh Minh-ha and Cornel West (eds), *Out There: Marginalization and Contemporary Culture*, Cambridge, MA: MIT Press, p.9.
39 Morgan, Michael and Leggett, Susan (1996). 'Introduction', in Morgan, Michael and Susan Leggett (eds), *Mainstream(s) and Margins: Cultural Politics in the 90s*, Westport, Connecticut: Greenwood Press, p.vii.
40 Pillai, Poonam (1996). 'Notes on centers and margins', in Morgan, Michael and Susan Leggett (eds), *Mainstream(s) and Margins: Cultural Politics in the 90s*, p.4.
41 Pillai: 'Notes on centers and margins', p.5.
42 Agamben, Giorgio (1998). *Homo Sacer: Sovereign Power and Bare Life*, translated by Daniel Heller-Roazen, Stanford: Stanford University Press, p.9.
43 Agamben: *Homo Sacer*, p.7.
44 Agamben: *Homo Sacer*, p.15.
45 Agamben: *Homo Sacer*.
46 Deleuze, Gilles and Guattari, Félix (1987). *A Thousand Plateaus: Capitalism and Schizophrenia*, Minneapolis: University of Minnesota Press, p.445.
47 Blanchot, quoted in Agamben, *Homo Sacer*, p.18.
48 Agamben: *Homo Sacer*, p.136.
49 Agamben: *Homo Sacer*, p.20.
50 Agamben: *Homo Sacer*, p.139.
51 Agamben: *Homo Sacer*, p.169.
52 Agamben: *Homo Sacer*, p.174.

Chapter Five

VIOLENCE AND MASCULINITY

Introduction: Masculinity as Spectacle

It has often been argued that 'war itself is a gendering activity, one of the few remaining true masculine experiences in our society'.[1] If war is a 'true' masculine experience, then '[v]iolence is often the single most evident marker of manhood'.[2] Violence as an affirmation of masculinity is most evidently played out in group struggle, where asserting one's manhood through terror serves 'as a means of drawing boundaries and making exclusions' between the Self and the Other.[3] Lebanese cinema is full of examples of male violence directed at bodies that act 'as representations of a collective trangressive other'.[4] In this sense, Lebanese cinema presents a classical representation of masculinity as spectacle.

Hollywood action cinema has established a tradition of representing masculinity as spectacle. As Tasker argues, there is a

> tendency of Hollywood action cinema towards the construction of the male body as spectacle. Together with an awareness of masculinity as performance, also evident in these films is the continuation and amplification of an established tradition of the Hollywood cinema space – play upon images of power and powerlessness at the center of which is the male hero. Within this structure, suffering – torture, in particular – operates as both a set of narrative hurdles to be overcome, tests that the hero must survive, and as a set of aestheticized images to be lovingly dwelt on.[5]

This tendency was intensified in the action films of the 1980s, where masculinity

> was largely transcribed through spectacle and bodies, with the male body itself becoming often the most fulfilling form of spectacle.

Throughout this period, the male body – principally the white male body – became increasingly a vehicle of display – of musculature, of beauty, of physical feats, and of a gritty toughness. External spectacle – weaponry, explosions, infernos, crashes, high-speed chases, ostentatious luxuries – offered companion evidence of both the sufficiency and the volatility of the display. That externality itself confirmed that the outer parameters of the male body were to be the focus of audience attention, desire, and politics.[6]

This exaltation of masculinity is then used in the context of a glorified hero whose suffering at the hands of the enemy only serves to strengthen his determination and commitment to a just cause. The spectacle of masculinity is a tool in a classic narrative of good and evil, where the audience is invited to gaze at the body of the hero as it undergoes hardship. Steve Neale argues that unlike the way the audience gazes at female characters on the screen, in this case 'our look is not direct, it is heavily mediated by the looks of the characters involved. And those looks are marked not by desire, but rather by fear, or hatred, or aggression'.[7] Such references to death and destruction, he argues, repress the eroticism of the male body.

It is not only action films that represent the male body as a spectacle. War films as well as Westerns revolve around melodramatic stories of men performing virile roles where good triumphs over evil.[8] As Newsinger argues:

> All war films are tales of masculinity. They are stories of boys becoming men, of comradeship and loyalty, of bravery and endurance, of pain and suffering, of the horror and the excitement of battle. Violence – and the ability both to inflict and to take it – is portrayed as an essential part of what being a man involves.[9]

In this context, Hollywood has traditionally represented 'real men' not as rebels but as conformists who serve God and country. This is manifested in the figure of the 'silent, solitary hero'.[10]

Examining the context of dominant representations of masculinity is revealing because it highlights the normalization of a certain representation of masculinity on the screen which both informs and is complicated by Lebanese cinema, especially Maroun Baghdadi's films *Little Wars*, *Land of Honey and Incense*, and *Outside Life*, which form the focus of this chapter. Baghdadi studied cinema in France, but he aimed to work in Hollywood and trained under Francis Ford Coppola after he left Lebanon in the mid-1980s.[11] He was known for his admiration of the work of Martin Scorsese, and his films reflected both American and French cinematic influences.[12] Like Scorsese in films like *Taxi Driver* and *New York, New York*, Baghdadi deviates from the classical representation of male heroes, instead depicting 'a fractured masculinity, a masculinity that is under pressure, that has been found wanting'.[13] The men we see in Baghdadi's films are more in line with those in films about the Vietnam War, like *Apocalypse Now*, *Full Metal Jacket* or *Platoon*, than with films about the Second World War where war is presented as righteous. There are no silent, solitary heroes in Baghdadi's films. There is no exaggerated masculinity to be admired. There is no good and evil. Instead, what we see in the films is a frustrated masculinity that is both a result of the war and a catalyst for it.

Militarized Bodies

One of the concerns of Lebanese cinema is the transformation of 'ordinary men' into militants. This is seen in films like *A Time Has Come*, *Lebanon in Spite of Everything*, *The Tornado*, *In the Shadows of the City* and *Little Wars*. John Armitage refers to this process of transformation as one resulting in the production of what he terms 'militarized bodies': 'The concept of militarized bodies ... indicates an assortment of practices consisting of the conversion of civilian bodies to military use and the inculcation into such bodies of military principles'.[14] The films do not only represent a process of transformation; they also show that involvement in the war is inevitable. The militarized body therefore is not a choice, but a matter of fate. René in *A Time Has Come*, for example, is characterized as having been an 'orphan who joined the family of war', in the words of his widow. A similar representation is found in *Lebanon in Spite of Everything* in the character Charbel, a young boy who joins a militia because he has a mother and younger sister to take care of and he has no other way of supporting them. Al-Ariss sees *The Tornado* as being about the war's stripping of innocence from people, even if they are not directly involved in its atrocities.[15] This is seen through the main character, Akram, a young man who returns from studying in Russia to Lebanon only to be sucked in by the war machine. Akram's nightmares and real life are merged on the screen as he tries to come to terms with his surroundings. Akram starts off as an engaged observer: he not only witnesses random acts of violence and paranoia, but tries to understand, interrogate and resist them. But he becomes a participant in the war after his friend is killed by a militiaman. Akram avenges his friend by killing the man who had shot him. Akram's stature changes. The bewildered look on his face disappears. He appears bigger. The way he walks gains a new swagger. We see him smoking a cigarette and then furiously throwing it on the ground, in the manner of militiamen. Akram transforms from a victim into a victimizer. A similar process happens to Rami in *In the Shadows of the City*, where he moves from a being a paramedic into a militiaman after his father is kidnapped by a militia.

The lives of the young people in *Little Wars* are also swallowed up by the Civil War. As in *The Tornado*, involvement in atrocities is presented as an inevitable consequence of living within Lebanon's war conditions. Baghdadi was careful not to identify the religious affiliation of the characters in this film, but presented three people (Talal, the son of a feudal chief who cannot escape from his ties to his – religiously undefined – clan; Soraya, a woman yearning to escape from the war but who cannot bring herself to leave Lebanon; and Nabil, a man caught in a paranoid dream world of his own creation), to make a statement on the way the war became a backdrop to personal alienation.

For all three characters, participation in the war is a matter of survival: they are either in it, or they cannot be there at all. Talal is romantically linked with Soraya. But unlike Soraya, he is drawn to the war machine from the start. After the death of their common friend Fouad, which was seen as either a war-catalyzed drug overdose or a suicide, Talal and Souraya discuss their status within the war. Talal tells Soraya, 'the war means nothing to me, I have no relation to it. But I do not want to be outside. We cannot be outside the war'. We soon find out that Talal's statement is due to his father's kidnapping by an unknown militia. Talal's first action in relation to his father's disappearance is contemplative. We see him going to his parents' house in an unnamed village in the Bekaa, and entering his father's room. Talal goes around his father's bed, and sits at his desk as he mindlessly turns a page in his father's diary. He stands in front of the mirror in his father's room, the scene marking the transformation of Talal into a version of his father. At first Talal thinks he can rescue his father, but he soon convinces himself that his father is dead, and becomes preoccupied with the idea of revenge. A mid-shot of Talal focuses on his stern face as he fires a gun repeatedly. Wearing the jeans and leather jacket outfit preferred by militiamen, Talal learns how to use the gun, and eventually recruits a small army of men to help him get revenge for his father's death – as he now believes that his father has been killed by a rival clan in the Bekaa Valley. We see Talal surveying his 'army' as he asks his confidant and aid Salim about one of the militants recruited:

> *Talal: Isn't he a bit too young?*
> *Salim: He is one of our fiercest fighters.*
> *Talal: How old are you?*
> *Militant: I'm 15 years old.*

Salim reassures Talal that his men have 'conquered' those of the rival clan. Using the language common during the war when referring to the massacring of those from rival groups, Salim says, 'in any case, we have cleansed the area'. This statement consolidates Talal's involvement in the war, and brings to

Little Wars

mind the memoirs of the thinker Said Takieddine in the 1960s: Kamal Salibi refers to Takieddine's remarks that

> the Lebanese are often people of the world, as urbane and sophisticated as any people can be. Back in their mountain villages, even those among them who had achieved the highest distinctions abroad immediately shed all sophistication and reverted to type, becoming thoroughly and shamelessly immersed in the pettiest mountain feuds. Takieddine ... spoke only of the Lebanese of the mountains; but the same applied to the Lebanese people in general, with the exception of only a select group of marginal outsiders. With the outbreak of the Lebanese civil war in 1975, even many of those shed their civility and reverted to a rash and wanton tribalism.[16]

Nabil's involvement in the war is presented as a result of his carelessly regarding the war as a game. A photographer by profession, he spends his time with militiamen, and enters a drug deal with some of them that results in his life being threatened by militiamen to whom he owes money. Nabil thrives on presenting himself as a fearless man, but in his solitary moments we find out that Nabil is weak, frightened, and incapable of facing reality, seeming to believe his own lies. Kennedy-Day sees Nabil and Talal as characters searching for their identity.[17]

Masculinity, War and Everyday Life

If Baghdadi's three films *Little Wars* (1982), *Land of Honey and Incense* (1987), and *Outside Life* (1991) are examined together as they were made and released, in chronological order, they make an interesting statement on masculinity and its relationship with the war. The men in *Little Wars* – as well as the main female character Soraya – are shown to be lost during the war. They search for their identities in a country that is falling apart, not knowing where they belong. The war sucks them into its monstrosity despite themselves. Baghdadi portrays his characters as fully human: fearful, dreaming, hesitating and anxious about their present and their future. The first man the film introduces us to is Fouad. Fouad is dead, killed by a drug overdose. As his friends mourn him, they cannot agree on whether his death was an accident or a suicide; others comment that 'the political party destroyed him'. Fouad's story sets the scene for the film and for the fate of the characters to come. Talal considers himself far from his father's feudal ties, abandoning the family home in the Bekaa Valley and living in Beirut. But – as we have seen – after Talal's father is kidnapped, he finds himself back in the Bekaa, trying to find his father, and then – convincing himself that his father is dead – seeking revenge. Talal is thus drawn into violence, and drawn into the war. We see him in a low-angle shot standing on a cliff practicing shooting his newly acquired gun, dressed in a leather jacket and jeans, like a cowboy in a Western film. Nabil is a photographer who is witness to the war's events without participating in them. But in his fantasy world he imagines himself as a macho hero; when Soraya suggests he helps her kidnap a man to exchange with Talal's father, believing Nabil's stories about him being 'well connected', Nabil finds himself enacting his fantasies in real life, with devastating results.

Land of Honey and Incense was filmed five years later, when the war was also five years older. The characters present in the film are not lost like the ones in *Little Wars*, but have progressed into becoming self aware about their involvement in the war's atrocities. They still retain their humanity, however. The central character in the film is Hassan, the 'Captain' of a Muslim militia. Hassan is a larger-than-life character, a heavily built man with wild hair and a bushy beard who looks more like a huggable bear than a frightening warlord. Although Hassan does not hesitate in verbally stressing his physical prowess, we never see Hassan inflict acts of violence in the film. Instead, we see Hassan protecting the French doctors of *Médecins Sans Frontières* working in West Beirut, listening to one of them as he plays the piano in a hospital ward, and eating traditional Lebanese raw liver with another as they drink Arak and crack drunken jokes. When one of the doctors, Fournier, is kidnapped by a faction belonging to the same militia as Hassan, he tries his best to rescue him.

But Hassan is also alienated by the war. Despite his influence in the militia and his role in the war, the film indirectly shows that Hassan did not benefit from it financially. Even his involvement in fighting during the war is shown to be fragile. The film shows us Hassan sitting around a dinner table drinking with the French doctors, before Fournier's kidnap. One of Hassan's fellow militiamen starts singing slow-paced traditional Lebanese songs. Hassan interrupts him and asks him to sing something in French to entertain his guests. Hassan then starts singing the French nursery rhyme *Frère Jacques*, after which everyone around the table joins him as they laugh and eat. Their merriment is interrupted with news of an Israeli landing on the beach. They abandon their dinner, heading towards the scene. But we do not see the men in battle. Nor do we see evidence of the Israeli landing. What we see instead is a surreal scene of the men dancing manically on the beach, shooting aimlessly at the sea. As morning breaks, we see Hassan standing still in the water, his trousers lifted to just above his knees, drinking a bottle of beer, as another militiaman throws stones in the water absent-mindedly.

When we finally reach *Outside Life*, filmed towards the final period of the Civil War at a time when no one could predict its end, we recognize the broken males we encountered in the previous films. But now they are even more engrossed in the war's madness. Baghdadi tried to maintain the human side to the characters in his portrayal of Muslim militiamen who kidnap a French journalist, Patrick. As he commented:

> it was better to find a common ground between the kidnappers and the kidnapped. The film's raw material comes from the characters' being human beings. The kidnapper is not just a militiaman but a person who is responsible for a family, who takes his little brother to school and who lives in a country that suffers from lack of water and electricity. In short, he lives under the circumstances of the Civil War ... What I wanted to say in the film is that we and they [the French] are both victims.[18]

Outside Life succeeds in hinting at the humanity of the kidnappers even as they inflict horrific acts of terror on Patrick. They inform him of the football star Platini's retirement. They bring him a photo of his wife at Christmas. Omar, one of the militiamen, takes Patrick to a room with a television where they watch Dalida perform and then sing a song by Fairouz (*Oudak Rannan*) together after Patrick says that he knows the Arabic lyrics. Patrick and another militiaman, Ali, are shown to have common visions. They play a game where Patrick chooses a French name for Ali and Ali chooses an Arabic name for Patrick, becoming 'Philippe' and 'Naoum'. Ali confides in Patrick of his dream of studying in France, and after Patrick's release we see him calling the place of his kidnap from France, perhaps hoping to find Ali, but certainly showing him to have achieved a greater understanding of the circumstances of his kidnapping and the lives of the militiamen.

Masculinity and Terror

Despite this representation of humanity, the militiamen in Lebanese cinema generally thrive on violence and the infliction of terror. *The Tornado* constructs the character of a nameless man who plants car bombs around Beirut, invoking terror in the audience every time we see him on the screen. *The Civilized* presents this in a slightly surreal manner through the character of the sniper. We are introduced to him as he surveys Beirut through binoculars, the camera zooming on people walking up and down a street, giving us the point of view of the sniper. When the camera turns to the sniper himself, we find him perched on top of a building, a poster of Jesus on the wall, playing cards with a corpse whom he had installed on a chair. The sniper is later shown conversing with the corpse, and pretending to be a dentist as he pulls a tooth out of the corpse's skull. This almost fantastical representation of masculinity and terror echoes that seen in *A Suspended Life*, which also constructs the character of a sniper who inhabits the top floor of an abandoned mansion. The sniper lurks behind a window, drinking alcohol, and singing songs from films as he manically recalls the days when he worked at a film theater. A teenage girl, Samar, climbs the grand staircase leading to where the sniper is. The sniper aims his rifle out the window and shoots. Samar simply asks, 'did you get him?', her flat tone contrasting with the violent act she has just witnessed. The next time Samar visits the sniper, she opens the door of a refrigerator only to find it filled with rifles. Every time she approaches the window, she is spotted by the rival sniper on the other side who then showers the mansion with bullets. The sniper eventually dies in an exchange of fire with the other sniper, with the mansion transforming into a place resembling the set of a horror film, with everything covered in spider webs.

Despite the human side of the militiamen in *Outside Life*, Baghdadi does not romanticize them. He shows us that Patrick 'is not the only victim' in the film, 'as I have insisted on portraying the Lebanese as victims too', but he also shows us the other side of the militiamen.[19] Violence in the film becomes the field for the performance of masculinity, where acts of terror against a helpless Other serve to emphasize the horrific nature of the war. The film can be classified as a thriller, where the audience is kept on their toes as they follow Patrick's story. The film's narrative is a rollercoaster of emotions: we are never given a hint at what might happen next, and the twists and turns in the story force us to identify with Patrick as we share his uncertainty about his fate.

Throughout this journey, the film presents militiamen who become more and more inventive in the infliction of terror on their victim. Thus, *Outside Life* can be seen as showing the war's effect on its victims at its fullest impact, thereby emphasizing a different aspect of the war's ugliness that goes beyond matters of good and evil. The war starts by threatening people's lives in *Little Wars*, closes up on them further in *Land of Honey and Incense*, and dehumanizes them in *Outside Life*. The monstrosity presented in the film, therefore, is not a matter of being but a matter of becoming, a result of a process and not a given. In this sense, the film departs from typical representations of heroes and villains, where characters are one-dimensional in their moral positioning.[20]

Patrick's first encounter with the kidnappers sees them severing his relationship with the outside world through covering his head with a paper bag as he is placed in the trunk of a car that is driven manically down the streets of Beirut. We then follow Patrick as he arrives at his detention place, an unmarked room with no furniture, where the paper bag is replaced by a blindfold that he is forced to keep on whenever any of his kidnappers enter his room. The stripping of Patrick's identity begins with the exchange of his clothes for striped pyjamas. His humiliation starts as he is given a bottle of water to drink from, and another to urinate in. In his confusion, Patrick urinates on the floor, and is reprimanded by one of the militiamen who makes him blot the floor with tissue paper, saying 'I was told the French are filthy, but not like this'. Patrick initially tries to defy his captors by refusing the food they offer him. Baghdadi aligns the viewer with Patrick as he kneels on the floor, not showing us the militiamen's bodies in full, but only their legs. Baghdadi uses this technique throughout the film, sometimes only allowing us to see fragments of images peeped at from the narrow space under Patrick's eye mask. The next time a militiaman brings Patrick food, all we see are the man's shoes.

The film presents escalating instances of physical terror. Patrick tries to remove one of the wooden planks blocking a window in his room. The plank falls onto the street below, prompting one of the captors, Moustapha, to hurry up to Patrick's room, place a knife on his throat, and eventually slit his ear. Moustapha drags Patrick across the corridor outside, and beats him as two men point their guns at him. Baghdadi chooses to partially shield us from this violent display as we only see the beating through the frosted glass panel of a door. But once we as an audience feel a tiny degree of relief at being spared the graphic horror, we are awakened by the sound of unrolling of adhesive packing tape. The next shot is one of Patrick mummified with tape. His voice is muffled as more layers of tape are placed over his mouth. Patrick is transported to another location in a trunk hidden underneath a truck. A high angle shot sees Patrick, adhesive tape covering him top to toe, looking small as he is placed in the corner of a tiled room.

Physical humiliation is coupled with psychological violence. Another prisoner is heard crying out for water. After establishing that the source of the 'noise' is not Patrick, the militiamen leave Patrick alone in his cell, and we see him pressing his ear against the wall, listening to the screams of the man as he is being beaten by them. The next day, the militia leader Walid enters the bathroom as Patrick is showering, forcing Patrick to lean naked against the wall as Walid interrogates him about a fellow militiaman, Ali, who had told Patrick of his desire to go to France. Patrick is then startled by another militiaman, Frankenstein, who suddenly enters Patrick's room, screaming and jumping around carrying a rifle, and puts a black tie around Patrick's neck, telling him that Ali would be executed that night. We later find out that Ali is alive and well. A similar mind game is played by Baghdadi on us as he epistemologically aligns us with Patrick in his encounters with Walid, who does not appear to speak French, and who torments Patrick by deliberately misunderstanding his pleas. In a moment of despair, Patrick asks Walid to interrogate him as a last resort to proving his innocence. But Walid's reply is to tell his assistant, in Arabic, to tell Patrick that they will bring him a chicken sandwich and mandarins, after which Patrick breaks down upon hearing the French translation. Only at the very end of the film do we find out that Walid speaks fluent French.

As Tasker argues, '[in] conceptualizing the relationship between masculinity and power the ability to speak is fundamental. Securing a position to speak from is crucial in order to invest the voice with authority'.[21] The ability to speak (or to decide which language to speak in) distinguishes the militiamen in Baghdadi's films from silent, mysterious heroes.[22] Their speech is peppered with expletives, with this use of language indicating an 'assertion of dominance'[23] that carries 'connotations of strength, masculinity and confidence'.[24] The use of extreme forms of slang also serves to establish the militiamen as challengers to traditional forms of authority, and to distinguish each set of militiamen as being 'part of a shared linguistic code, reinforcing group membership'.[25] Expletives are also used to refer to the 'enemy'. The enemy is therefore demonized, which justifies acts of terror against him.[26] He is also dehumanized. As Kaplan argues:

> military logic works to accomplish its missions through a process of dehumanization. The enemy is depersonalized and objectified – as a target to be hit or as an obstacle to be dealt with. Focusing on the technical, machine-like performance of military action against the enemy reduces that human aspect of another man's death.[27]

Ultimately, the representation of violence towards the Other shows men usurped by the power the war has granted them, but also tells us something about their own victimization by the war. As Baudrillard argues:

> These scenes are the illustration of a power which, reaching its extreme point, no longer knows what to do with itself – a power henceforth without aim, without purpose, without a plausible enemy, and in total impunity. It is only capable of inflicting gratuitous humiliation and, as one knows, violence inflicted on others is after all only an expression of the violence inflicted on oneself.[28]

War as Performance

War is presented as a space for the performance of masculinity. In *In the Battlefields*, we see two teenage militiamen smoking marijuana and chatting to another man, Marwan. One of the militiamen says, 'last week, we burned some of the bastards. There were some foreigners amongst them. They're so fucking huge they'd pluck your heart out'. Marwan sarcastically responds, 'I've been told they found some strange footprints down there, so fucking huge!' The militiman answers seriously: 'If I'd seen them, I would have beaten the shit out of them'. Marwan continues his sarcasm: 'I would have beaten the fuck out of their whole family'. The film therefore mocks the construction of a macho Self by the militiamen. This is emphasized as Marwan finishes the conversation only to start French kissing his girlfriend. All the teenage militiamen can do in response is to stare.

The affinity between man and machine transforms violence into an erotic fantasy and a celebration. Men in all three Baghdadi films pose with their guns as if they are trophies, and derive erotic ecstasy from combat.[29] In *Outside Life*, Frankenstein dances as he recites 'rah tidbuk!' (literally, 'it will start pounding', meaning the fighting will start). Likewise, Hassan, the chief militiamen in *Land of Honey and Incense*, announces to one of the French doctors, 'we're going to get high on the smell of gunpowder. Badda tidbuk!' Sometimes the eroticism of the war is more literal. This is seen in the film's references to women. As Donald argues:

> [i]n most war films, men relegate women to three basic roles: mothers to revere and respect, chattel to acquire and use legally in marriage or illegally via rape and pillage, or whores to provide temporary satisfaction while the men are away from home. In each case, women are clearly the 'out-group', a separate entity men find distracting to the task at hand, but a commodity to think, dream, and make plans about.[30]

Land of Honey and Incense

Little Wars presents this point through a conversation between Nabil and Soraya, whom he tries to seduce. Showing her pictures of militiamen posing with guns, Nabil comments to Soraya, 'See? They are all fake. They all just want to show off in front of their girlfriends'. Later in the film, Nabil's statement is confirmed as Soraya chats with a female friend of hers. As she brushes her hair, Soraya's friend dreamily tells her that she missed out on a photo shoot that day when Soraya was away: 'there were so many good looking fighters'. *Land of Honey and Incense* also references a similar role played by women. We see Hassan speeding along an unpaved road in an orange car. The car skids along the road as dust is blown up in the air. The scene cuts to a shot of a group of women smiling and clapping at Hassan's 'performance' in appreciation, and the camera cuts back to Hassan as he emerges from the car to further applause. The war becomes an erotically-driven spectacle of men and machines.

Baghdadi uses references to the media to emphasize this performative aspect of the war. Having studied political science at university, Baghdadi worked in journalism before entering the domain of cinema. Baghdadi's journalistic eye never left his cinematic work, and he often went further in emphasizing this synergy through films that contain overt references to the role of the media in mediating the Civil War. The three films stand out in their use of this relationship between the camera and the war. In *Little Wars*, we see a group of American journalists standing in front of a bombed building with a group of militiamen, arguing whether they got a good shot of a sniper positioned in the building opposite. As one journalist says he needs more people on the street to make the photograph more 'credible', the Lebanese photographer, Nabil, becomes frustrated with him, and shouts 'if he wants shooting, I'll give him shooting!' Nabil runs across the street to the other side of the road, crossing through the sniper's firing range. Nabil zigzags and almost dances as he dodges the sniper's bullets while he crosses. The journalists and militiamen cheer when he arrives at the other side. He crosses back in the same way, and the camera shows us the appreciating journalists photographing Nabil's escapade.

Later, we witness the journalists interviewing one of the militiamen. When he answers a question on the logistics of a battle his militia engaged in with the opposing side by saying 'can we not talk a bit about the political motive behind the battle and that our fight is democratic?', Nabil interrupts and says that the journalists 'don't want a lecture, they want action'. The scene then cuts to a shot of Nabil directing a group of six militiamen in green uniforms as he takes their photo. Mockingly calling one of them 'Guevara', Nabil lifts the tip of another militiaman's rifle to enhance the pose for the photograph. As he cries out 'photograph!', the men point their guns forwards, with the man in the middle smiling broadly as he creates a victory sign with his left hand, his rifle in the other. Later in the film, the American journalist is shown filming a report on a kidnapped man. After a false start, he orders the militia to 'take it from the top'. The journalist talks to the camera: 'In two minutes this man will be killed unless he is exchanged with a kidnapped victim from the other side'. His assistant, who is carrying the microphone, goes over to where a man holds a gun to the head of a blindfolded person. Soraya, translating from English to Arabic, tells the man with the gun, 'speak', and he goes on to say 'this man, we've kidnapped him. We'll kill him unless they release my brother', after which he cocks his gun. Soraya refuses to translate the statement into English. The journalist becomes furious and starts shouting like a director at the set of a film scene: 'Cut, cut, this is not good'. *Little Wars* here hints at the way the performance of the war was further played out for the Western gaze. This Western way of seeing the war is criticized for focusing on the spectacle without analysis or true understanding. Sensationalism, action, and the death and brutality of Others: that is what is sought, what sells and what matters. History is reduced to a series of spectacular images. The media become a machine that itself produces this spectacle.

Outside Life also highlights the mediated nature of the war through the depiction of photo-journalists who are shown as cannibalizing the scenes of destruction around them. All aspects of the war are shown to be open to media scrutiny: even death ceases to be a private affair. Journalists are first shown taking photos of released detainees as they first encounter their families. Their cameras focus on a woman wailing for her son who was not among the men as she carries a Quran in her hand. The photographers are then shown shooting helicopters landing and picking up militiamen, as well as photographing people carrying the dead and the injured at a bomb site. A French journalist goes as far as riding in a car where a woman sits cradling a wounded person, directing his camera at her, and then photographing a man being shot by a militiaman. Horrific acts of violence are played out for the camera. We see a photographer shooting the scene of a man tied to a car by his legs who is dragged on the ground as the car drives around a group of cheering militiamen. After the militia raids a building, we see the body of a dead man hanging upside down inside the building as the French photographer Patrick enters the site. A militiaman urges Patrick to take a photo of the scene. Patrick takes the photo, but then throws the camera film on the floor in disgust. Death therefore becomes a game; playing it becomes proof of one's masculine standing. And the war itself becomes almost surreal, its acts of terror played out like film scenes – a point made more poignant through Baghdadi's self-awareness as a filmmaker: the war is like a film within his films.

Masculinity as Performance

In commenting on war as a performance, Baghdadi's films follow the tradition of Hollywood action films and Westerns, where violence is a masculine spectacle. In discussing the Western genre and its relationship to masculinity, Warshaw says:

> it is not violence at all which is the 'point' of the Western movie, but a certain image of man, a style, which expresses itself most clearly in violence. Watch a child with his toy gun and you will see: what most interests him is not (as we so much fear) the fantasy of hurting others, but to work out how a man might look when he shoots if shot. A hero is one who looks like a hero.[31]

Warshaw's last sentence can be perfectly linked to the character De Niro in *Outside Life*, a disturbed and disturbing character who symbolizes the war victims' search for themselves. As Patrick lies on the floor in the dark in his cell, a man enters the room. A high-angle shot makes the man dominate the screen. 'Are you sick?', we hear him address Patrick in American English. Patrick replies in French, 'I'm cold'.

> De Niro: *You speak English, don't you?*
> Patrick: *I'm cold* [in English].
> De Niro: *You know why I speak English? Because I've been living in the States. For five years. I was an actor.*

VIOLENCE AND MASCULINITY

Patrick: *Fantastic...*
De Niro: *Yeah, man! De Niro! You know Bobby De Niro? I was his bodyguard. Look.*

The man proceeds to recreate the scene from *Taxi Driver* where Travis talks to himself in the mirror. Turning his back on Patrick, De Niro, bearded and wearing a Hawaiian print shirt, twists to the right to face Patrick. 'You're talking to me?' He points a finger at himself. 'Are you talking to me? But who the hell else are you talking to? Are you talking to me? But I am the only one here!' He drags his pistol and points it at Patrick. 'But who the fuck you think you're talking to? Oh yeah?' De Niro places the tip of his gun under Patrick's nose. 'Shit head!'

By re-presenting the scene, Baghdadi creates different levels of signification. On one level is the direct reference to the character of Travis Bickle, where film images act as icons of virility to be emulated.[32] As Page writes about the scene:

> [i]n addressing himself in the mirror Travis Bickle is asserting, questioning and reshaping his identity and masculinity. He wants to be hard ... Travis Bickle's words reinforce the make-believe image which he is presenting to himself. He combines his loneliness and his crucified maleness into a play-acting performance that connotes an obsessive and narcissistic fixation. The gunslinger/tough cop pose, drawing on movie imagery, is both text and test of his will to act. He becomes his own pin-up. The mirror image presents Travis as both his own antagonist and as his ideal other. Although he is on his own in the room, Travis is not alone in his imagination because he shapes both

Outside Life

images which are under his control and gaze. Each image reinforces the other and they become the identity that he desires to realize, the image that he desires others to see and recognize. However, whilst the mirror serves to complete him, it also divides him. His identity is split, his 'real me' is fractured.[33]

On another level, the scene in *Outside Life* references the 'obsession [of Scorsese's characters] with performance as a way of defining their identities'.[34] Page writes:

> Scorsese's male protagonists have much in common. They combine restless energy with a penchant for violence. They hurt themselves and others in their obsessive need to perform and to be recognized as somebodies. As Peachment states 'they are all marked down by the overbearing hunger for celebrity'.[35]

Both Travis and Baghdadi's De Niro are

> violent men and frightened little boys. They are beset by anxieties. Their fears are nurtured within their imaginations. In acting out their desires they perform within a structure of violence and obsession. Both characters are prepared to relinquish self-control to satisfy their need to dominate, even if it is at the cost of their humanity. They are trapped in a state of maleness that is neither stable nor desired.[36]

Outside Life therefore presents a masculinity that is grotesquely disturbing.[37] De Niro continues performing his exalted identity as he leads Patrick out of the building and onto the front line. They reach a wall of sandbags. He addresses Patrick: 'Don't listen to the devil ... He tells you: Take a horse, move the barrier and run! Don't do it, man! Don't! I'm here to protect you from yourself'. De Niro pushes Patrick forwards: 'Go! Go! Go! Go! Go! Go man! Go! You know where we are? On the front line!' In a surreal scene, De Niro grabs a white horse and directs it at the street that lies beyond the sandbags. It is promptly shot dead by a sniper. As the dead horse's legs go up in the air as it falls down, De Niro continues his movie speech, smiling manically as Patrick collapses with horror: 'This is Lebanon, man! Don't trust your eyes ... Things are never the way they look! There's always a snake behind the rock!' In a scene that shortly follows, we see De Niro adopting the identity of another film character. This time, he performs karate movements down the corridor as he heads to the room where Patrick is sitting on the floor blindfolded. 'You know karate?' 'I know what?' 'Karate. Come on, man. Get up. Let's have some action'. De Niro starts hitting Patrick provocatively, asking him to hit him back. Despite Patrick's protests that he cannot see, he is forced to punch aimlessly in front of him, until he desperately declares defeat. 'OK. You won! You're the strongest'.

This grotesque performance of masculinity is also seen in the character Frankenstein. The *nom de guerre* of the character is an obvious reference to a non-human monster. Frankenstein, like De Niro, is a hallucinating character to whom violence is an amusing game. A scene in which this is played out shows Patrick led down the corridor outside his cell, and struck by Frankenstein's sudden appearance and manic laugh. In this sense Baghdadi references Hitchcock's use of terrifying characters who appear on the screen out of nowhere (such as in *Rebecca*). Frankenstein proceeds to follow Patrick down the corridor, shooting at him with a pellet gun. Frankenstein's performance only ends with his death. Black and white posters bearing his image are created, and Frankenstein's humanity is restored. He is no longer Frankenstein, but Ahmad once again. Only in his death is the war over for him. Only in his death can he escape war's dehumanization. Baghdadi further emphasizes this by introducing us to Ahmad's sister towards the end of the film. She cries over him when she finds about his death, collapsing with grief.

Death of Masculinity

Patrick's masculinity is eliminated in the face of that of his captors. In this sense, violence is presented in the film as an element of hegemonic masculinity. Hegemonic masculinity is usually constructed with respect to women. It is

> the ideology that justifies and naturalizes male domination. As such, it is the ideology of patriarchy. Masculinism takes it for granted that there is a fundamental difference between men and women, it assumes that heterosexuality is normal, it accepts without question the sexual division of labour, and it sanctions the political and dominant role of men in the public and private spheres.[38]

However, what is more pertinent in the construction of hegemonic masculinity, and its representation in Baghdadi's films, is its relationship with other masculinities. As R.W. Connell argues, '[w]e must also recognize the *relations* between the different kinds of masculinity: relations of alliance, dominance and subordination. These relationships are constructed through practices that exclude and include, that intimidate, exploit, and so on. There is a gender politics within masculinity'.[39] Therefore, what is of relevance here is how hegemonic masculinity is defined as 'a particular idealized image of masculinity in relation to which images of femininity and other masculinities are marginalized and subordinated'.[40]

In *Outside Life*, as well as in *Land of Honey and Incense*, hegemonic masculinity is played out through the feminization of the Other.[41] In a scene in *Land of Honey and Incense*, the Muslim militia chief Hassan takes the French doctor Fournier to the front line. Hassan uses a loudspeaker to taunt a Christian militiaman, Joseph, who is positioned on the other side of a high mud wall separating the two zones. In a high-pitched voice mocking Joseph's sexuality, Hassan shouts: 'Zouzou! Where are you, Zouzou? Why aren't you answering? You are proud that you carry a rifle, Zouzou? It doesn't suit you'. As Joseph replies, 'Go to hell', Hassan continues, 'In three or four days we will attack you and destroy the hell out of you'. In this sense, Hassan's character follows the way 'movies have defined manliness in terms of getting the "enemy" before he gets you'.[42] Joseph's subsequent silence establishes Hassan as the alpha male.

Frankenstein in *Outside Life* suddenly asks Patrick if he wants anything: 'You don't want anything. You are also handsome, rosy and cute and you have hair like a woman's'. Patrick recoils as Frankenstein tries to touch his hair. Patrick wonders if Frankenstein is homosexual, which horrifies Ali, Frankenstein's fellow militiaman. 'No, he is a fierce fighter'. So it seems only suitable that when Patrick is finally released at the end of the film, he is made to dress as a woman. Patrick is given a black chador that covers his whole body and head except for his eyes. The last scene of Patrick in Lebanon is a wide shot of him running on the beach, his chador flapping in the wind.

Little Wars also depicts the figure of the emasculated male through the character Nabil. The difference between Nabil on the one hand, and Patrick and Joseph on the other, is that Nabil is not presented as a defined enemy. His character is used to show how the war results in a crisis of masculinity as men lose control of their lives. Viewed in the context of the film as a whole, Nabil's masculinity is contradictory. On one hand, he dwells on performing ultramasculine roles in front of the camera. On the other hand, he slowly recognizes his weakness in the war environment. We see Nabil transform from a macho impersonator into being symbolically impotent. During his first interaction with Soraya, he plays the role of macho protector. As he shows her some of his photos, he narrates stories of real and imagined near-death experiences and of evading bullets. When they leave his apartment and enter the hall of her building, he comes closer to Soraya to 'shelter' her from an imaginary explosion. Later in the film, Nabil calls Soraya from a bar, but pretends to be at the front line. He asks his friend to fire a round of bullets in the air as he says to Soraya 'it's quite tense over here. Listen!' Nabil's delusion reaches its peak when Soraya asks him to help her kidnap a man. Having presented himself to her as a fearless fighter, he finds himself going through with the kidnapping as if it is another fragment of his imagination.

Nabil's engagement in the war slowly leads to his decline. His involvement in a drug deal that goes wrong transforms him from a performing macho man into an emasculated one. He can no longer appeal to Soraya through bravado alone, so he resorts to victimization as a way of attracting her by generating sympathy for himself. After causing a fight in a bar, Nabil runs to Soraya's apartment and tells her that 'they' want to kill him. The figure of the mysterious threatening 'they' was common during the Civil War. Baghdadi recreates this paranoia to emphasize its deep impact on the Lebanese psyche, where the word 'they' serves as a blank space on which the fear of multiple Others is projected. 'They' is in the eye of the beholder. Sitting next to Soraya, Nabil invents a story where he casts himself in the role of the renegade hero. 'There was a suicide attack against me ... five or six men tried to attack me. Check if there is anyone downstairs. Have you closed the door? It's a political conflict that they are trying to entangle me in'. He puts his hand on Soraya's thigh as he says this, and she tells him to remove it. Nabil tries again by clutching Soraya's shoulder as he reacts to the sound of her elderly, blind uncle suddenly walking through the apartment, oblivious to Nabil's presence, by pointing his gun at him. Soraya in turn reacts by laughing at Nabil, and gets up from the sofa. The camera focuses on Nabil's gun as his grip on it weakens, and the gun is lowered gradually in his hand until it is completely flaccid.

Here Baghdadi makes a more overt statement about guns being a representation of the penis. The gun is also a prop hinting at the potential carrying out of violence, where such a performance is a means of asserting a masculinity under threat. As Clark Mitchell argues:

> Violence ... is less a means than an end in itself – less a matter of violating another than of constituting one's physical self as a male. The purpose is less defeat or destruction than (once again) display. And if this celebration of violence confirms it as a masculine emotional prerogative (that is, as an activity released and controlled by men), it does so by putting the male body distinctively on show ... allowing us to gaze at masculinity in action.[43]

Nabil's failure to use the gun as such a prop is symbolic of the evolution of his character within the film, but also of Baghdadi's characters across the three films. As the context of the war deteriorates, the masculinities come under further threat.

Another example of a man broken down by the war is found in *The Belt of Fire*. The film shows Shafik encountering different examples of war madness that end up in him losing his mind. Shafik tolerates living without necessities like water or electricity. He puts up with Abdo's harassing him for money. Shafik learns to cope with staring into empty desks at the university as his students abandon their classes to join the militias. The militias themselves also impose on Shafik, constantly stopping him at a checkpoint near his house as he drives his car to check his papers. The war even intrudes on Shafik's fantasies. As he sits on a rocking chair in the dark on his balcony, fantasizing about a girl, his daydream is interrupted by the start of shelling. As Shafik goes to his bedroom, bullets penetrate the door. Shafik's descent into breakdown intensifies as he encounters another hysterical character. As he gets into a shared taxi, a female passenger glances at him and manically accuses him of killing her son, saying that he is going to pay. Shafik gets out of the car, and arrives home only to find that the building's new gate is locked. Referring to Abdo's latest scheme to accost money from the building residents, Abdo informs him that 'only those who paid get a key'. The film ends with Shafik's complete breakdown as he arrives at where the checkpoint usually is, but finds that it is not there any more. Shafik is filmed in a high-angle shot, screaming that he will not move until the militiamen examine his papers. He only stops screaming when an elderly man living nearby feels sorry for him and offers to 'be' the checkpoint. The man checks Shafik's papers, and then goes back to playing backgammon as if nothing happened.

Conclusion

Brittan argues:

> The main actors in history were men, they were the conquerors, the explorers, the soldiers, the statesmen, the inventors ... The writing of history has been a privileged male activity ... History, from this perspective, is the history of warfare.[44]

He goes on to say that '[m]en have not only written history, they have appeared in it as the authors of atrocity and massacre'.[45] Lebanese cinema – and Baghdadi's films in particular – revolves around the stories of such 'authors'. The Civil War is shown as being fought by men in a masculine arena.

However, Baghdadi's films complicate the representation of men and masculinity on the screen. They use elements of Hollywood films, namely Westerns and war films, to present masculinity as a spectacle. But they push the parameters of representation beyond that as they depict the male caught in a liminal space outside heroism and villainess. Masculinity in the films is in crisis, but this is far from the crisis of masculinity that is based on modern life's threat of emasculation. The crisis is not about men losing their social standing as women become more emancipated. Here, the crisis is political. In all three films, the male body is highlighted as 'a site of political conflict, and a limit point at which ideological oppositions collapse ... the body is invested and colonized by power mechanisms ... it is both a means and an end of social control'.[46] The stories of men, whether as victims or victimizers, act as a reflection of the cruelty of the war. The violence inflicted by men on each other highlights the way the war dehumanized the Other as well as the Self.

Endnotes

1. Donald, Ralph R. (2001). 'Masculinity and machismo in Hollywood's war films', in Whitehead, Stephen and Frank J. Barrett (eds), *The Masculinities Reader*, Cambridge: Polity Press, p.172.
2. Kimmel, Michael S. (2001). 'Masculinity as homophobia: fear, shame, and silence in the construction of gender identity', in Whitehead, Stephen and Frank J. Barrett (eds), *The Masculinities Reader*, Cambridge: Polity Press, p.278.
3. Connell, R.W. (2001). 'The social organization of masculinity', in Whitehead, Stephen and Frank J. Barrett (eds), *The Masculinities Reader*, Cambridge, Polity Press, p.44.
4. Peteet, Julie (2000). 'Male gender and rituals of resistance in the Palestinian intifada: a cultural politics of violence', in Ghoussoub, Mai and Emma Sinclair-Webb (eds), *Imagined Masculinities: Male Identity and Culture in the Modern Middle East*, London: Saqi Books, p.105.
5. Tasker, Yvonne (1993). 'Dumb movies for dumb people: masculinity, the body, and the voice in contemporary action cinema', in Cohan, Steven and Ina Rae Hark (eds), *Screening the Male: Exploring Masculinities in Hollywood Cinema*, London: Routledge, p.230.
6. Jeffords, Susan (1993). 'Can masculinity be terminated?', in Cohan, Steven and Ina Rae Hark (eds), *Screening the Male: Exploring Masculinities in Hollywood Cinema*, London: Routledge, p.245.
7. Neale, Steve (1993). 'Prologue: masculinity as spectacle: reflections on men and mainstream cinema', in Cohan, Steven and Ina Rae Hark (eds), *Screening the Male: Exploring Masculinities in Hollywood Cinema*, London: Routledge, p.18.
8. Donald: 'Masculinity and machismo'.
9. Newsinger, John (1993). ' "Do you walk the walk?": aspects of masculinity in some Vietnam war films', in Kirkham, Pat and Janet Thumim (eds), *You Tarzan: Masculinity, Movies and Men*, London: Lawrence and Wishart, p.126.
10. Mellen, Joan (1978). *Big Bad Wolves: Masculinity in the American Film*, London: Elm Tree, p.11.
11. Daoud, Hassan (2003). 'The final scene in the cinema of life', *BabelMed* [Online]. Available: http://www.babelmed.net/index.php?menu=162&cont=534&lingua=en
12. Soueid, Mohamad (1992). 'Maroun Baghdadi', *An-Nahar newspaper supplement*, 5 September.

13 Newsinger: 'Do you walk the walk?', p.126.
14 Armitage, John (2003). 'Militarized bodies: an introduction', *Body & Society*, 9(4), p.1.
15 Al-Ariss, Ibrahim (2000). 'A look into Lebanese war cinema on the Civil War's twenty-fifth anniversary', *Al-Hayat*, April 14 (Arabic).
16 Salibi, Kamal (2005). *A House of Many Mansions: The History of Lebanon Reconsidered*, London: I.B.Tauris, p.193.
17 Kennedy-Day, Kiki (2001). 'Cinema in Lebanon, Syria, Iraq and Kuwait', in Leaman, Oliver (ed), *Companion Encyclopedia of Middle Eastern and North African Film*, London: Routledge, p.369.
18 Baghdadi, Maroun (1993). 'Republished 1992 interview with Mohamad Soueid', *An-Nahar*, December 18.
19 Baghdadi, Maroun (1992). 'Interview with Mohamad Soueid', *An-Nahar*, September 5.
20 Khatib, Lina (2006). *Filming the Modern Middle East: Politics in the Cinemas of Hollywood and the Arab World*, London: I.B.Tauris.
21 Tasker: 'Dumb movies for dumb people', p.238.
22 Clark Mitchell, Lee (1996). *Westerns: Making the Man in Fiction and Film*, London: University of Chicago Press.
23 De Klerk, Vivian (1997). 'The role of expletives in the construction of masculinity', in Johnson, Sally and Ulrika Hanna Meinhof (eds), *Language and Masculinity*, London: Blackwell, p.145.
24 De Klerk: 'The role of expletives', p.147.
25 Ibid.
26 Kaplan, Danny (2000). 'The military as a second Bar Mitzvah: combat service as initiation to Zionist masculinity', in Ghoussoub, Mai and Emma Sinclair-Webb (eds), *Imagined Masculinities: Male Identity and Culture in the Modern Middle East*, London: Saqi Books, pp.127–46.
27 Kaplan: 'The military as a second Bar Mitzvah', p.133.
28 Baudrillard, Jean (2006). 'War porn', *Journal of Visual Culture*, 5(1), p.86.
29 Barrett, Frank J. (2001). 'The organizational construction of hegemonic masculinity: the case of the US Navy', in Whitehead, Stephen and Frank J. Barrett (eds), *The Masculinities Reader*, Cambridge, Polity Press, pp.77–99.
30 Donald: 'Masculinity and machismo', p.175.
31 Warshaw, Robert (1962). *The Immediate Experience: Movies, Comics, Theater and Other Aspects of Popular Culture*, Garden City, New York: Doubleday, pp.151–2.
32 Cohan, Steven (1997). *Masked Men: Masculinity and the Movies in the Fifties*, Bloomington: Indiana University Press.
33 Page, Ken (1993). 'Going solo: performance and identity in *New York, New York* and *Taxi Driver*', in Kirkham, Pat and Janet Thumim (eds), *You Tarzan: Masculinity, Movies and Men*, London: Lawrence and Wishart, pp.142–3.
34 Page: 'Going solo', p.137.
35 Ibid.
36 Page: 'Going solo', p.143.
37 Page: 'Going solo'.
38 Brittan, Arthur (1989). *Masculinity and Power*, Oxford: Basil Blackwell, p.4.

39 Connell, R.W. (1995). *Masculinities*, Oxford: Polity Press, p.37.
40 Barrett: 'The organizational construction of hegemonic masculinity', p.79.
41 Barrett: 'The organizational construction of hegemonic masculinity'.
42 Mellen: *Big Bad Wolves*, p.11.
43 Clark Mitchell: *Westerns*, p.169.
44 Brittan, *Masculinity and Power*, p.80.
45 Brittan, *Masculinity and Power*, p.81.
46 Shaviro, Steven (1993). *The Cinematic Body*, Minneapolis: University of Minnesota Press, p.134.

Chapter Six

MOTHERS, FIGHTERS AND TABOO BREAKERS

As presented in the previous chapter, the main roles in Lebanese war films are given to men. But women were at the heart of the conflict. The war seemed to be orchestrated by men, but women both bore its impact and took part in its operation. Lebanese cinema however has generally chosen to ignore the role of women as active agents in the Civil War. Films such as *Letter from a Time of Exile* and *Outside Life* present the war as a masculine arena. Women in those films are relegated to the position of victims, or are not there at all. I asked Borhan Alawiyeh, the director of *Letter from a Time of Exile*, why his film does not include a single female character. His reply was that he could not imagine the experiences of women.[1] In other words, this dominant representation of women as passive or silent is supplemented by a marginal reference to the role of women as active agents in combat. Although women did take part in military activities during the Civil War and in context of the conflict with Israel, Lebanese cinema largely shies away from representing women in such roles. The only exceptions are Roger Assaf's film *Ma'raka* (1985), which represents the civil resistance of women against Israel in the South of Lebanon, and Leyla Assaf's (no relation) film *Martyrs* (1988), which is the only Lebanese film representing a woman in a combat role, although again this role is within the context of anti-Israeli resistance. Perhaps the most interesting representation of women, however, is that of films like *Little Wars*, *The Civilized*, *West Beyrouth*, and to a lesser extent, *In the Battlefields*. Those films present female characters outside the victimhood/resistance binary. What they show instead are women who reveal the social taboos of wartime Lebanese society.

Victims and Peacekeepers

Traditionally, war is conceived of as a masculine arena, or a male activity that is associated with masculine traits.[2] War stories are full of male fighters whose relationship to women is reduced to either victimizers or protectors. Men are presented as the builders of a nation and its defenders. War creates a male sphere where separation from females becomes a condition for male fraternity.[3] Women in this context are either essentialized or idealized. The first constructs them as weak, subjected to the horrors of war that culminate in rape by male aggressors, or in witnessing the death of their children helplessly. The second sees them in their roles as devoted mothers or wives. Both tropes construct their identity only in relation to that of men. Or they are romanticized as peacekeepers; Morokvasic quotes Virginia Woolf as saying 'scarcely a human being in the course of history has fallen to a woman's rifle'.[4] In all cases, the dominant imagery of women in this traditional discourse is of being on the margin, of being silent, their experiences rendered 'unimportant' compared to the stories of men.[5] Lebanese cinema presents examples merging all three tropes, where women are characterized by their helplessness.

Anthias and Yuval-Davis argue that citizenship constructs men and women differently. They state five ways in which women participate in national processes. First, women are constructed as biological reproducers of members of an ethnic group. Second, they are constructed as reproducers of boundaries of ethnic or national groups. This has necessitated the establishment of codes determining women's acceptable sexual behavior, limiting this behavior within the group. Third, they are ideological reproducers of collectivity and transmitters of culture. Fourth, they signify national difference, and therefore act as symbols in ideological discourses used in the construction, reproduction, and transformation of the nation. And finally, women are constructed as participants in national, economic, political and military struggles.[6]

In the latter case, often the participation of women is passive rather than active, so that 'women... become the battleground of [national] group struggles'.[7] This is represented in a number of Lebanese films where women, namely in their roles as mothers and wives, are constructed as observers and victims of the war. An early example of this representation is found in the film *The Shelter* (1980). The first time we see women in the film is through a shot of two families listening to the news on the radio in an underground shelter. A young man, As'ad, gets up and states that it is his turn to fetch water. When a fellow young man, Hanna, tries to contest that, Hanna's mother tries to dissuade him from going, fearing for his life. Oum Hanna (Hanna's mother) then turns to the other woman in the shelter, who expresses her concern about her husband, Ibrahim, who is supposed to return from Kuwait that day. Thus, the film establishes the role of the two mothers as nurturing the men. The men in turn are the active participants. The film maintains this dichotomy after Ibrahim's and As'ad's return. When the men decide to take on their neighborhood's sniper, the women stay indoors in the shelter. Joined by As'ad's wife, Jamilah, we see the men leaving the shelter as the three women hug one another, concerned about them. The shelter's only access to sunlight is

The Shelter

through a street-level window covered in wrought iron. The camera often shows us the women looking out the window, behind the wrought iron, observing events happening outside.

The only two times the women participate in those events, they do so as victims. The first such time happens as Jamilah arrives in the neighborhood. As the street outside the shelter is controlled by a sniper, she is unable to cross the road to join her husband. Jamilah is urged by Ibrahim to cross quickly, but as she attempts to do so she stumbles and falls to the ground. The film here presents an extended scene of Jamilah, frozen with fear. As she lies on the muddy ground, with her head down, the camera zooms on her face as she sobs and tries to get up in vain. The camera lingers as Jamilah is forced to crawl to get to the shelter, and is eventually shot by the sniper. The film emphasizes Jamilah's victimization through cutting her crawling scene to one of her husband As'ad watching her through the wrought iron. We see a close-up of As'ad smiling and saying how happy he is now that Jamilah cannot control him any longer. When Jamilah finally reaches the shelter, As'ad makes fun of the way the sniper's bullet landed in her bottom, saying the sniper must have aimed it there deliberately. He reprimands Jamilah for leaving their children behind with her mother, and she in turn reprimands him for leaving her and the children behind. Jamilah can therefore be seen as a victim of both the war and patriarchy.

The second incident of female participation in events outside the shelter occurs towards the end of the film, after the men finish their mission to kill the sniper. Although they succeed in killing him, the men are chased by the sniper's fellow militiamen who shoot one of them – Mahmoud – dead, injure Ibrahim, and shoot As'ad. The women witness As'ad falling onto the ground from the window, and the camera again zooms on their faces as they cry, sigh and scream. Oum Hanna decides to go out to collect As'ad, and like Jamilah, she is forced to crawl on the ground in an attempt to avoid being shot. However, both she and As'ad are shot dead as soon as she reaches him, and the film ends with both their bodies lying on the muddy ground. The wrought iron of the window becomes a defining element in the role of the women: the only woman who survives unscathed is Ibrahim's wife, who stays behind the wrought iron, thereby not crossing her assigned boundary.

Two more examples of female victims are found in *The Belt of Fire* and *In the Battlefields*. The first introduces us to Amal, a university professor. Amal is a disturbed woman who keeps on scratching her skin, proclaiming that she has caught 'the belt of fire, a disease that burns the skin and causes extreme pain'. Amal says that she is not crazy, but that the disease caused her to 'stop shaking hands because I don't trust anyone anymore'. *In the Battlefields* presents another example of female victimization in the character of Thérèse, the mother. The film parallels *The Shelter* in its linking of war and patriarchy, but presents this duality in a much more sophisticated manner: the film's focus on internal conflict within a family mirrors the external conflict of the Civil War. Our first introduction to Thérèse – heavily pregnant – is when she asks her daughter Lina to go fetch the priest. Thérèse sits silently as the priest reprimands her husband Fouad for gambling, asking him to swear on the Virgin Mary and his daughter's life that he would stop. Fouad responds by storming out. Thérèse's helplessness is here established, and is later confirmed when Fouad's debtors come to her house looking for him and demanding money. Fouad again responds by leaving, and all Thérèse can do is sit by the window, crying, and holding her stomach. When Fouad returns, he removes a rug from the floor, rolls it and tries to take it outside to sell it. Thérèse stands at the front door, and tries to block his way. He ignores her, and in frustration, she starts throwing ashtrays and other glass objects on the floor in the living room, shouting that she cannot take it anymore. The next shot shows Thérèse packing, having decided to leave.

Although Thérèse does leave, we see her with Fouad a little while later in the film. By choosing not to announce Thérèse's return, Arbid presents her quiet, even silent, arrival as a strong symbol of her helplessness. She is now confirmed as someone who has no control over her life, or her destiny. She has no choice, and no voice. This is emphasized in a sequence where a dog is tied up by militiamen to the railings of the front door of the building where Thérèse and Fouad live. The dog's pain causes it to bark and whine during the night, and Fouad's outrage leads him to come downstairs to shoot the dog, ignoring Thérèse's pleas not to do it. The camera only shows us Thérèse in the background as Fouad shoots the dog in the head. The next day, we see Thérèse trying to calm down the militant owners of the dog who had come to her house looking for Fouad. After the men leave, we see Thérèse standing by the window. As in *The Shelter*, the window is blocked by iron bars. Thérèse stands with her eyes downcast. The scene is almost overexposed as it is flooded by white light. This white light, along with the window's white bars and Thérèse's pale clothes, work well to emphasize Thérèse's paleness and vulnerability.

The climax of Thérèse's helplessness arrives at the end of the film. We see Fouad leaving a gambling table at a café without paying. He is followed by his fellow gamblers and beaten. We later find out that Fouad is killed. At Fouad's funeral, we see Thérèse shrouded in black, crying silently over the situation his death has put her in. Women are heard talking about Thérèse, whispering 'look at her, poor woman. She is pregnant'. What is interesting about the construction of the character Thérèse is that she is rarely referred to by her first name in the film. Only once do we hear Fouad's sister Yvonne pronounce her name. The rest of the time, she is referred to as either 'his wife' or 'your mother', the latter being whenever Fouad talks to his daughter Lina about Thérèse. In one scene, Fouad tries to snatch Lina's grandmother's ring from his daughter's hand in order to sell it. When Lina tries to prevent him, hitting him in the process, his response is 'you're becoming just like your mother'.

Even women's involvement in violence is often constructed through their victimization. In *Little Wars*, Soraya is a character linking the stories of Talal and Nabil, being the object of their affection. However, unlike the two men, she starts off in the film as a detached observer. We see Soraya riding in a car and witnessing a group of men stopping another. Her driver comments that 'they probably had someone kidnapped, so they are kidnapping in return'. Soraya and the driver are soon stopped by militiamen who check the driver's ID card. All Soraya does is stare at the man at the checkpoint, who in turn stares back at her silently.

When Soraya reaches her house, where she meets Talal, her position as observer continues. We see them stand on her balcony, watching as militia jeeps roam the neighborhood. When she walks down the street with a friend the next day, she seems oblivious to the jeeps that casually pass by, and to the bombed buildings surrounding her. Later, a nighttime scene set outside Soraya's house shows a militiaman shooting at the letters of a neon sign spelling the word 'Thomson' until the letters T, H, O and M are gone. The camera cuts to a shot of Soraya looking on, smiling. She descends from her balcony and joins two militiamen in their jeep as they travel through Beirut at night. Soft, non-diegetic music is heard as Soraya rides in the jeep, surrounded by the city lights, as if riding in a fairground.

However, Soraya's detachment ends as soon as she finds out that she is pregnant with Talal's child. Her plan to leave Beirut is shattered as she tells Talal that she cannot leave without him. When she finds out about Talal's kidnapped father, she decides that the only way to resolve this problem (and therefore free Talal to leave the country with her) is by kidnapping a man herself to exchange with Talal's father. Soraya slowly starts learning the dynamics of the war. She approaches Salim to ask for advice.

> *Soraya: What if the father is dead?*
> *Salim: Then we'll have to get revenge.*
> *Soraya: From whom?*
> *Salim: It doesn't matter.*

Soraya proceeds with the kidnapping operation. Imagination and reality blur in an almost surreal sequence where we witness the kidnapping of the man. The sequence is set at the front line among the ruins of downtown Beirut. We first see a young child with one of Soraya's accomplices. He explains to Soraya and Nabil that he had to bring his son Maher with him as there is no one to look after him at home. As Maher plays with a football on the street, a mid-shot shows Soraya standing with a gun and stopping an unfortunate man in a car. She and Nabil, Maher and his father jump into the man's car. Soraya recreates the sequence in her head in a nightclub where they take the man. The kidnappers sway to the magical-sounding music, bathing in the club's red lights, as the kidnapped man stands alone, blindfolded. This merging of reality and fantasy serves to detach Soraya from the act of violence she had committed, and emphasizes her position as a victim whose fate is to participate in the war.

Women are also sometimes presented as peacekeepers who exist outside the war system. Roach Pierson argues that this kind of representation has led second-wave feminists to argue for the existence of separate spheres for males and females where women's position towards war was seen as distinct from that of men. She adds that this idea was based on women's exclusion from arenas of power and involvement in motherhood.[8] This argument is represented in the character of Talal's mother in *Little Wars*. When Talal acquires a gun for the first time to avenge his father, his mother reprimands him for training 'like thugs', accusing him of having no sense of responsibility. As Talal ignores his mother and leaves, the camera shows her through the door frame, looking small and slight. After Talal assembles his army of men, his mother is used to indicate his criminal actions. We hear his mother saying to him 'you have only been here a month and you have already orphaned five families'. Baghdadi later references a similar mother figure in the opening sequence of *Outside Life*. The first thing we see is what appears to be a Muslim funeral, with a crowd of men and veiled women carrying photos of young men high above their heads. The non-diegetic sound of the radio is heard announcing the number of the injured, dead, handicapped, missing, exiled and displaced during the war. The camera zooms in on some of the photos carried by the veiled women, and on the women's faces. The scene is then cut to a mid-shot revealing a group of soldiers standing in front of the crowd. A car stops and men emerge from it, and we realize that the scene is not a funeral, but the day of the release of some kidnapped men by militias. We see some of the women embracing the men who have been released, while others wail over the sons, husbands and brothers they had been waiting for but who have not returned. A woman cries over her missing son Khaled as she carries a Quran in her hand. Suddenly, militiamen arrive and round people up, forcing them to stand with their hands up against a wall. One man is made to kneel on the ground, his arms crossed behind his head. A man is heard saying 'this is Khaled's brother'. The mother comes closer and calls after one of the militiamen by name. 'Hussein! What are you doing my son?' She turns to the rest of the militiamen as she tries to disperse them: 'What are you doing, my children? I raised you to fear God. Go home, go to your mothers. What is this anger, God? Blood brings blood. Relieve us from this war'. The figure of the mother here – whether it is the mother we see on screen or the one invoked in 'go to your mothers' – is that of complete detachment from evil.

'Resistant' Women

Anthias and Yuval-Davis have argued that 'in national liberation struggles... generally [women] are seen to be in a supportive and nurturing relation to men even where they take most risks'.[9] This traditional role of women has been represented in Arab cinemas like those of Egypt and Palestine, and is reflected in the Lebanese film *Ma'raka* – a film about the Shiite resistance to the Israeli occupation of Southern Lebanon, set in the village Ma'raka. The men in the film are the main characters; they are the narrators of the story. But the film presents women who support the men in defying the enemy. We see a woman confronting a man known in the village as being a spy for Israel. He threatens her that the Israelis might arrest her son as a result, and she responds by throwing a stone at him. When Israeli soldiers raid a house looking for weapons, the mother confronts the soldiers, cursing them and telling them that her son is in the Ansar prison and that her husband is dead. When the soldiers ask the woman where the weapons are, she goes inside and brings a Quran, saying, 'this is our weapon'. The women are also presented as agents in the Adha Intifada, an incident where women marched towards the Israeli-run Ansar prison camp, where hundreds of Lebanese and Palestinian people were held and tortured by Israel in the village of Ansar in South Lebanon. The scene starts with women talking to television cameras about their oppression by Israel. An Israeli soldier tries to stop them from approaching a tank. The women persist and continue marching forwards towards the prison of Ansar, clashing with the soldiers outnumbering them. They push the soldiers back, and one woman manages to climb the hill overlooking the prison. The prisoners riot. When Israel invades the village, it is the women who are shown throwing stones, household objects and boiling water and oil at the Israeli soldiers. With this representation of low-key resistance, the women in Ma'raka become a symbol of the ability of the powerless to fight.[10]

Roach Pierson says that contemporary feminists have argued against the separation of roles of men and women in this context, and called for full equality between men and women both in and outside of battle, which led to the creation of a visible discourse on women's role as combatants fighting alongside (and sometimes without) men.[11] Leyla Assaf's film Martyrs is an illustration. The film's main character, Nadia, can be seen as an example of women who 'have broken through traditional prejudices to become fighters'.[12] The film's opening sequence presents a shock to the viewer as we see the image of a pretty young woman, in full makeup and military uniform, reciting a martyrdom statement on television, as her stunned parents watch the broadcast. The film then becomes a long flashback showing us how Nadia, an ordinary girl from the South of Lebanon who was forced to become a refugee in Beirut, became a 'martyr'.

The film is the only one commenting overtly on the engagement of Syria in conflict in Lebanon. It is also the only one where Lebanese cinema has represented the Syrian Social Nationalist Party and the issue of suicide operations in the South of Lebanon. Leyla Assaf says she chose to represent this party 'because it was the first to send young people to kill themselves in Lebanon. And they were stronger than the Communist party that followed them in such operations'.[13] Leyla Assaf chose to represent Nadia as a Christian

> because I wanted to show a phenomenon, how young people can be manipulated regardless of their origin (like Hitler used people, and Japan used the Kamikaze). I wanted to show that if there is a war, and there are people with no work, no money, no food – and Nadia's father is humiliated on top of everything else – it makes those young people vulnerable. She is a Christian to counter the stereotypes: to say this can happen in any country under the same circumstances; it's universal.[14]

Nadia's transformation into a 'martyr' is shown through a familiar method. Nadia undergoes a process of political awakening whereby her 'incorporation into the military body is achieved via a cancellation of the feminine. Women, it is argued, can either be playthings or else quasi men'.[15] The first time we see Nadia in the flashback, she wears a pretty blue dress, her long hair tied back. Nadia's feminine appearance is maintained whenever we see her with her parents who we find out are oblivious to her political involvement with the Syrian Social Nationalist Party. Nadia sheds one element of this 'femininity' when she consolidates her military role in the party, by cutting her long hair. Nadia's short hair becomes a visible sign of her embrace of a new identity. However, due to her parents' suspicion towards all political parties in Lebanon, Nadia is forced to perform a different identity when she is at home. The dresses that she used to wear on a daily basis become a mask hiding her 'new' Self. The film emphasizes this in a scene where Nadia's mother comments on Nadia's suntanned skin. Nadia explains the tan by pretending that she spent the day on the beach. But we know that the tan is a result of her spending long hours in the sun in military training. However, Nadia is not presented as someone who has left her 'old' Self behind. When Nadia decides to perform an anti-Israeli suicide operation, we see her carefully applying make up to her face as she prepares to record her martyrdom statement. This act can be seen as a method to tone down Nadia's toughness and to 'reassure the audience that... [she] is a "normal" woman'.[16] At the same time, the film constructs Nadia as someone with self-awareness regarding this issue: when Nadia's Party Chief shows her the martyr posters the Party had printed for distribution after her death, Nadia expresses her delight at the result, adding 'of course, I am not becoming a martyr for the color photograph!'

The film's strength lies in its use of this clichéd representation to produce a twist in the narrative. While we find out that Nadia's first introduction to the Syrian Social Nationalist Party is through her friend Susanne whom she is reacquainted with when Nadia decides to volunteer at a clinic where Susanne is a nurse, we only discover Nadia's plan to perform the suicide operation after a similar operation is conducted by her fellow party member, Samir. When Nadia first joins the Party, she has no idea that Samir, her childhood sweetheart whom she had not seen for years, is in the Party too. When Samir and Nadia finally meet, their romance is rekindled, and the film lingers on shots of them reliving the past as they embrace. They discuss marriage, and although Samir tries to tell Nadia that they cannot marry 'under the current circumstances', the impression we get is that the reason for this is either because Nadia is a Christian and Samir is a Muslim, or because of Samir's devotion to the Party. Samir's televised martyrdom statement that Nadia witnesses in her parents' living room comes as a shock both to her and the epistemologically aligned audience. We cannot help but assume that her decision to follow suit is driven by her love for Samir. This is emphasized when we see how Nadia records the audio from Samir's televised statement on a cassette tape that she listens to on her Walkman repeatedly.

However, only towards the end of the film do we find out that Samir's death was only a catalyst in Nadia's decision. The real reason for her choosing to perform the suicide operation lies elsewhere. In another flashback, we see Nadia as a child in her village house in the South of Lebanon. An Israeli fighter jet is shot down by Palestinian *fedayeen*, and its pilot lies outside Nadia's parents' house, still alive, but wounded. Nadia's father agonizes over whether he should rescue the soldier. On one hand, he says, if he hands the soldier back to the Israelis and the *fedayeen* find out, he and his family could be slaughtered by the Palestinians. On the other hand, if he delivers the soldier to the Palestinians, the Israelis would probably do the same. In the end he decides to regard the soldier simply as a human being in agony, and brings him home. The *fedayeen* roam the village looking for the soldier, and as they ask Nadia's father whether he has seen the soldier, which he denies, we see Nadia running to the door to loudly inform her father that 'the soldier has woken up'. We realize that the reason why Nadia and her family had to leave their village is because of Nadia's outburst. Nadia's suicide operation then becomes an act of redemption, and a way to try to restore her father's reputation that she is blamed for destroying.

The film also succeeds in critiquing the patriarchy that rules Nadia's life. Susanne asks Nadia if she is a virgin; Nadia says she is, and Susanne confesses that she is not. Nadia's first reaction to this news is 'do your parents know?' Susanne answers: 'we are an island, and our parents are another'. This patriarchal generational gap is emphasized later in a scene where we see Nadia going to the video shop to rent the latest American war movie. When she arrives home, however, she has to endure a conversation among her parents and relatives where they criticize Syria. When Nadia expresses her offense at their remarks, her father responds by demanding, 'leave the discussion of politics to the men. Follow your mother to the kitchen; can you not see that the kibbeh plate is empty?' Nadia reacts by breaking the kibbeh plate. The Party becomes a refuge from patriarchal shackles. When Nadia is in military training, she is dressed in the same uniform as her male counterparts, and performs the same roles. Assaf ensures that we see Nadia engaging in the same activities as the men: we see her loading guns, shooting at targets, performing tough physical exercises. As Nadia passes in front of the video shop again, she stops outside, listening to Samir's statement on her Walkman. We cannot help but notice that behind her is a poster for the film *Rambo*. Leyla Assaf explains that this film reference is not just aesthetic; it also stems from the process of researching the film, where she interviewed 'parents of martyrs, and they said those young people liked watching *Rambo*. It was escapist, but also, they loved war

Martyrs

films because they represented things they wanted to do but could not do out of frustration. [Through martyrdom operations], those young people are allowed to become "heroes", like the ones seen on television: "if you do this, tomorrow you will be a hero. Today no one knows you; tomorrow everyone will know who you are"'.[17]

Indeed, the film represents this point through conversations between the Party leaders, where they emphasize the way recorded martyrdom statements will transform their fighters into heroes. They use this point to convince Nadia to record such a statement, saying, 'television is the only way we can get our message across. Nothing is real unless it is broadcast on television'. Nadia's existence therefore becomes unreal; she can only be validated through death. It is this complex representation that undermines the status of Nadia as a resistance fighter. In the end, and despite her convictions, she is a victim of the war and a political tool in the hands of men.

Women as Markers of Difference

The role of women in war and peace is complex as '"women" cannot be considered a category of analysis across contexts, regardless of class, race-ethnicity, nationality and sexual orientation'.[18] Challenging the representations of women as victims and of resistant women within patriarchy are films that represent women in between. Those films do not represent female combatants. They are not limited to presenting a classical victimization of women during the war. What they do is something other Lebanese films do not do, and that is use women to depict not only the condition of difference to which those outside the Lebanese nation were relegated during the war, but also difference within the nation itself. Lebanon in those films is a multi-ethnic, multi-religious place, but the people within it do not perceive themselves and Others as equals. Racial, class, and ethnic-religious divisions are rife. The Civil War had brought into the open and was a consequence of deeply embedded differences in Lebanese society. But difference in Lebanese society has never been fully confronted. In a country where political representation and personal legal rights are firmly based on the idea of difference (through the system of confessionalism), it remains difficult to address this issue head on. Those films are a step forward in that they bring this issue out to the open. The films use women as the voice of the taboos of Lebanese war society.

The films are interesting to examine because they depict women during the Lebanese Civil War who represent the different encounters of people from different backgrounds. From prostitutes to maids to rich, high society 'madams', the women speak about the divisions in war-torn Lebanese society. Despite the involvement of women in combat in the war, the films choose to concentrate instead on mediating the experiences of women trying to cope with 'ordinary' life during the war. Therefore, although the women in the films are used to comment on Lebanese society at large, their experiences are unique to them being women and cannot be replicated by substituting the female characters for male ones. That is not to essentialize the women; this uniqueness stems from the women's existence in a patriarchal society, where '[w]omen are divided by class, culture and ethnicity, by sexuality and family, but are bound together by being women'.[19]

Speaking through the women, the films present a challenge to what Cooke calls the 'War Story' – the story of war based on gender binaries that prioritize men's experiences.[20] Writing about Lebanese war novels, Cooke observes that 'women's descriptions of the war seemed to preclude the possibility of arranging the chaos into a coherent narrative, whereas most men's war stories lined up oppositions'.[21] It is precisely this resistance to reducing the war to an 'us and them' story that is mediated through the women in the films. The female characters then present a challenge to a dominant discourse on the war that has been propagated through Lebanese society since the end of the conflict, a discourse that blames the war on an undefined Other. As Randa Chahal says about *The Civilized*, 'It was our war, and we should not play the innocent. Unless we accept responsibility for every bullet, we will never become a nation'.[22]

Women's *Different* Stories

The prominent women in those films are those living on the margin: the prostitutes in *West Beyrouth* and *The Civilized*, and the maids in *The Civilized* and

In the Battlefields. The representation of those women sends several messages about Lebanese war society – messages emphasizing all Lebanon's inhabitants' involvement in the war and the country's racial and religious divisions, but also the tension of building bridges between Self and Other. *In the Battlefields* constructs a relationship of Otherness in its representation of the tension between the maid Siham and the family matriarch, Yvonne, on one hand, and Lina on the other hand. Our first introduction to Lina sees her plaiting Siham's hair in the film's opening sequence, and saying to Siham 'you and I are the same'. The film indulges the viewer in scenes representing the closeness between Lina and Siham. They peep on a neighbor as he watches television while lying half naked on a bed and smoking. They playfully splash each other with water as Siham cleans a stairway. They steal moments where they stare at the young man living opposite them, and who takes off his clothes as he stands on his balcony, parading his body to the girls who respond by intense giggling.

But Siham and Lina's relationship is destabilized when Lina finds out that Siham is planning on running away to marry a man called Marwan. This is where we discover that Lina's link with Siham is not one of friendship, but one of possession. She confronts Siham about her plan to leave by literally telling her 'but you cannot go because we have bought you'. Lina here converges with her aunt Yvonne's view of Siham. The relationship between the aunt and the maid is revealed as such from the start. The first time we see them together is during a family lunch, where Yvonne persistently reprimands Siham for not setting the table properly, eventually slapping her for 'not

In the Battlefields

putting oil on the moutabbal'. When Lina informs Yvonne of Siham's plan, Yvonne reacts by locking Siham up. It is only towards the end of the film, when we see Marwan asking Lina where Siham is, that we find out that Siham is Syrian from Lina's lie to Marwan: 'Siham's father took her back to Syria to marry her off'.

The Civilized tells the stories of different marginal characters living in Beirut during the war after the rich inhabitants of the city fled abroad, leaving their servants behind. The film introduces us to Thérèse, an elderly Lebanese Christian maid living in her bosses' abandoned grand house with their chauffeur (Michel) and another young maid (Bernadette); Nouna and Soussa, two Egyptian lesbian servants; and Mali and Rachika, Sri Lankan maids living in the same apartment block housing the Egyptian women. The harsh life of the servants is contrasted with that of the rich Lebanese Madame Viviane, who only returns to Beirut from Paris to meet her lover and is seemingly oblivious to the war going on around her. As Viviane enters her apartment, she smiles and is greeted by her two Filipina maids. The scene is cut to that of two militiamen beating up and then shooting a man outside Viviane's building. A swift cut brings us back to Viviane, talking on the phone to her lover and drinking coffee prepared by the maids. When we next see Viviane in the film, she is lying in a bath with a beauty mask on her face, telling her maids that she is waiting for an important phone call from her lover. This scene is juxtaposed with the sound of the radio announcing the commencement of shelling on the green line. Viviane eventually leaves Beirut and heads back to Paris, almost untainted by the war.

Viviane's ridiculously idyllic existence is in sharp contrast to that of the servants, highlighting the class divisions in Lebanon where money can buy anything, even peace. Indeed, Viviane's only relationship with the Other is one of superiority, through her maids whom she orders around. It seems that it is only the poor who have to suffer from the war's cruelty. When Rachika falls ill, Nouna says she will knock on people's doors in the building to collect money to admit Rachika to hospital as 'money solves everything'. However, Nouna fails and Rachika dies. Rachika's illness and death are used to highlight another division in Lebanese society, that of race. When Mali asks Nouna and Soussa for help after Rachika falls ill, Soussa's first thought when Nouna suggests they take Rachika to hospital is 'do you think they'd let a Sri Lankan in with all those wounded?' Sri Lankan maids in Lebanon are 'imported' in their thousands and are subjected to different levels of abuse. Some are sexually abused, others have their passports confiscated by their employers, and many are denied personal freedom. The Sri Lankan maids are looked down on as second-class human beings, unworthy of the most basic rights enjoyed by Lebanese citizens.[23] This division was heightened during the war, with the prioritizing of the Lebanese body over the body of the 'foreigner'. The body of the foreigner is invested in meaning that renders it grotesque, not to be touched by 'us'.[24] Thus, Mali can only seek comfort through approaching those who inhabit similar bodies to hers and Rachika's – the Egyptian maids. The maids are Othered not only through their social position, but also through their sexual orientation. In fact, the representation of lesbians was one reason behind the banning of the film in Lebanon. In a nation traditionally defined in heterosexual terms, homosexuality is considered outside the social order: threatening, abnormal and profane.[25] This division is a manifestation of boundaries, of difference and of separate social spaces in Lebanese society, where the boundaries of bodies have to be policed as they signify social boundaries. As Ahmed argues, 'different bodies come to be lived through the very habits and gestures of marking out bodily space, that is, through the differentiation of "others" into familiar (assimilable, touchable) and strange (unassimilable, untouchable)'.[26]

But the body is 'always inscribed within particular cultural formations'.[27] The relationship between the Lebanese body and the bodies of the maids in the film is also a comment on Lebanon's colonial past and its connection with the present. Viviane speaks in French to her lover and to a Lebanese friend who visits her, but to her Filipina maids in English. Viviane embodies a perceived superiority identifying the Lebanese Self with the French colonizers. By not speaking to the maids in French, Viviane further distances herself from the Other, reserving the 'superior' language for those she regards as her equal. The film's ridicule of Viviane therefore adds another dimension to its critique of Lebanese society. Lebanon's ironic identification with the colonizer becomes an example of Frantz Fanon's argument in *Black Skin, White Masks*, where the colonized perceive themselves as positively 'different'.[28] *West Beyrouth* also engages with critiquing the playing out of colonial authority in Lebanese society. Towards the beginning of the film, we see its central character, the teenage boy Tarek, defying his French headmistress ('mother France') by refusing to sing La Marseillaise in the playground before the start of the day at his French school in Beirut. Instead, Tarek grabs a loudspeaker and sings the Lebanese national anthem, which all the schoolchildren eventually join him in chanting.

Women and the Boundaries Within

It is not only the 'racialized bodies' that are policed in Lebanese war society in the films.[29] Boundaries exist within the national body as well. The films revolve around the conflict over what constitutes the national body in Lebanon. What complicates this situation is that the spatial distribution of different religious groups in Lebanon intersects. Beirut – the setting of *The*

Civilized and *West Beyrouth* – is a prime example of this intersection, a space linking unrelated bodies.[30] The division of the city into a Christian East and Muslim West during the war was an attempt to demark the Self from the foreign body, only that the foreign body is always within. *West Beyrouth* emphasizes the intersection by showing how a Muslim family at the beginning of the war did not know which Beirut they were in, East or West. However, the war was to soon set fixed physical and symbolic boundaries for Beirut's dwellers. The body was again at the heart of this setting: kidnapping of Christians by Muslims and vice versa became a familiar practice of control over the Other. *The Civilized* represents this through the Christian character Michel whose 16-year-old son was kidnapped by a Muslim militia. Michel in turn kidnaps two Syrian Muslims and keeps them in his basement, believing he would be able to get his son back this way. But Thérèse complains about the presence of the Muslims. She says she cannot handle their screams, and has had enough of 'cleaning their shit'. Thérèse decides to get rid of the Syrian men and manages to smuggle them out of the basement. But Thérèse's act is not out of compassion; she screams at Michel 'I will kill them and relieve myself and God forgive me'. Thérèse and her friend Ousmane carry the Syrians – their bodies flaccid with hunger – and dump them on the side of a road. Thérèse therefore becomes as much a participant in the atrocities of the war as a victim; as Cooke argues, during the Lebanese war the distinction between civilians and combatants was blurred.[31] Thérèse's actions are also an example of the way the body is geopolitical, 'its location ... marked by its position with[in] specific historical and geographical circumstances', so that the bodies of Muslims and Christians that used to exist in the same space are now marked as 'different' and separated.[32] But perhaps more importantly, Thérèse's expulsion of the bodies of the Muslim Syrians is a direct materialization of abjection.[33] 'The abject relates to what is revolting, to what threatens the boundaries of both thought and identity. The abject is expelled – like vomit – and the process of expulsion seems to establish the boundary line of the subject'.[34]

The abandonment of the Muslim bodies is therefore a symbolic act of purifying the Self from contact with 'dirty' Others. It refers to Lebanon's society that is based on multiple exclusions, whereby each group claims to be Lebanese and yet objects to the presence of (Lebanese) Others on national land. Kristeva argues for the recognition of Otherness within ourselves, that we all have the capacity to be abject.[35] Only if we do so, if we recognize the stranger within ourselves, can we live with strangers.[36] Both films present situations complicating Kristeva's call. However, 'the abject holds an uncanny fascination for the subject, demanding its attention, and desire'.[37] Thérèse's repulsion by the Muslim body is complicated as she finds herself attracted to the Muslim Ousmane. Thérèse's discomfort with her desire is projected onto

Ousmane's racial identity, as he is a Sudanese black man. Thérèse looks at herself in the mirror and says 'if only he weren't black! I would love him till the end of my life!' Ousmane therefore embodies two tropes of Otherness for Thérèse: race and religion.

Thérèse furthermore disapproves of Bernadette's confession that she is in love with a Muslim man. Bernadette is used in the film to build a bridge between the Self and the Other. Bernadette can only pass through a Muslim checkpoint after she attracts one of the militiamen, Moustapha. Moustapha's fascination with Bernadette is similar to Thérèse's fascination with Ousmane: when he first sees Bernadette, Moustapha declares to his companion that he finds her attractive although she is a brunette. His friend replies by saying 'I thought all Christian women were blonde'. The body is therefore fetishized as a symbol of essential Otherness, both feared and desired. But Bernadette is used in the film as an example of hybridity. Passing through the checkpoint a second time, Bernadette is given a golden necklace with a Quran pendant by Moustapha that she proceeds to wear around her neck. She then runs away from home and joins Moustapha who says that he can never get used to her 'strange' name, and willfully allows him to change it. When she calls Thérèse to inform her of her decision to stay with Moustapha, she introduces herself as Bernadette/Yasmin. But Bernadette's hybrid identity is not acceptable. As she crosses a bridge from the Muslim side of Beirut to the Christian side, Bernadette/Yasmin is shot dead by Michel. Here is where the body ceases to be just a body and becomes gendered. The woman's death is a manifestation of how ethnic nationalism demands tight control over women's sexuality in order to 'define and maintain the boundaries of the ethnic community'.[38] Michel's act can be read as a defense against the destruction of his community by the access of Others to the community's women. The women in the community are constructed as subordinates and subjected to what Moghadam calls the 'patriarchal gender contract' that allows men to define the women's identity and behavior.[39] Access to the women's bodies by Others is deviant and condemned.

Randa Chahal returns to this point in her later film *Kite*. The film also uses the body of a woman as a bridge between the Self and the Other. In a divided village in the South of Lebanon (part Lebanese, part Israeli) where passage to the other side is only permitted to the dead, the newborn and brides, it is the latter who bear the burden of maintaining the community's cohesion. Such women are expected to behave according to a patriarchal contract, whereby they do not choose who to marry, but must obey the elders in their families and – when married – their husbands. But it is as if Chahal uses the film's main character, Lamia, to avenge Yasmin in *The Civilized*. Both Yasmin and Lamia step outside the patriarchal circle: like the former, Lamia falls in love with an Other. We see her stealing glances at Youssef – a young Israeli-Arab

Kite

reservist soldier positioned at the border – and he in turn channels his fascination with her through daydreaming and staring at her through his binoculars. When Lamia crosses the border to be united with her husband-to-be, she simply ignores him, and lives a life of her own as if in an enclosed bubble that baffles both their mothers. The mothers' attempts at bringing the two young people together fail, and the film ends with a dream sequence that sees Lamia magically crossing the barbwire to be with Youssef. Lamia takes off his outer army jacket, removes the star of David from his army cap, and asks him to take off his military boots. With the removal of such overt signs of national/political affiliation, Youssef is once again only human. Lamia's dream thus metaphorically succeeds in building the bridge that Yasmin was condemned for.

The Woman's Body as the National Body

West Beyrouth also contains a representation of the woman's body as a bridge between Self and Other. This is done through the characters of prostitutes working on the green line in Beirut, who are visited by militiamen from both the Christian and Muslim sides. Traditionally, prostitutes are represented as silent Others whose social degradation is used to emphasize the respectability of mothers and virgins. Prostitutes have also been romanticized as 'independent sexual tradeswomen' (as seen in *Pretty Woman* for example).[40] But *West Beyrouth* celebrates the prostitutes as the voices of reason in a country consumed by madness. After getting caught up in a demonstration on the streets of Beirut, Tarek hides on the back seat of a car whose driver heads towards the famous Oum Walid brothel. Our first contact with Oum Walid, the madam, is when Tarek hears her screaming at two militiamen: 'This war of yours stops right here on my doorstep! Let Gemayel [Christian militia leader] and Arafat know who they're dealing with!' The two men sheepishly collect the rifles they had left outside her door and leave. When Oum Walid discovers the underage Tarek in the brothel, she demands that he goes back home. But Tarek exhausts her patience, trying his best to stay in this alluring place, leading her to wonder aloud 'what planet are you from?' Tarek replies that he is from West Beirut, to which Oum Walid responds 'West Beirut? What is this East West Beirut shit? Here, there's no East or West! At Oum Walid's, it's Beirut, period!' Later in the film Tarek sneaks into the brothel again, saying to Oum Walid 'I think I have a solution to the Middle East problem. Make Gemayel and Arafat meet right here!' Oum Walid agrees and disapprovingly tells Tarek how the night before her clients 'brought the war in here', as a Christian militiaman refused to have sex with a prostitute who had just slept with a Muslim man.

The prostitutes therefore are not depicted as aberrant. The film speaks through the bodies of those women, engaged in a social taboo, about issues deemed to be of greater threat to the nation. Far from being subjugated by the men they service, the prostitutes provide perhaps the last space where men are regarded as equal despite their ethnic-religious affiliation. Being outside the realm of acceptable moral behavior, the prostitutes are cast a privileged position that enables them to confront 'normal classifactory structures'.[41] The women thus use their bodies not only materially but also symbolically to send a nationalist message. This use of the body stems from the women's marginal position; as Macdonald argues, 'symbolic use of the body is more likely to come from those who lack an effective political voice'.[42] But the women's role as 'mediators of space' means that their marginal position is transformed into a position of power.[43] As bell hooks argues, the margin itself can be chosen by its inhabitants and used as a space of resistance.[44] The margin is also used for the preservation of the Self and the nation. *The Civilized* briefly depicts a Beiruti prostitute called Marika who, like the prostitutes in *West Beyrouth*, is visited by men from all factions. Marika advertises her brothel by writing the words 'Chez Marika' in red capital letters on a concrete wall constructed on her balcony to protect her apartment from bullets and shrapnel. The film depicts a sniper (Samir) pointing his rifle at the building, and shows us Samir's point of view as he surveys Marika's apartment through the viewfinder of his weapon. But Samir never shoots. The concrete wall becomes more than just a physical barrier, for it is its red letters that act as a more important symbolic barrier. Similarly, in *West Beyrouth*, a driver can only pass through the green line by attaching a red bra to the antenna of his car, signaling to the snipers that he is visiting the brothel. The body of the prostitute therefore becomes of symbolic importance, succeeding in maintaining national unity when all else has failed.

The representation of women in those films goes beyond the traditional mother/virgin/whore triad. The woman's body signifies the nation, but does not do that through exaltation over the nation's pride or disparagement of its demise. Women in the films are not essentialized, not idealized. They are part of the war as much as the war is a part of them. In doing so, the women break down the binaries of good and evil. By narrating their stories, the films challenge 'masculinist ways of knowing [that] marginalize women'.[45] The experiences of women on the margin unearth unspoken taboos in Lebanese (war) society. The women in the films are finally speaking. It is their stories that 'rearrange the possibilities of voicing that in turn open up new configurations of identity'.[46] It is the women's voice that makes the films an important constituent in the process of creation of a much-needed national discourse in Lebanon.

Endnotes

1 Alawiyeh, Borhan (2004). *Interview with the author*, Beirut, April.
2 Macdonald, Sharon (1987). 'Drawing the lines: gender, peace and war: an introduction', in Macdonald, Sharon, Pat Holden and Shirley Ardener (eds), *Images of Women in Peace and War: Cross-Cultural and Historical Perspectives*, London: Macmillan Education, pp.1–26.
3 Benton, Sarah (1998). 'Founding fathers and earth mothers: women's place at the "birth" of nations', in Charles, Nickie and Helen Hintjens (eds), *Gender, Ethnicity and Political Ideologies*, London: Routledge, pp.27–45.
4 Morokvasic, Mirjana (1998). 'The logics of exclusion: nationalism, sexism and the Yugoslav War', in Charles, Nickie and Helen Hintjens (eds), *Gender, Ethnicity and Political Ideologies*, London: Routledge, p.65.
5 Macdonald: 'Drawing the lines', p.17.
6 Anthias, Floya and Yuval-Davis, Nira (1989). 'Introduction', in Yuval-Davis, Nira and Floya Anthias (eds), *Woman-Nation-State*, London: Macmillan, pp.1–15.
7 Spike Peterson, V. (1999). 'Sexing political identities/nationalism as heterosexism', *International Feminist Journal of Politics*, 1(1), p.48.
8 Roach Pierson, Ruth (1987). '"Did your mother wear army boots?": feminist theory and women's relation to war, peace and revolution', in Macdonald, Sharon, Pat Holden and Shirley Ardener (eds), *Images of Women in Peace and War: Cross-Cultural and Historical Perspectives*, London: Macmillan Education, pp.205–27.
9 Anthias and Yuval-Davis: 'Introduction', p.10.
10 Waylen, Georgina (1996). *Gender in Third World Politics*, Buckingham: Open University Press.
11 Roach Pierson, 'Did your mother wear army boots?'
12 Holt, Maria (1996). 'Palestinian women and the Intifada: an exploration of images and realities', in Afshar, Haleh (ed), *Women and Politics in the Third World*, London: Routledge, p.190.
13 Assaf, Leyal (2007). *Interview with the author*, London: April.

14　Ibid.
15　Höpfl, Heather J. (2003). 'Becoming a (virile) member: women and the military body', *Body & Society*, 9(4), p.13.
16　Inness, Sherrie A. (1999). *Tough Girls: Women Warriors and Wonder Women in Popular Culture*, Philadelphia: University of Pennsylvania Press, p.98.
17　Assaf: *Interview with the author*.
18　Lentin, Ronit (1997). 'Introduction: (en)gendering genocides', in Lentin, Ronit (ed), *Gender and Catastrophe*, London: Zed Books, p.5.
19　Ledwith, Sue, Woods, Roberta and Darke, Jane (2000), 'Women and the city', in Ledwith, Sue, Roberta Woods and Jane Darke (eds), *Women and the City: Visibility and Voice in Urban Space*, Basingstoke: Palgrave, p.4.
20　Cooke, Miriam (1996). *Women and the War Story*, Berkeley: University of California Press.
21　Cooke: *Women and the War Story*, p.16.
22　Hoang, Mai (2004). 'Lebanese filmmaker: Randa Chahal Sabbag', *World Press Review*, 51:3 (March) [Online]. Available: http://www.worldpress.org/Mideast/1803.cfm
23　Abu Khalil, As'ad (2005). 'The ugly (real) face of Lebanon', *The Angry Arab News Service* (Thursday August 18) [Online]. Available: http://angryarab.blogspot.com/2005/08/sushar-rosky-lest-she-dies-namelessly.html
24　Ahmed, Sara (2002). 'Racialized bodies', in Evans, Mary and Ellie Lee (eds), *Real Bodies: A Sociological Introduction*, New York: Palgrave, pp.46–63.
25　Charles, Nickie and Hintjens, Helen (1998). 'Gender, ethnicity and women's identity: women's "places"', in Charles, Nickie and Helen Hintjens (eds), *Gender, Ethnicity and Political Ideologies*, London: Routledge, pp.1–26.
26　Ahmed, Sara (2000). 'Embodying strangers', in Horner, Avril and Angela Keane (eds), *Body Matters: Feminism, Textuality, Corporeality*, Manchester: Manchester University Press, p.91.
27　Ahmed: 'Embodying strangers', p.88.
28　Fanon, Frantz (1991). *Black Skin White Masks*, New York: Grove Press.
29　Ahmed: 'Racialized bodies'.
30　Grosz, Elizabeth (1998). 'Bodies-cities', in Pile, Steve and Heidi Nast (eds), *Places Through the Body*, pp.42–51. London: Routledge.
31　Cooke: *Women and the War Story*, p.16.
32　Nast, Heidi J. and Pile, Steve (1998). 'Introduction: MakingPlacesBodies', in Nast, Heidi J. and Steve Pile (eds), *Places through the Body*, London: Routledge, p.2.
33　Kristeva, Julia (1982). *Powers of Horror: An Essay on Abjection*, New York: Columbia University Press.
34　Ahmed: 'Embodying strangers', p.93.
35　Kristeva, Julia (1991). *Strangers to Ourselves*, London: Harvester Wheatsheaf.
36　Smith, Anna (1996). *Julia Kristeva: Readings of Exile and Estrangement*, London: Macmillan.
37　Ahmed: 'Embodying strangers', p.93.
38　Charles and Hintjens: 'Gender, ethnicity and women's identity', p.6.

39 Moghadam, Valentine (2000). 'Economic restructuring and the gender contract: a case study of Jordan', in Marchand, Marianne and Anne Sisson Runyan (eds), *Gender and Global Restructuring*, London: Routledge, p.102.
40 Jones, Vivien (2000). 'Eighteenth-century prostitution: feminist debates and the writing of histories', in Horner, Avril and Angela Keane (eds), *Body Matters: Feminism, Textuality, Corporeality*, Manchester: Manchester University Press, p.134.
41 Macdonald: 'Drawing the lines', p.19.
42 Macdonald: 'Drawing the lines', p.20.
43 Ardener, Shirley (1993). 'Ground rules and social maps for women: an introduction', in Ardener, Shirley (ed), *Women and Space: Ground Rules and Social Maps*, Oxford: Berg, p.9.
44 hooks, bell (1990). *Yearning: Race, Gender, and Cultural Politics*, Boston: South End Press.
45 Spike Peterson, V. (1996). 'Shifting ground(s): epistemological and territorial remapping in the context of globalization(s)', in Kofman, Eleonore and Gillian Youngs (eds), *Globalization: Theory and Practice*, London: Pinter, p.18.
46 Cooke: *Women and the War Story*, p.298.

PART III

REFLECTIONS

Chapter Seven

WAR AND MEMORY

Introduction: The Different Faces of Memory

Cinema has been looked at as contributing to imaginings sustaining the nation. It has also been perceived as constituting part of the debate about a nation's history. In this sense, cinema can be argued to put forward different memories of the nation. The analysis of the relationship between cinema and memory is pertinent because cinema can function as a link between the personal and the public. It offers both an insight into the complex world of individual memories, and an expression of shared ones. Often the line between the two is blurred, making cinematic expression an interesting case of the personal as the political. This stance has not always been supported in 'traditional' studies of history, where personal/popular memory has been juxtaposed as a subjective account against the objective 'reality' of history. This juxtaposition is noted by Reading, who says that there is a perception of history as being a more objective recollection of the past than memory.[1] This perception defines memory as the 'images, beliefs and feelings which arise primarily from *individual* experience'.[2]

However, Reading says that 'how we consider the past is no longer in terms of a singular authoratitive historical record by scholars, but it is recognized as an historical record created in conjunction with personal memories which then as a whole form our collective or social memories'.[3] Therefore, 'our memories of the past are constructed dialectically; they develop in part through history and from historical accounts which in turn are fed back into collective and popular memories of events'.[4] Raphael Samuel echoes this argument, saying that '[h]istory has always been a hybrid form of knowledge … Its subject matter is promiscuous'.[5] Samuel argues that history draws on several sources, both public and private.[6] Public and private recollections often work together to form what is known as collective memory:

> 'Collective memory' ... usually refers to the making of a group memory so that it becomes an expression of identity, and accepted by that group as the 'truth' of experience. Collective memory can be set in stone as an unquestioned myth or it can be continually renegotiated across time ... [Therefore], 'collective memory' helps us to understand the 'continued presence of the past' in public debates ... as well as the 'politics of time' that has become evident in the contest over the meaning of past events.[7]

The above arguments tell us that, first, we need to acknowledge the role popular memory – whether individual or collective – plays in the creation of history; and second, we need to pay attention to the issue of interconnectedness that governs the transformation of individual memories to collective, cultural memories. This means that cultural memory is determined by the frameworks constructed by a certain group – frameworks that dictate what is acceptable and what is not, what is representable and what is not.[8] Those frameworks are a result of the interplay between the official and the popular or the vernacular. Burgoyne terms the outcome of this process 'public memory'. He says that

> '[p]ublic memory can be understood as a form of organized remembering'.[9] Public memory is the body of beliefs and ideas about the past produced from the political give and take of competing groups, each of which has a distinct claim on the past and an interest in its representation ... Public memory serves to mediate the 'competing restatements of reality' that emerge from the clash of vernacular, official and commercial interpretations of past experiences.[10]

In this sense, paralleling the distinction between history and popular memory is one between popular (vernacular) memory and official memory. Burgoyne defines vernacular memory as 'memories carried forward from firsthand experience in small-scale communities; it conveys the sense of what "social reality feels like rather than what it should be like"', while he says that official memory is 'a commemorative discourse about the past that offers an overarching, patriotic interpretation of past events and persons ... It seeks to neutralize competing interpretations of the past that might threaten social unity, the survival of existing institutions, and fidelity to the established order'.[11] Burgoyne's concept of official memory echoes Hellmann's description of the expression of dominant ideology in a nation-state as 'public myth'.[12] Shaw defines myth as 'the specific stories and beliefs about the past which are commonly constructed and play a part in a culture'.[13] Hellmann argues that public myths serve to reconcile nations with historical catastrophes to guide them into the future.[14] Public myths therefore are mechanisms of maintaining unity and cohesion in a nation at a time of crisis. One of the most prominent public myths in Lebanon during and after the Civil War is the idea of the war being that of 'others on our land'. This myth serves to absolve the Lebanese people or state from any blame or responsibility for the war. Lebanon is here imagined as a land victimized by foreign warring factions, due to its strategic location, both geographically and politically.

Scholarship on history and memory is therefore constructed in a series of overlaps between different concepts. On one hand, public myths and official memory are seen not as objective accounts of history, but as elements of contestation to popular memory. On the other hand, official memories, popular memory and history are shown to be inevitably linked. As Samuel argues, the expression of popular memory also takes place in the public and private realms; and popular memory may have different priorities in the recall of history than official memory.[15] This scholarship is however problematic when it idealizes popular memory against official memory. This idealization, found above in Burgoyne's definition of the vernacular, constructs popular memory in terms of authenticity versus the falsity of official memory. Official memory is seen as having an ulterior motive, whereas popular memory is perceived as resisting notions of how things 'should' be presented, and is therefore constructed as being more 'free', and consequently, more 'real'. As Sue Harper argues, 'it is important not to canonize the popular, or to present it as the hero in the battle against the forces of darkness'.[16] Lebanese cinema is an illustration of Harper's point. It can be argued that Lebanese cinema is an example of popular memory; however, as we have seen from the analysis of the films, Lebanese cinema does not always contest notions of official memory and public myths. While some films challenge the Othering of the war, others subscribe to this notion of victimization of the Self, absolving Lebanon of responsibility for the war and its atrocities.

Cinema and Memory

Cinema, with its link between the personal and the collective, the private and the public, the real and the imagined, is an ideal tool to illustrate how memory is 'a complex construct'.[17] It illustrates how we cannot write about memory as a coherent set of images or histories. Scholarship on cinema and memory has addressed this relationship from different angles. First, cinema is seen as a process of recreating the past. As Joyce writes, '[r]emembering reinforces what is known, because to retrieve a memory is actually to create it anew'.[18] Cinema here becomes a way of 'returning home', providing comfort to the viewer by representing shared memories.[19] Sue Harper uses Gramsci's

The Veiled Man

theory on individual consciousness to argue that film contains 'fossils' of the past, just like consciousness does. Thus, Harper sees film as a public extension of mass consciousness, where the recognition of the 'fossils' represented in film by the viewer is a source of pleasure.[20]

This is seen in films depicting familiar aspects of Lebanese society, such as in *Bosta*, *Land of Honey and Incense*, *The Veiled Man* and *West Beyrouth*. All four films use food as a representation of shared memories. *Bosta* weaves a scene around a large tray of *knafe*, a traditional dessert often eaten at breakfast. *Land of Honey and Incense* and *The Veiled Man* offer scenes of people drinking *arak* and consuming Lebanese *meze*, especially dishes like raw *kibbeh* and *sawda* (liver). *West Beyrouth* shows the teenagers eating the Lebanese confectionary *Ras al-Abed*. The representation of food sharing and Lebanese hospitality ascribes the materiality of food 'affective qualities of home'.[21] This process of homing is an important mechanism that resists the fragmentation of war: 'homing, then, depends on the reclaiming and reprocessing of habits, objects, names and histories that have been uprooted'.[22] This presentation of shared meaning can be seen as an attempt to 'establish a sense of national belonging'.[23]

Second, cinema is seen as having its own specificity that allows it to represent things other forms of communication cannot. Hayden White distinguishes between historiography, or the verbal and written representation of history, and historiophoty, the 'representation of history and our thoughts about it in visual images and written discourse'.[24] He sees film as being 'capable of telling us things about its referents that are both different from what can be told in verbal discourse and also of a kind that can only be told by means of visual images'.[25] This emphasis on the visual is also because cinema is a realm of fantasy and desire, and therefore can blur processes of remembering and fantasy both at the level of representation and at the level of spectatorship.[26] Films often provide spectators with images substituting actual memories, and therefore take part in what Sorlin calls 'metahistory'.[27] At the same time, 'film seems to actually shape and define the terrain of popular memory'.[28] Lebanese cinema's construction of the war as an alienating experience serves to fix this image of the war in the Lebanese imagination. More than a decade and a half after the end of the Civil War, Lebanon is witnessing internal instability that is bringing memories of the war back to life. The way the war memory is excavated in the present constructs the elements of war as alien: there is a fear of repeating history that is being translated on the ground through a process of denial. Shops in Beirut have put up signs warning their customers not to discuss politics, and even Lebanese expatriots have subscribed to the same process of blindness. The young organizers of a Lebanese charity film night in London in April 2007 expressed wariness about screening films they regarded as 'political'. 'Politics' became associated with divisiveness and, consequently, avoiding 'politics' was seen as the only way the Lebanese could work collectively and seamlessly. In this sense, the Lebanese people have come to put into practice the problematic fantasy created by Lebanese films such as *A Country above Wounds* and *In the Shadows of the City*, where the war is constructed as an external aggressor that can be countered through mere non-recognition.

This is an illustration of how cinema can be a method of creation of public history. Custen defines public history as both 'the product and … the process in which members of the mass public – the "public-at-large" – obtain their definitions of the symbolic universe from watching and talking about the communications media'.[29] While he acknowledges that films are not the primary medium through which people cultivate their historical images, he maintains that 'film still exerts a powerful influence on people's notions of what counts as history'.[30] Winter and Sivan argue that history has often separated individual and official memories.[31] However, 'individual memory is inseparably bound up with cultural memory'.[32] Lebanese cinema brings together personal memories and transforms them into collective memories.[33] In their different representations of the Civil War, the filmmakers become witnesses to history; however, their films do not show *what really happened* but what they *saw*.[34] Collectively, their films' different stories are marked by the subjectivity of experience and recollection, which submit history to a process of interpretation.[35] By merging the two seemingly contrasting elements of personal and public memory, cinema becomes part of history itself. Thus we have a cycle of remembering where cinema as a product of history is only a step in the performance of memory. In other words, cinema as an expression of personal (individual and collective) narratives both participates in the creation of myth and preserves it.[36]

The Past as a Haunting Presence

Cinema's relationship with the 'past' is marked by the context of the present. Greene cites how General Charles de Gaulle had linked France's 'past glories' with 'what he saw as its inherent *grandeur*'.[37] This invocation of grandeur is a reference to how 'history was not merely the study of the nation's past but also a means by which to create a new sense of national unity and purpose. The memory of the nation's past glories, it was hoped, would point the way to a brighter future'.[38] This example illustrates how '[m]emory can create the illusion of a momentary return to a lost past; its operations also articulate the complex relationship between past, present and future in human consciousness'.[39] But it is not only through invocation that the past plays a role in the present. As Lowenthal argues, '[t]he past is everywhere. All around us lie features which, like ourselves and our thoughts, have more or less recognizable antecedents. Relics, histories, memories suffuse human experience ... Whether it is celebrated or rejected, attended to or ignored, the past is omnipresent'.[40] Or, as Gilles Deleuze puts it, '[t]he present and former presents are not, therefore, like two successive instants on the line of time; rather, the present one necessarily contains an extra dimension in which it represents the former and also represents itself'.[41]

Al-Sheikha (1994) is a film commenting on the presence of the past in Lebanese society, despite the inattention to this past. Made in the immediate postwar period, the film is set during the last days of the Civil War, and depicts the story of a ten-year-old girl from a poor background known as al-Sheikha who leads a gang of thieves, all of them fellow poor children. The children are abused and exploited by everyone from their parents to strangers, and struggle to survive on the margin of society, ignored and unseen by the mainstream. Leyla Assaf's intention behind making the film was to highlight a social problem that is a particular indirect outcome of the Lebanese Civil War.[42] But the film's presentation of the war is complex. The war is not shown as directly contributing to the children's misery. For most of the film, the devastation of the war is almost irrelevant to the children's everyday lives. The film even shows the children taking advantage of the panic accompanying the start of shelling: we see the children stealing a man's wallet as they all shelter from bombs behind a wall. The general sidelining of the war in the film highlights its tackling of a problem 'created by the war that persisted after the war ended'.[43]

Al-Sheikha

The film ends with a potent scene critiquing the inattention to the presence of the past in postwar Lebanese society. We see a group of schoolchildren, all dressed in clean uniforms, approaching a boat on a school trip in the immediate postwar era. The children are led by their teacher in a rendition of a song called *yalla naa'mer ya ashabi*. As the children sing, we see al-Sheikha and her brother Ahmad wearing rags, trying to sell them chewing gum. The children ignore them, and go on board the boat where they sing French nursery rhymes. The camera shows the boat slowly departing out to sea, leaving al-Sheikha and Ahmad standing alone with their trays of gum, as the schoolchildren sing *yalla naa'mer* again. The song's lyrics ironically state: 'Let's build, my friends, small houses in our country. Tomorrow we will grow up, my friends, and the whole world will grow with us'. The children's ignoring of al-Sheikha and Ahmad and the visual disappearance of the siblings as the boat departs present a strong statement on their status of invisibility. This invisibility is further emphasized by locating the two children as inhabitants of Wadi Abu-Jmil, a neglected area in downtown Beirut (which, today, is being transformed into a luxury residence as downtown Beirut is being rebuilt). The film therefore presents a critique of the concept of national space, showing that 'being internal to a given space is not always emancipatory', and how people can be 'marginalized in spite of being *within* the nation space'.[44]

Other postwar Lebanese films also comment on the presence of the past. The characters in *Bosta* try to come to terms with the past as they carve their future. The film revolves around the story of a young man, Kamal, who returns to Lebanon after the Civil War and tries to re-assemble the dance group he used to lead at school. As the group gathers, its members find themselves fighting the past: Vola and Toufic struggle with reigniting their romance which never materialized during the war because one of them is a Muslim and the other a Christian; Omar stuggles to convince his traditional father of the validity of his chosen career as a dancer, which the father had considered unacceptable; and Khalil goes back to his village in the North where he fights for his family's acceptance of his homosexuality. The group as a whole also find themselves caught between modernity and tradition: they negotiate this tension through creating a form of dance that merges Western dance music and moves with traditional Lebanese dabke, which they call 'digi-dabke'. Throughout the film, the group tries to assert a changing Lebanese identity that has not abandoned tradition, but that is hybrid, as the country tries to step out of the shadow of the Civil War. The film utilizes a bus to make a more overt statement on this issue: the group's method of transportation is an old bus from their school. The school is set in the town of Aley, known in Lebanon as a Muslim/Christian/Druze area, thereby signifying the diversity of the group. The bus's bringing together of diverse people presents a message of hope for a unified, tolerant Lebanon, especially when viewed in context of the Ain el-Rimmaneh massacre which started the Civil War, and which took place on board a bus.

In contrast, *Around the Pink House* presents a mocking statement on the past, through the character of a young man, Maher, who resides in the pink house selected for demolition by a reconstruction company. Maher parades through the neighborhood with his mates, running through traffic in military uniform, chanting for an unnamed leader, and posting posters of martyrs on the doors of his wardrobe. Maher suggests getting support from 'the militia' to

Bosta

defy the reconstruction company, but his brother responds, 'the militia is over'. Despite the film's optimism about the cessation of militias in postwar Lebanon, it hints at the war's persistent presence through a conversation between Maher and a fellow party member, where the latter informs Maher that 'war can be done without guns'.

An elaboration on this point – the past as a haunting presence – is represented in four other Lebanese postwar films. *A Perfect Day*, *Beirut Phantoms*, *Terra Incognita* and *Falafel* depict a Beirut enveloped in darkness and inhabited by creatures of the night. Young people wander aimlessly around the city. They waste their youth smoking, drinking and taking drugs. They do not speak of a brighter future but seem to be forever haunted by a lingering past that colors their everyday existence.

A Perfect Day represents the repercussions that wartime kidnapping has had on families living in Lebanon today. The film is inspired by the real-life story of the uncle of its director Khalil Joreige, who disappeared during the war and was never found. The film portrays the tense relationship between Claudia and her son Malik in today's Beirut after the disappearance of Malik's father Riad in April 1988. Claudia is reluctant to declare her husband dead after all those years; she resigns herself to live forever in the past, refusing to acknowledge that her husband is almost certainly dead, and awaits his return every night. When Malik takes her to see a lawyer to sign papers declaring her husband dead, her first reaction is not to sign the papers but simply to do nothing. However, even after she and Malik eventually sign the papers, their lives continue to be ruled by the shadow of the disappeared father. Riad's office is frozen in time, still displaying the family photos he used to surround himself with, and containing the same dusty desk with its old-style dial telephone set. Claudia does not know whether she now has to mourn Riad, and wonders whether he will hate her for not waiting for him. Claudia lives in the past, fondling Riad's clothes and rehanging them in the closet as if he is still around.

Malik on the other hand tries to break away from being haunted by his father's absence, but seems unable to detach himself from the memory of his disappeared father. He drives through the streets of Beirut, bleary-eyed and almost unaware of his surroundings due to endless sleepless nights. His zombie existence seems to mirror that of a city resurrected from the dead but that is still not detached from the underworld. Malik is alienated: from his lover, who chooses to leave him and indulge in a fantasy existence of nighttime pleasure, drinking, smoking and dancing in Beirut's nightspots with others from her generation who have also chosen the same escapist path; from his mother; and from himself, as he tries to run away from the shackles of his father's presence/absence, without really succeeding. One night Malik returns home to find Riad's jacket laid on his bed, looking like it is inhabited by the father's ghost. The film ends without closure: we do not see Claudia or Malik moving on. Khalil Joreige says that the open-endedness deliberately parallels that of the war.[45] The lack of closure emphasizes the connection of people in Lebanon with a past they have not yet come to terms with.

Beirut Phantoms is also concerned with the figure of the ghost from the past. It is loosely structured around a group of young men and women who encounter a friend of theirs, Khalil, who they had assumed was dead. We find out that Khalil faked his own death during the Civil War and assumed a new identity in order to escape (this echoes the story of Nabil in *Little Wars*). Khalil returns to Beirut as the war is ending, hoping he could regain his freedom in a postwar city marked by indifference. The film presents postwar Beirut as a city where the sense of community has disappeared, thereby offering Khalil 'the lonely liberty of knowing that no one is looking, nobody is listening'.[46] However, Khalil finds out that he cannot reclaim his old identity. Even when his friends see him on the street by chance, they start questioning both his existence as well as their own, reaching a state where they find themselves unable to detach their presence from the war.

Ghassan Salhab carries this vision forward in his next film *Terra Incognita*, but in a more oblique way. The film does not follow a linear narrative, instead presenting the moods, feelings and experiences of a group of young Lebanese people who either live in present-time Lebanon or have just returned to the country from abroad. The characters in the film are all alienated, and spend much of their screen time staring blankly at the camera, or engaging in gloomy existential conversations. Their alienation is also represented through their daily lives. Tarek returns to Lebanon only to be faced with his friends' desire to leave the county. Nadim – an architect involved in reconstruction projects in downtown Beirut – spends his time on the computer creating imaginary

Terra Incognita

versions of the city he cannot relate to in reality, while Soraya tries to fill the void in her life by spending her nights with different men. Carole Abboud says about this character: 'In the film the director wanted to make parallels between the body of Soraya and that of Beirut, because they both give themselves up to others'.[47] The characters' daily lives are presented in the context of the political instability and uncertainty in Lebanon: the sound of the radio is omnipresent in the film, announcing Israeli violence towards Palestinians, endless meetings among Lebanese politicians and religious figures, and news of Israeli warplanes roaming the air space of Lebanon. Thus, although the film does not deal with the topic of the Civil War directly, it comments on the war's destabilizing and disorienting presence that has prevented the country from moving forward. Salhab comments:

> *Terra Incognita* reflects a frozen time, a country stuck in the present, but not in a positive way. It's because it does not want to face the past, or the future. It's imprisoned by the present. That's why people come back and don't know where they are. This is reflected in both space and time in the film. The film is 'defragmented' deliberately. Living here, you get a different cinematic structural orientation. I wanted to make the viewer uncomfortable when watching people being lost, to enter the viewer into a physical experience of being lost through the film's structure. I wanted to remove the viewer from the comfort zone of linear structures.[48]

Falafel presents the theme of escape, or the difficulty of it. The main character in the film, Toufic (or Tou, as he is known to his friends and family), is a young Lebanese man eager not to follow the crowd and to be his own man.

However, he is dragged into the very dark hole he is trying to avoid. We first meet Tou as he zooms around Beirut late at night on a scooter borrowed from his boss at the computer shop he works at. Tou smiles as the scooter takes him around the mostly empty streets of the city, evoking a sense of freedom that Tou, as we later find out, thinks he has. The city at this point does not appear menacing. Rather, it seems to embrace Tou, his hair ruffling in the wind as he rides his scooter, bathed in the city lights. Kammoun weaves a Beirut that is instantly recognizable to a Lebanese viewer, giving the audience a glimpse of Downtown, the Manara promenade, Hamra Street and other familiar places. Kammoun could have easily showcased Beirut's 'icons', with panoramic shots of prominent areas for example, or lingering scenes by some of the city's 'gems'. Yet he chooses to show only as much of the city as is necessary to breed a sense of familiarity and comfort, without taking a quasi-touristic 'isn't-Lebanon-beautiful?' stance as seen in *Bosta* for example. This familiarity works to contextualize the character of Tou as an 'ordinary Lebanese man'. But no sooner do we revel in this comfort than it is shattered. Seeing things from Tou's point of view, we are soon introduced to Beirut's underworld that emerges without warning.

Tou witnesses, from a short distance, a kidnapping operation where a man is dragged from his car by a group of men who suddenly emerge from a black jeep and block his way. Kammoun presents this scene with no explanation or prior warning, and all we can do, like Tou, is watch helplessly. Such kidnapping incidents were common during the Civil War, and the use of this scene serves to shatter our image of a stable postwar Lebanon. The scene is the first of several where Tou faces such ugliness, which stands in sharp contrast to the seemingly carefree existence of Tou's friends, who spend their nights at parties drinking and chasing lovers. Tou finds himself torn between the two worlds. On one hand, he wants to enjoy the irreverence of youth. He flirts with a beautiful young woman, Yasmin, and succeeds in taking her on his scooter to the shut computer shop, where they make love. At a party at his friend Nino's house, Tou is amazed as he sees two women and a man emerge one by one from a closet in the bedroom. Tou enters the closet only to find that it is being used as a marijuana smoking den, where he joins the rest of the smokers. On the other hand, Tou is driven towards the madness of the city when he is beaten up by a gangster who accuses Nino of scratching his parked car. Tou's rage at his treatment by the man drives him to seek revenge, and he roams the streets of Beirut searching for the gangster. His search leads him to a car mechanic whose garage is, mysteriously, the only shop open in the early hours of the morning. The mechanic listens to religious hymns on the radio, but we later find out that he tells Tou where to buy a handgun in order to assassinate the gangster who wronged him. Such twists in the plot are effective in their evocation of the days of the Civil War, when gangsters ruled the streets, and men killed while praying. We realize that the Civil War is very much still with us.

Falafel is unique in its invocation of the war in that it is the only Lebanese film offering a postmodern comment on the naturalization of its representation in Lebanese cinema. As we have seen in this book, the Civil War is almost an obsession for Lebanese films, present in different forms, in the foreground and the margins of the cinema. Kammoun acknowledges this by presenting a playful scene where we see Tou's living room while we hear the sounds of bombs and firing of bullets. Such scenes are so familiar to the Lebanese audience that we immediately assume that the sounds are those of the Civil War in some form. But the camera cuts to the TV set in the living room as it shows images of Saddam Hussein being captured by American troops in Iraq, while Tou's mother sleeps on the sofa. An American soldier is heard through the television saying 'we will fight them till we get rid of the terrorists'. Later in the film, as Tou's friends Nino and Abboudi drive around Beirut looking for him, their car radio announces that 'Chirac welcomes UN Resolution 1559' – the resolution calling for the withdrawal of Syrian troops from Lebanese land that was supported by the Cedar Revolution of 2005. In this way, the film sends a subtle message linking instability in the Middle East region with internal Lebanese politics. Its representation of bleak characters – from the sinister car mechanic, to the mad gun seller whom Tou encounters in a cheap nightclub, to the gangster – becomes a warning against the easiness of involvement in the violence, and the way the underworld is not hidden, but present around every corner.

George Ki'di compares *Falafel* with Martin Scorcese's *After Hours* and *Taxi Driver*, the first because of the similarity of its all-in-one-night presentation of events, the second because of *Falafel*'s references to 'repressed internal and expressed external violence' that mark *Taxi Driver*'s character Travis.[49] Like Travis, Tou is going through a living nightmare, and is driven to a dark fate by the circumstances surrounding him. However, perhaps a more recent comparison can be made between the film and Maroun Baghdadi's *Little Wars*, where young Lebanese people are driven to participate in the Civil War's madness despite themselves. More than 20 years separate *Falafel* and *Little Wars*, yet the convergent messages of both films are telling. The Civil War is not just a memory in *Falafel*; it is part of the subconscious that can emerge to the surface and take over with little encouragement. The way Tou becomes consumed by the madness of revenge can be seen as a warning against the presence of war in the Lebanese psyche. As a review of the film in *Variety* states:

> hidden beneath the entertaining action is the point that 16 years after the civil war, life in Lebanon has never normalized. Violence seems to be lying in wait for the innocent ... Though shot before the recent

Israeli conflict, the film seems to hold a prescient warning of conflict lurking around every corner.[50]

This view is echoed by Michel Kammoun himself, who describes the character Tou as discovering 'that having a normal life, in this country, is a luxury out of his reach. 15 years after the war had ended; [sic] a volcano is lying dormant on every street corner, like a ticking bomb that is ready to explode ...'[51]

Those comments add another dimension to postwar Lebanese cinema's obsession with the past. The obsession is not simply a matter of recreating the past as it is; rather, it is about using the present to reveal what history was blind to at the time of its creation. Anne King cites Freud's term Nachträglichkeit, which has been translated as 'afterwardsness',[52] to refer to the way memory, 'operating as it does in the present, must inevitably incorporate the awareness of "what wasn't known then"'.[53] She says that this concept 'unsettles the belief that we can recover the past as it was and unproblematically reunite our past and present selves'.[54] The war is therefore not presented without contestation. 'But to contest the past is also, of course, to pose questions about the present, and what the past means in the present'.[55] In this sense, the films pose questions about the role that the war, now invisible, still plays in the Lebanese psyche, and about ways of taking this past forward.

War Nostalgia

In *Nation and Narration*, Homi Bhabha introduces the notion of 'double time' to point out the way nations pay attention to both the past and the future simultaneously.[56] Edensor criticizes this temporal conception because it ignores the present.[57] Lebanese cinema is an arena where the past, the present and the future are tied together by the Civil War. As Ibrahim al-Ariss argues, 'the war has transformed from something to be documented to something to be lived. War has become part of the new generation's identity. Baghdadi's *Little Wars* was saying it was a witness to the war without being involved in it. Baghdadi wanted to criticize the war and distance himself from it. The new generation, on the other hand, has been shaped by the war'.[58] The war not only inhabits the identity of the new generation in Lebanon. It is also present in the memory of those who lived through it, and who find it impossible to live in the present.

Some Lebanese films articulate this through the representation of nostalgia towards the war. This war nostalgia is generated out of postwar emptiness. As Westmoreland observes, '[n]ostalgia for the past exists alongside the death-time of the present; the irony is that the peace of the postwar situation is perceived much like a living death-time, as if the war left no survivors, only ghosts'.[59] *Beirut Phantoms* constructs a nostalgia 'for an imagined simpler past'.[60] It echoes Jeremy Bowen's statement about being faced by peace after living with war on a daily basis. Jeremy Bowen writes:

> I began to understand the relationship that humans have with war, their greatest vice. Wars are horrendous and awful but when they are happening they are not always terrible, as long as the worst things are happening to other people, who you don't know and better still don't love. Life stops drifting along and suddenly has a sharp purpose. It gets reduced to a very simple and fundamental equation about death and survival, and the complications and the nonsense fall away. Peace is better, but it is complicated and it can be dull.[61]

Bowen's statement parallels those of two actresses in *Beirut Phantoms*, Darina al-Joundi and Carole Abboud. The film breaks its narrative through the presentation of a series of monologues by the actors delivered while they sit in a white room facing the camera. Salhab comments that those characters represent the disenchanted, those who had dreamt during the war but found that their dreams amounted to nothing.[62] Darina al-Joundi says:

> War is not over for me. There is still war inside me. I don't believe the lie that the war is over. I was not consulted when it ended, nor when it began. I was happier during the war. Then, I did not care. I did not care about the moments to come, only about the moment

Beirut Phantoms

I was living. Now, I think about everything: work, tomorrow ... Things were easier during the war. People loved each other more then. Now everyone is on their own ... During the war I used to dream about all the things I would do when it ended. I was disappointed when it ended; suddenly everything looked smaller.

Carole Abboud's statement is similar:

> Our problem is that we want to be reborn, but we are not dead. We are dying... I try to erase it [the war], like everyone else. But in my subconscious I long for it. Everything had a better meaning then. My relationships with my parents, friends and myself were better. There was real friendship. Now, there is chaos and uncertainty. There is something broken.

Both statements articulate a sense of loss, but also a romanticization of the past. As Boym argues, '[n]ostalgia ... is a longing for a home that no longer exists or has never existed. Nostalgia is a sentiment of loss or displacement, but is also a romance with one's own fantasy'.[63] She says that this sentiment emerges out of the urgency of the present: 'Nostalgia is not always about the past; it can be retrospective but also prospective. Fantasies of the past determined by needs of the present have a direct impact on realities of the future'.[64] In this sense, Lebanon is imagined as a place unable to escape from the shadow of the war. What is frightening about this imagination is that it becomes almost prophetic when the instability that is plaguing Lebanon after the Cedar Revolution is considered. This 'warning' was presented by Ziad Doueiri when he was interviewed for this book back in 2004. He said at the time:

> the war has not been dealt with smartly. There has not been a national reconciliation process. Everything is done overnight, and everything has been kicked under the bed, and then we 'move on'. There has not been a process of healing and discussing and bringing about what everybody feels about the other. The situation can fall any time – maybe not to a Civil War, but chaos. Lebanon has not healed yet.[65]

Doueiri has been seen as articulating a certain romanticization of the war in *West Beyrouth*. The film presents the war as playful (although it does end with Tarek's longing for the mundane prewar reality by wishing he was back at school). When making the film, Ziad Doueiri says that he 'imagined Lebanon as a country that still has a joi de vivre. There were problems in Lebanon during the war, but the Lebanese still know how to have fun'.[66] Hirsch and

Spitzer argue that although nostalgia has often been criticized for its idealization of the past, it can nevertheless be useful as a 'creative inspiration and possible emulation within the present, "called upon to provide what the present lacks"'.[67] *West Beyrouth* can thus be read not as a longing for the war, but as a search for those elements that made human life possible during the Civil War – elements that need to be kept alive in the present.

Remembering and Forgetting

Nicola King argues: 'Reading the texts of memory shows that "remembering the self" is not a case of restoring an original identity, but a continuous process of "*re*-membering", of putting together moment by moment, of provisional and partial reconstruction'.[68] When the war ended, it became an urban myth. The Lebanese people seemed to choose to forget – the memory of the war was deemed too painful and guilt-inducing to be resurrected. Al-Ariss says that cinema was one of the few arenas that interacted with the war, and that the Civil War contributed to shaping Lebanese cinema as we know it today.[69] Filmmakers like Randa Chahal resisted the sidelining of the memory of the war, and continued to make films about their war experiences. She has been quoted as saying 'Everyone said to me, "Why do you want to talk about the war?"… There has been a huge national effort to erase and forget all traces of the war'.[70]

Indeed, Lebanese cinema has confronted the war's demons, and has sometimes been audacious in its references to issues otherwise silenced. For example, in 1982, Samir Nasri pointed out that *Lebanon in Spite of Everything* was the only film referring to the Syrian presence in Lebanon at the time.[71] The film constructs a scene where the radio announces that the Syrians are the only Arab force left on Lebanese land from the original multi-Arab Deterring Forces (*rade'*) sent by the Arab League to control the situation in Lebanon. The radio broadcasts that the Syrian forces have installed rocket launchers in Lebanon, hinting at Syria's active military involvement in the war. In 1988, *Martyrs* represented the Syrian intervention in Lebanon boldly, constructing scenes where characters criticized Syria's involvement openly, and even including one where a character cracks a joke about Syria's head of intelligence in Lebanon at the time, Ghazi Kanaan: the character only refers to him as 'Ghazi', but the hint is easily understood by the local audience. *A Country above Wounds* tackles the issue of unification of history textbooks in Lebanon. Both during and after the war, schools in different areas of Lebanon taught their students wildly diverging accounts of Lebanon's history through using subjectively-written history textbooks. Thus students in East Beirut would learn 'facts' depicting their dominant factions favorably, while those in West

Beirut would learn the opposite. The film represents this through a scene of students demonstrating and demanding the unification of the curriculum and school textbooks.

A Time Has Come comments on the absence of national belonging in Lebanon during the war and the reduction of patriotism to empty symbols. The film shows Kamil, a musician residing in Paris, being approached by an organization called the Global Union of Lebanese Emigrants to compose a nationalist song about Lebanon to be accompanied by a video illustrating different tourist areas in Lebanon. The Union's delegate warns Kamil of the importance of the task: 'your country's image is at stake! Everything has to be perfect'. Kamil responds by singing the tune to a well-known soft cheese advert in the scale of a folkloric Lebanese song: 'La vache qui rit! A cream cheese with a delicious taste, soft like butter!' Kamil later drops out of the project when he discovers that the video idea has been changed to one depicting an old man on his death bed, surrounded by all his immigrant grandsons who have 'buried their differences to be with him'.

West Beyrouth and *In the Battlefields* are both unafraid to depict the localized experiences in divided Beirut. While Danielle Arbid stresses that her film *In the Battlefields* 'is cinema, not politics or propaganda', she defends her choice of setting the film in a Christian community:

> I am telling my own story. This is not a film about political commitment. I grew up in a Christian community where people wore crosses. I write about what I know. And I know the Christian sector of Lebanese society, so why should I hide this background? I did not know people called Rami and Nawal, I knew George and Georgette.[72]

Remembering is also about the futility of the war. This is seen in the character René in *A Time Has Come*, and Rami in *In the Shadows of the City*. René shoots himself after witnessing his militiamen murdering a group of Muslims. Though forced into joining a militia after his father is kidnapped, Rami is later shown leaving the militia to become a primary school art teacher after being disgusted with the violence and profiteering the militia is engaged in. Both characters serve a wider role in commenting on the war; as Jean-Claude Codsi says about René:

> René was a militant in 1975, a time when people thought the war was necessary. At the time people were idealists, and believed in a cause, and that they were defending Lebanon. But when René witnesses the killing of the Muslims, he realizes that there is no cause to defend.[73]

The war is revealed as a misleading game of destruction.

But memory is an act of forgetting as well as remembering, and Lebanese cinema has engaged in a process of forgetting.[74] Forgetting is articulated on several dimensions. Forgetting is constructed in political terms. It is remarkable that the prominent roles played by Israel and the Palestinians in the history of conflict in Lebanon are largely marginalized in Lebanese cinema. Very few films have references to Palestinians, and even then the references are extremely marginal. There is an unnamed Palestinian woman in *The Shelter* (who is known as a Palestinian only from her accent). *Lebanon in Spite of Everything* obliquely hints at the Palestinians as agents of blame in the Civil War, in a scene where a radio news bulletin is heard announcing that 'Palestinian resistance fighters have kidnapped ...' before the radio is abruptly turned off. *West Beyrouth* presents oblivion to the Ain el-Rimmaneh massacre of 1975 by Tarek's parents, where the father Riad is heard saying the incident 'is between the Israelis and the Palestinians, nothing to do with us'. The film does present documentary footage of Arafat and Rabin, but this choice of political leaders is informed by the need to present 'icons whom a variety of audiences will recognize',[75] and not to make a political statement. *Beirut Phantoms* comments on the forgetting of Palestine in the Lebanese psyche by placing the characters Khalil and Hanna on the beach, where they see the remnants of a train track. Khalil says to Hanna: 'Did you know that this train track used to go all the way to Egypt and Palestine? Palestine that occupied our memory for so long. A place that still dreams of becoming a country, with a government, police, borders and a football team?' Hanna responds, 'soon we will all play the amnesia game. To pretend that we are not responsible for anything'. *Once Upon a Time, Beirut* has a fleeting reference to the Arab-Israeli conflict through the juxtaposition of a song about the Six Day War with documentary footage of Palestinian refugees arriving in Lebanon. The film follows this with an audio announcement of an imminent Israeli attack on a village in the South of Lebanon in 1975.

This fleeting reference to the South of Lebanon is an example of how forgetting in Lebanese cinema is also constructed in spatial terms. While Beirut is prominent in its cinematic presence, the South of Lebanon is spatially marginalized. *A Suspended Life* presents a longing for the prewar South through speeches by Samar's father who reminisces about his time as a fisherman in Saida, and through the presentation of the main characters as refugees from the South. *Beirut, The Encounter, Lebanon in Spite of Everything, In the Shadows of the City* and *Martyrs* also present Haydar, Rif'at, Rami and Nadia respectively as Southern refugees. *West Beyrouth* only hints at the migration of Southerners to Beirut in a short scene depicting an argument between the mother Hala and her neighbor, whom Hala instructs to 'go back to the South'. *The Explosion* refers to the South as a place of suffering, showing Akram's mother being killed in the area by an air raid, and Samir commenting that 'people are resilient in the South, despite their suffering'. Although *Terra Incognita* and *Bosta* both show the South visually, their representations of the area remain tokenistic. *Terra Incognita* presents the South as the place where Soraya is physically attacked. *Bosta* on the other hand celebrates the South in staging one of its dance sequences in the town of Hasbayya. However, Hasbayya in the film does not have a specificity beyond being a ring in the chain of picturesque Lebanese towns and villages that form the backdrop to the dance sequences. In fact, none of the places featured in *Bosta* are engaged with. The South therefore is largely a place of departure that is not given a visual presence. Its absence sits uncomfortably with the large role the South has played in Lebanese conflict, being the only area of Lebanon 'at war' for almost ten years after the Civil War was over. *Beirut, The Encounter* comments on the absence of the South from living memory. Haydar is shown picking up a magazine carrying the headline 'In Lebanon, there is no space for divisions of East and West', and comments, 'what about the South?'

Only three films attempt to give the South of Lebanon a visual cinematic presence (as opposed to a reference). The first is *The Rebelling South* (Al-Janoub al-Thaer), of which I could not find a copy, and the second is *Beirut ya Beirut*, made by Maroun Baghdadi on the eve of the war. Set between 1968 and 1970, *Beirut ya Beirut* revolves around four characters: a bourjois woman; two men (another bourjois and an 'ideologically-committed man'[76]), who fail in their relationships with her; and a third man, a refugee from the South who rejects Beirut and goes back to the South to participate in the resistance movement. The third film is *Ma'raka*, the only film to give a substantial visual presence to the South of Lebanon (although, ironically, the film was shot in the suburbs of Beirut and the Bekaa Valley, due to the occupation of the South by Israel at the time).[77] *Ma'raka* focuses on the Shiite resistance to the Israeli occupation in the South through paralleling the narration of the story of the martyrdom of Hussein during Ashoura's *majlis al-ta'ziyah* with the narration of stories of resistance by Southern Shiites. Roger Assaf acknowledges the limitation of focusing his film exclusively on Shiite resistance, when in 1985 resistance to the Israeli occupation was not limited to any particular group (the Syrian Social Nationalist Party and the Communist Party are examples of other active participants in this movement at the time).[78] However, the film makes a positive connection between religion and resistance. The film is keen to present everyday life in the South to stress the way life goes on regardless of hardship, with images of farmers working, people getting married, and religious events being commemorated. This is paralleled by lengthy depictions and narration of stories of suffering, where we either see or hear about people being arrested, tortured, wounded or killed by Israel. This is balanced with references to resistant acts, again either visually represented or narrated. Ashoura transforms from a religious event to one where stories of defiance are told. Visually, we witness scenes such as one presented towards the beginning of the film, where we see a family being stopped at an Israeli checkpoint on their way to their village. An Israeli soldier tries to intimidate the grandfather by asking him, 'where are you from?' The grandfather responds, 'From the village. Where are *you* from?'

Stuart Hall argues that 'our identity is partly shaped by recognition or its absence ... Non-recognition of misrecognition can inflict harm, can be a form of oppression imprisoning someone in a false, distorted and reduced mode of being'.[79] *Ma'raka* is an exception in Lebanese cinema. The lives of the people in the South are largely cinematically forgotten, and the lives that are represented are usually those of refugees, reducing the South to a tokenistic gesture at the representation of deprivation.

Forgetting is also applied to the representation of intra-Lebanese conflict. This is seen in the abstract construction of the war in films like *A Country above Wounds*, *Little Wars*, and *The Belt of Fire*. Those films present characters with no religious affiliation, and who are given religion-neutral names like Ghoussoun, Samir, Fouad, Nabil, Talal, Soraya, Abdo and Shafik, although critics have inferred the religious leanings of characters in *Little Wars* (Mohamad Soueid for example argues that Soraya cannot not be seen as a Christian).[80] Bahij Hojeij defends the vagueness of his characters and of Beirut in *The Belt of Fire* by saying:

> I wanted to avoid clichés about the war: East Beirut, West Beirut, Muslims and Christians. Those were like abbreviations of the war in the Western society's mind. I wanted to make a film set in Beirut – it doesn't matter if it's East or West; about a person's experiences – it doesn't matter if he is Muslim or Christian or Druze. The same problems took place in East and West Beirut and among Muslims and Christians. I did not want the main character to have a defined identity like that. I wanted him to remain a bit abstract, but I wanted to emphasize the environment that he lived in, which stifled human beings, oppressed the expression of love, oppressed freedom, prevented progress. I wanted the film to present the war existentially, to present it as a virus that attacks humans and society. That's why I made a parallel between the war and Camus' novel *The Plague* in the film. This virus destroys society. During war, people are prevented from communicating, one cannot realize one's identity, one cannot dream.[81]

The involvement of outside players in the war game is also subject to forgetting. In *The Shelter*, characters with obvious Muslim and Christian names (Mahmoud and Hanna) are shown hiding from snipers in the same shelter.

Mahmoud in turn is shown addressing the sniper terrorizing their neighborhood, asking, 'who has sent you? Who is supporting you?' The film also starts with a voice-over declaring, 'this is not the first war. Others came before it. Whoever won the wars, the people were always the losers'. In *A Country above Wounds*, the melodrama descends into farce with a narrative thread that is supposed to be full of symbolism and surrealism but which is one of the worst executed threads in a Lebanese film. The thread starts with a scene of a wedding, where the bride is crying out in agony for an unknown reason. Her groom rushes to consult a group of Lebanese men in the neighborhood. Each man advises him to see a different doctor: a Chinese one, a French one, a British one, a Russian one, and an American one. The men disagree over which doctor would be the best one, with each insisting that 'his' doctor would be the one. Later in the film, we see the same men, emerging one by one from two rows of buildings lining a street, and putting on white gowns on their way to examine the woman in unison. We then see a panning shot of the men as they sit in a semicircle, smiling as the bride has been 'cured' due to their unity. This caricaturish way of dealing with issues of foreign intervention denies the film any credibility. One might speculate that the reason for this method of representation is to generalize the experience of victimization of those characters, to say that the war's atrocities were shared by all in Lebanon, no matter what their background is. But at the same time:

> just as cinema lends itself to the expression of dreams, so, too, is it a powerful medium for the transmission of historical and political myths that, frequently, soften or obscure the most brutal or unpalatable of historical truths even as they give rise to compelling visions of the national past.[82]

Lebanese cinema has also taken part in a process of displacement through the focus on the issue of victimization. In this sense, 'film and other forms of popular representation ... parallel one of the principal features of ideology: concealing certain features or parts of reality while simultaneously disclosing certain aspects of that same past, present, and range of conceivable futures'.[83] Displacement is a strategy for coping with unpleasant pasts. It replaces questions of responsibility with more comfortable ones.[84] As Leila Fawaz writes about *The Tornado*, *A Time Has Come*, *Once Upon a Time*, *Beirut* and *A Suspended Life*, the 'films all portray the randomness, cruelty, and waste of a civil war. Those who live through it are victims: even when they seem to take the initiative and make choices, those choices are limited and mainly out of their control'.[85]

A Country above Wounds presents the most simplistic representation of victimization. The film is an over-the-top melodramatic construction that 'symbolizes' the war as an evil-looking man who appears every now and then in the film, and who we see laughing as he witnesses incidents of conflict among Lebanese citizens. The film couples this with lengthy speeches by its different characters where they declare their patriotism ('My love is for my country above all. I am loyal to it above all else') and blame the war on mysterious Others ('Who is playing with this country?'). *The Explosion* is clear in its blame, presenting a character declaring 'there are outside forces playing with the country. It's bringing back sectarian divisions between Muslims and Christians'. The film even blames Lebanon's booming drug trade during the Civil War on victimization: in the article that Samir writes about marijuana fields in the Bekaa Valley, he argues that the phenomenon is a result of the Bekaa being 'a forgotten area of Lebanon whose people's only means of living is drugs'.

Lebanon in Spite of Everything dedicates almost half its screen time to sequences representing the imagination of the ten-year-old girl Joumana. The sequences are a visual representation of what Joumana writes in her Arabic language essay assignments. They depict scenes of horror, death and fear as they revolve around the story of a man looking for a son he lost during the war. We follow this fictional man on his journey as he encounters different examples of terror. Images of bombs, snipers, wounded people and children running away from a playground being shelled merge with stories of displacement and futile ceasefires. The visual sequences are complemented by the reading out of Joumana's essays by characters in the film (her teacher, her father, her aunt and herself). However, the intricacy of Joumana's essays makes her character less and less convincing as the film goes along, as it becomes impossible to imagine a ten-year-old child who is capable of such a fine articulation of issues of loss, pessimism and despair. It therefore becomes clear that Joumana is merely used as a narrative device enabling the film to comment on sensitive topics that could have been otherwise controversial to represent. For example, the film shows a sequence where Joumana's teacher reads out a segment of an essay where she describes the Lebanese Civil War as 'the great Lebanese world war'; the teacher, Rif'at, responds that 'world wars are those involving different major states, but the Lebanese war is...' Rif'at pauses, lost for words, as Joumana reacts to his feedback with questioning eyes. Later in the film, Joumana reads a letter from her brother in Germany that states, 'why has this happened to us? It's international politics'. At the end of the film, Rif'at reads another essay by Joumana, where the lines said by the fictional man she has invented state, 'They say it's the Arabs, the Jews, the Communists, the attempt at nationalizing Palestinians ... I'm lost'.

Even postwar films about the war like *West Beyrouth* and *Beirut Phantoms* – which were made by the newer generation of filmmakers – 'located their filmmakers themselves outside the war: the war was that of the previous generation, not their generation, so they see no need for apologizing for it'.[86] For example, Westmoreland comments that the character Tarek in *West Beyrouth* – who can be seen as mirroring Ziad Doueiri – 'is an innocent witness, passively watching the country spiral into war'.[87] In this sense, the filmmakers are detaching their whole generation from the preceding one. This process can be seen as an example of what Forty and Kuchler call the 'art of forgetting'.[88] Lebanese cinema presents a tension between, on one hand, the need to represent the war, and on the other hand, to detach oneself from it.

What is problematic in those films is that they externalize the war. By this I mean that they present the war as something *happening to us*, i.e. when the films do not construct 'us' as an agent, only as a passive receiver. The films in this respect follow the tradition of using the terms 'they'/'them' during and after the Lebanese Civil War. It was never 'us' who engaged in atrocities, it was always 'them' who did it. Who are those mysterious 'they'? This question was never answered. Whether through presenting militiamen as outsiders or through the representation of 'the war of others on our land', Lebanese cinema can be seen as a response to Portelli's statement that '[t]oday, history has been replaced (effaced) by myth, and above all by the question: who do we blame?'[89] The blame is detached from 'us'. As Studlar and Desser argue, '[m]odern societies, of course, are cognizant of a past, but frequently find it filled with unpleasant truths and half-known facts, so they set about rewriting it. The mass media, including cinema and television, have proven to be important mechanisms whereby this rewriting – this re-imaging – of the past can occur'.[90]

Forgetting is also a reflection of the present. As Van Dyke and Alcock argue, '[p]eople remember or forget the past according to the needs of the present, and social memory is an active and ongoing process'.[91] Lowenthal says that '[m]emories are not ready-made reflections of the past, but eclectic, selective reconstructions'.[92] While Passerini reminds us that historical narratives are about words as much as they are about silences: 'the art of memory cannot but be also an art of forgetting, through the mediation of silence and the alteration of silence and sound'.[93] Perhaps the best illustration of this tension is *In the Shadows of the City*. Jean Chamoun constructs the film as a comment on the necessity of remembering the war. He even weaves a sequence into the film where the wife of a kidnapped man, Siham, confronts Abu Samir to ask about her husband. Abu Samir tells her to forget about her husband and move on, to which Siham responds, 'who counts on forgetting, is building the basis for a new war'. Jean Chamoun comments that this scene is critical of how 'people want to forget to "build a new Lebanon". But the problem with Lebanon is this amnesia'.[94]

But this process of remembering is undermined in three ways. First, the film tries to distance itself from sectarian tensions by giving the characters religiously-neutral names and by only hinting at their religious affiliations. Chamoun defends this by saying that 'it is not necessary to name Muslims and Christians to depict sectarianism'.[95] While this is true, the constructed neutrality becomes unnecessary as the film presents other, more effective, means of representing sectarianism and its resistance by people. For example, Rami's family is shown helping Yasmin's as they are forced to evacuate their home in West Beirut. Second, the film presents the war as an abstraction and does not present any historical 'facts' overtly. Instead we get oblique statements like those pronounced by Yasmin's brother Nadim. Nadim disapproves of Yasmin's friendship with Rami, and tells her 'you will become like his people. You are old enough to realize who you are hanging out with'. Later Nadim announces that he is leaving his family to go and join 'the militia'. Finally, the film's main weakness lies in the way – like *A Country above Wounds* and *The Explosion* – it blames the war on mysterious Others. We see a musician in the film, Nabil, saying that he is skeptical that the problems in Lebanon in 1975 are sectarian: 'how come it is only *now* that the sects can't tolerate one another? Someone is behind this'. A man responds to him by saying, 'I'm sure they are foreigners'. Even Nadim is heard talking about the need to 'get rid of the foreigners'. One can read the response to Nabil's statement in a multitude of ways (can the foreigners be Israeli for example?), while Nadim's can be read as a hint at the Christian right-wing militias' intolerance of the presence of Palestinian *fedayeen* in Lebanon.

When I asked Jean Chamoun about the film's stance towards the war, he replied that 'the war divided society in Lebanon. The characters in the film refer to ordinary civilians, whom the war was imposed on'.[96] While it is true that not everyone in Lebanon took part in the war machine, this construction of the war as an outsider is problematic as discussed earlier in this chapter. *In the Shadows of the City* is therefore symptomatic of the tension between the need to remember and the guilt of the memory. It is symptomatic of Lebanon in the post-Civil War period, a country still looking for its identity in the past and the future. As Stuart Hall says:

> identities are about questions of using the resources of history, language and culture in the process of becoming rather than being: not 'who we are' or 'where we come from', so much as what we might become, how we have been represented and how that bears on how we might represent ourselves. They relate to the invention of tradition as much as to tradition itself.[97]

Trauma Cinema

But there is another need in the present that triggers Lebanese cinema's relationship with the memory of the Civil War. Pierre Nora has suggested that 'the contemporary preoccupation with memory is prompted by the fear that what has been called the national "substance" or "essence" is fast disappearing'.[98] Lebanon's problem is not that the national essence is disappearing; it is that Lebanon is a country without a national essence. Moreover, the Civil War jeopardized the fragile ties stitching the country together. As Dolores Hayden argues, '[m]emory ... becomes more important when losses accumulate. The inability to forget traumatic experiences may become as much of a problem as wanting to remember positive ones'.[99] Oklowski elaborates on this: '[t]he trauma produced by a tragedy in childhood should not be construed as a sign of a past wound; it is a present fact, that of having had a tragedy, having been wounded'.[100] The films' focus on the war can therefore be seen as an illustration of its presence as a persistent trauma.

As Walker argues, a symptom of individual trauma is the recurring recollection of traumatic events.[101] The obsession with representing the war can be looked at as a case of collective trauma. In this sense, Lebanese cinema becomes an example of 'trauma cinema'. Walker defines 'trauma cinema' as 'a group of films, drawn from various genres, modes and national cinemas, each of which deals with world-shattering events ... in a non-realist style that figures the traumatic past as meaningful, fragmentary, virtually unspeakable, and striated with fantasy constructions'.[102] Lebanese cinema complicates this definition by not exclusively drawing on non-realist styles of representation. However, even through realism, Lebanese cinema is not concerned with representing truth. Westmoreland for example points out that the Ain el-Rimmaneh incident of 13 April 1975, which catalyzed the Civil War, is represented in *West Beyrouth* as disrupting school, whereas 'critics argue that students would not have been in school because this event was on a Sunday'.[103] He adds, 'we quickly realize the precedent of character over history in the narrative flow of this film'.[104]

The Civil War in Lebanese cinema is a mixture of reality and fantasy. The cinema is not concerned with documenting the war, but reflecting on it, while also sometimes shying away from confronting this reflection. But whether it is translated or imagined, the Civil War remains Lebanese cinema's main concern, and main trauma. The different ways in which the cinema deals with the war present a challenge to trauma theory. Hodgkin and Radstone write that while trauma theory is concerned with determining the origin of trauma, its focus on the traumatic event blinds it to

> the way the mind makes its own meanings. Trauma from this point of view is a response not so much to an event as to the meaning given to

that event. And even the event itself is not a precondition: trauma may be the product of fantasy, of things that did not happen as well as of things that did.[105]

In this sense, the importance of Lebanese cinema in the context of the Civil War is that the cinema can be looked at as a memory project giving a voice to a silenced past.

As Merridale argues, narratives of war are open to 'periodic reassessment',[106] and memory is continuously revised.[107] The different versions of memory are in constant contest, generating competing images and historical memories of war.[108] As we have seen, in Lebanon the 'attempted destruction of social memory' through the creation of public myths has served to sanitize the war and induce forgetfulness of its monstrosity.[109] While Lebanese cinema is sometimes complicit in this position, it nevertheless serves an important function in highlighting the central role that the Civil War plays in the Lebanese imagination.

In the Lebanese context, there is no clear cultural center. Lebanon is composed of different religions, sects and ethnicities, where everyone is a minority. The tumultuous history of Lebanon shows how almost every group in Lebanese society has been, at one moment or another, an Other. Lebanon is a place still searching for an ultimate formula for unity. Paradoxically, the Civil War has been one of the few events that the Lebanese people have experienced collectively – almost as a 'nation'. The centrality of the war in Lebanese cinema can therefore be seen as one way in which the '"entropic" obsession with the past' is channeled.[110] War drove the Lebanese apart, but its memory is bringing them together. Lebanese cinema's importance here is that it does not present a coherent narrative of the war, but multiple, sometimes conflicting narratives:

> Collectively, these narratives contribute, by a sifting process that is gradual and probably not conscious, to the emerging, evolving story of their wars, a story that is neither history nor memory, but myth – a compound war-story that gives meaning and coherence to the incoherences of war-in-its-details, which is what each narrative separately tells.[111]

But perhaps most prophetically, the centrality of the war in postwar Lebanese cinema is an indirect expression of the social and political instability that still permeates Lebanon. As Melling argues, it is the *prospect of war* that 'invariably creates a fixation with history'.[112]

Endnotes

1. Reading, Anna (2002). *The Social Inheritance of the Holocaust: Gender, Culture and Memory*, New York: Palgrave.
2. Shaw, Martin (1997). 'Past wars and present conflicts: from the Second World War to the Gulf War', in Evans, Martin and Kenneth Lunn (eds), *War and Memory in the Twentieth Century*, Oxford: Berg, p.192, my emphasis.
3. Reading: *The Social Inheritance of the Holocaust*, p.33.
4. Ibid.
5. Samuel, Raphael (1994). *Theatres of Memory*, London: Verso, p.x.
6. Samuel: *Theatres of Memory*.
7. Hamilton, Paula (2003). 'Sale of the century? Memory and historical consciousness in Australia', in Hodgkin, Katharine and Susannah Radstone (eds), *Contested Pasts: The Politics of Memory*, London: Routledge, p.142.
8. Taylor, Diana (2003). *Performing Cultural Memory in the Americas*, Durham: Duke University Press.
9. Burgoyne, Robert (2003). 'From contested to consensual memory: the Rock and Roll Hall of Fame and Museum', in Hodgkin, Katharine and Susannah Radstone (eds), *Contested Pasts: The Politics of Memory*, London: Routledge, p.208.
10. Burgoyne: 'From contested to consensual memory', p.209.
11. Burgoyne: 'From contested to consensual memory', p.210.
12. Hellmann, John (1997). 'The Vietnam film and American memory', in Evans, Martin and Kenneth Lunn (eds), *War and Memory in the Twentieth Century*, Oxford: Berg, p.177.
13. Shaw: 'Past wars and present conflicts', p.191.
14. Hellmann: 'The Vietnam film and American memory'.
15. Samuel: *Theatres of Memory*.
16. Harper, Sue (1997). 'Popular film, popular memory: the case of the Second World War', in Evans, Martin and Kenneth Lunn (eds), *War and Memory in the Twentieth Century*, Oxford: Berg, p.164.
17. Eley, Geoff (1997). 'Foreword', in Evans, Martin and Kenneth Lunn (eds), *War and Memory in the Twentieth Century*, Oxford: Berg, p.ix.
18. Joyce, Rosemary A. (2003). 'Concrete memories: fragments of the classic Maya past (500–1000AD)', in Van Dyke, Ruth M. and Susan E. Alcock (eds), *Archaeologies of Memory*, Oxford: Blackwell, p.107.
19. Eley: 'Foreword', p.viii.
20. Harper: 'Popular film, popular memory'.
21. Ahmed, Sara et al (2003). 'Introduction: uprootings/regroundings: questions of home and migration', in Ahmed, Sara et al (eds), *Uprootings/Regroundings: Questions of Home and Migration*, Oxford: Berg, p.9.
22. Ibid.
23. Edensor, Tim (2002). *National Identity, Popular Culture and Everyday Life*, Oxford: Berg, p.20.
24. White, Hayden (1988). 'Historiography and historiophoty', *The American Historical Review* (December), 95(5), p.1193.

25 Ibid.
26 Eley: 'Foreword'.
27 Sorlin, Pierre (1999). 'Children as war victims in postwar European cinema', in Winter, Jay and Emmanuel Sivan (eds), *War and Remembrance in the Twentieth Century*, Cambridge: Cambridge University Press, p.107.
28 Healy, Chris (2003). 'Dead man: film, colonialism and memory', in Hodgkin, Katharine and Susannah Radstone (eds), *Contested Pasts: The Politics of Memory*, London: Routledge, p.223.
29 Custen, George (1992). *Bio/Pics: How Hollywood Constructed Public History*, New Brunswick, New Jersey: Rutgers University Press, p.12.
30 Ibid.
31 Winter, Jay and Sivan, Emmanuel (1999). 'Setting the framework', in Winter, Jay and Emmanuel Sivan (eds), *War and Remembrance in the Twentieth Century*, Cambridge: Cambridge University Press, pp.6–39.
32 Hodgkin, Katharine and Radstone, Susannah (2003a). 'Introduction: contested pasts', in Hodgkin, Katharine and Susannah Radstone (eds), *Contested Pasts: The Politics of Memory*, London: Routledge, p.8.
33 Shaw: 'Past wars and present conflicts'.
34 Young, James (2003). 'Between history and memory: the voice of the eyewitness', in Douglass, Ana and Thomas A. Vogler (eds), *Witness and Memory: The Discourse of Trauma*, London: Routledge, pp. 275–84.
35 Bradley, Richard (2003). 'The translation of time', in Van Dyke, Ruth M. and Susan E. Alcock (eds), *Archaeologies of Memory*, Oxford: Blackwell, pp.221–7.
36 Hynes, Samuel (1999). 'Personal narratives and commemoration', in Winter, Jay and Emmanuel Sivan (eds), *War and Remembrance in the Twentieth Century*, Cambridge: Cambridge University Press, pp.205–20.
37 Greene, Naomi (1999). *Landscapes of Loss: The National Past in Postwar French Cinema*, Princeton, New Jersey: Princeton University Press, p.3.
38 Greene: *Landscapes of Loss*, p.14.
39 King, Nicola (2000). *Memory, Narrative, Identity: Remembering the Self*, Edinburgh: Edinburgh University Press, p.11.
40 Lowenthal, David (1985). *The Past is a Foreign Country*, Cambridge: Cambridge University Press, p.xv.
41 Deleuze, Gilles (1994). *Difference and Repetition*, London: The Athlone Press, p.80.
42 Assaf, Leyla (2007). *Interview with the author*, London: April.
43 Ibid.
44 Pillai, Poonam (1996). 'Notes on centers and margins', in Morgan, Michael and Susan Leggett (eds), *Mainstreams(s) and Margins: Cultural Politics in the 90s*, Westport, Connecticut: Greenwood Press, p.8.
45 Joreige, Khalil (2005). Introduction to the screening of *A Perfect Day*, London Film Festival, October 26.
46 Tonkiss, Fran (2003). 'The ethics of indifference: community and solitude in the city', *International Journal of Cultural Studies*, 6(3), p.300.

47 Carole Abboud, quoted in Al-Hajj, Nada (2002). 'Carole Abboud on her cinema, television and theater experiences', *An-Nahar*, December 22 (Arabic).
48 Salhab, Ghassan (2004). *Interview with the author*, Beirut, April.
49 Ki'di, George (2006). 'Falafel', *Al-Balad*, December (Arabic).
50 Variety (2007). *Falafel*, January 5 [Online]. Available: http://www.variety.com/review/VE1117932397.html?categoryid=1270&cs=1
51 Kammoun, Michel (2006). 'Falafel', *Michel Kammoun Official Website*. Available: http://www.michelkammoun.com
52 King: *Memory, Narrative, Identity*, p.11.
53 King: *Memory, Narrative, Identity*, p.12.
54 Ibid.
55 Hodgkin and Radstone: 'Introduction: contested pasts', p.1.
56 Bhabha, Homi (1990). 'DissemiNation: time, narrative, and the margins of the modern nation', in Bhabha, Homi (ed), *Nation and Narration*, London: Routledge, p.294.
57 Edensor: *National Identity*.
58 Al-Ariss, Ibrahim (2006). *Interview with the author*, Beirut, April.
59 Westmoreland, Mark (2002). 'Cinematic dreaming: on phantom poetics and the longing for a Lebanese national cinema', *Text, Practice, Performance*, issue IV, p.37.
60 Van Dyke, Ruth M. and Alcock, Susan E. (2003). 'Archaeologies of memory: an introduction', in Van Dyke, Ruth M. and Susan E. Alcock (eds), *Archaeologies of Memory*, Oxford: Blackwell, p.2.
61 Bowen, Jeremy (2006). *War Stories*, London: Simon and Schuster, p.51.
62 Salhab: *Interview with the author*.
63 Boym, Svetlana (2001). *The Future of Nostalgia*, New York: Basic Books, p.xiii.
64 Boym: *The Future of Nostalgia*, p.xvi.
65 Doueiri, Ziad (2004). *Interview with the author*, London, April.
66 Ibid.
67 Hirsch, Marianne and Spitzer, Leo (2003). '"We would never have come without you": generations of nostalgia', in Hodgkin, Katharine and Susannah Radstone (eds), *Contested Pasts: The Politics of Memory*, London: Routledge, p.83.
68 King: *Memory, Narrative, Identity*, p.175.
69 Al-Ariss, Ibrahim (2000). 'A look into Lebanese war cinema on the civil war's twenty-fifth anniversary', *Al-Hayat*, April 14 (Arabic).
70 Hockstader, Lee (1999). 'Lebanon's forgotten civil war', *Washington Post Foreign Service* (Monday December 20) [Online]. Available: http://www.library.cornell.edu/colldev/mideast/civwr1.htm
71 Nasri, Samir (1982). 'The Lebanese filmmakers' excuse is that they are passionate', *An-Nahar*, December 30 (Arabic).
72 Arbid, Danielle (2006). *Interview with the author*, Paris, April.
73 Codsi, Jean-Claude (2004). *Interview with the author*, Beirut, April.
74 Hellmann: 'The Vietnam film and American memory'.
75 Doueiri: *Interview with the author*.
76 Khalaf, Ghazi (1994). 'Documentary cinema: a true human testimony to the harshness of war', *Ad-Deyar*, October 18 (Arabic).

77 Assaf, Roger (2006). *Interview with the author*, Beirut, April.
78 Ibid.
79 Hall (2000), quoted in Taylor, Gary and Steve Spencer (2004). 'Introduction', in Taylor, Gary and Steve Spencer (eds), *Social Identities: Multidisciplinary Approaches*, London: Routledge, p.3.
80 Soueid, Mohamad (1986). *The Postponed Cinema: Films of the Lebanese Civil War*, Beirut: The Arab Research Organization (Arabic).
81 Hojeij, Bahij (2005). *Interview with the author*, Beirut, April.
82 Greene: *Landscapes of Loss*, p.6.
83 Williams, Doug (1991). 'Concealment and disclosure: from *Birth of a Nation* to the Vietnam war film', *International Political Science Review* (January), 12(1), p.30.
84 Studlar, Gaylyn and Desser, David (1988). 'Never having to say you're sorry: *Rambo*'s rewriting of the Vietnam war', *Film Quarterly* (Autumn) 42(1), pp.9–16.
85 Fawaz, Leila (1997). 'Once Upon a Time, Beirut; A Suspended Life; The Tornado; Time Has Come', *The American Historical Review* (February) 102(1), p.252.
86 Al-Ariss, Ibrahim (2000). 'A look into Lebanese war cinema'.
87 Westmoreland, 'Cinematic dreaming', p.40.
88 Forty, Adrian and Kuchler, Susanne (eds) (1999). *The Art of Forgetting*, Oxford: Berg.
89 Portelli, Alessandro (2003). 'The massacre at the Fosse Ardeatine: history, myth, ritual and symbol', in Hodgkin, Katharine and Susannah Radstone (eds), *Contested Pasts: The Politics of Memory*, London: Routledge, p.32.
90 Studlar and Desser: 'Never having to say you're sorry', p.10.
91 Van Dyke and Alcock: 'Archaeologies of memory', p.3.
92 Lowenthal: *The Past is a Foreign Country*, p.210.
93 Passerini, Luissa (2003). 'Memories between silence and oblivion', in Hodgskin, Katharine and Susannah Radstone (eds), *Contested Pasts: The Politics of Memory*, London: Routledge, p.250.
94 Chamoun, Jean (2004). *Interview with the author*, Beirut, April.
95 Ibid.
96 Ibid.
97 Hall, Stuart (1996). 'Introduction: who needs "identity"?', in Hall, Stuart and Paul du Gay (eds), *Questions of Cultural Identity*, London: Sage, p.4.
98 Greene: *Landscapes of Loss*, p.4.
99 Hayden, Dolores (1999). 'Landscapes of loss and remembrance: the case of Little Tokyo in Los Angeles', in Winter, Jay and Emmanuel Sivan (eds), *War and Remembrance in the Twentieth Century*, Cambridge: Cambridge University Press, p.144.
100 Olkowski, Dorothea (1998). *Gilles Deleuze and the Ruin of Representation*, Berkeley: University of California Press, p.110.
101 Walker, Janet (2003). 'The traumatic paradox: autobiographical documentary and the psychology of memory', in Hodgkin, Katharine and Susannah Radstone (eds), *Contested Pasts: The Politics of Memory*, London: Routledge, pp.104–19.

102 Walker: 'The traumatic paradox', p.109.
103 Westmoreland: 'Cinematic dreaming', p.39.
104 Westmoreland: 'Cinematic dreaming', p.40.
105 Hodgkin, Katharine and Radstone, Susannah (2003c). 'Remembering suffering: trauma and history', in Hodgkin, Katharine and Susannah Radstone (eds), *Contested Pasts: The Politics of Memory*, London: Routledge, p.97.
106 Merridale, Catherine (1999). 'War, death, and remembrance in Soviet Russia', in Winter, Jay and Emmanuel Sivan (eds), *War and Remembrance in the Twentieth Century*, Cambridge: Cambridge University Press, p.61.
107 Meskell, Lynn (2003). 'Memory's materiality: ancestral presence, commemorative practice and disjunctive locales', in Van Dyke, Ruth M. and Susan E. Alcock, (eds), *Archaeologies of Memory*, Oxford: Blackwell, pp.34–55.
108 Merridale: 'War, death, and remembrance in Soviet Russia'.
109 Merridale: 'War, death, and remembrance in Soviet Russia', p.63.
110 Edensor: *National Identity*, p.25.
111 Hynes, 'Personal narratives and commemoration', p.220.
112 Melling, Phil (1997). 'War and memory in the new world order', in Evans, Martin and Kenneth Lunn (eds), *War and Memory in the Twentieth Century*, Oxford: Berg, p.255.

Epilogue

ON NATIONAL CINEMA

The relationship between the nation and art in general, and the nation and cinema in particular, has been theorized in two different ways. Theorists like Anthony Smith see the arts as an expression of the nation as an enduring entity,[1] while others like Gellner 'assume that nations are constructed in a process of myth-making' which includes artistic expression.[2] Both tropes are linked by a focus on the role of communication. Different theorists have expressed overlapping views on this issue. Benedict Anderson stresses the centrality of the role of communicative space in the process of nation formation.[3] Hobsbawm adds to this argument that communication functions not only in the creation of a nation, but also in maintaining it.[4] While Gellner argues that in such communication, it is

> the language and style of the transmission [that] is important, that only he who can understand them, or can acquire such comprehensions, is included in a moral and economic community, and that he who does not and cannot, is excluded ... What is actually *said* matters little.[5]

This has led Hastings to conclude that '[n]ationhood can survive only through an exercise in imagination, both collective and personal'.[6] There has been a degree of disagreement over what this imagination means. Benedict Anderson criticizes Ernest Gellner's categorizing of imagination as 'falsity' and 'fabrication', saying that all communities are imagined.[7] In this sense, national cinema can be looked at as a space for the creation and maintenance of an imagined community whose members imagine themselves as a coherent community with a secure shared identity and sense of belonging.[8]

Andrew Higson has come up with a typology of national cinema where he lists four elements, each of which can be used to define what national cinema means. The first element defines national cinema economically, with this definition encompassing the infrastructures of production, distribution, and exhibition within a particular nation-state; the scale of capitalization and integration, the patterns of ownership and control and the size and make-up of the workforce of these infrastructures; the size of the domestic market and the degree of penetration of foreign markets; the extent of foreign intervention; and the relative economic health of the industry.[9]

As we have seen in this book, Lebanese cinema fails on almost all counts within this definition. Lebanese cinema has no production infrastructure to speak of, being almost completely reliant on foreign funding. Its distribution is limited both within Lebanon and abroad, and the same applies to exhibition, which includes both cinematic exhibition and video. While Lebanese films do utilize the local talent for things like camera work and editing, films shot on 35mm are usually processed abroad. The size of the Lebanese domestic market is too small to sustain a healthy industry under current conditions, whereby Lebanese cinema enjoys virtually no government subsidy.

The second element defines national cinema

in terms of exhibition and consumption. In this case, the major questions are: which films are audiences watching? How many foreign films, and especially American films, are in distribution within a particular nation-state? How do audiences use these films and what are the effects of this diet on their well-being? Should these viewing practices be regulated? Often, what is at stake here is an anxiety about the nation's cultural standing, and about the assumed effects of foreign cultural intervention.[10]

Lebanese cinema does not exist comfortably within this definition. Over the last 30 years, the vast majority of films exhibited and distributed in Lebanon have been American, followed by Egyptian and then French films. Even before the Civil War, the Lebanese audience was primarily a consumer of European and Egyptian films. Lebanese films have never been an essential part of the national cultural diet, unlike Lebanese music for example. So while almost every Lebanese person, of any age, can recognize a song by Fairuz, very few people can relate to, or even recall, Lebanese films they have encountered. An incident I have been involved in is an example of this detachment. In 2007, a London-based Lebanese charity asked me to act as an adviser for a Lebanese film night it was planning. I was asked to provide a list of suggested films to screen, under the condition that the films should come from the 1960s – a decade thought to be, by the event organizers, a nostalgic one for the Lebanese cinema audience, which would particularly appeal to 'our parents' generation' who would have been in their twenties in that decade. I struggled to come up with nostalgia-invoking titles from the period, and eventually settled on the three Rahbani productions from the 1960s: *Safar Barlik*, *Bint al-Hariss*, and *Bayya' al-Khawatem*. I emailed the suggestions to the organizers, and they decided to test the titles on one of the organizers' mothers, a woman in her sixties. They replied to me disappointedly, saying that while she recognized the film titles, her reaction was that 'she didn't really seem to know them that well. She had heard of them, but there wasn't that nostalgic reaction we were hoping for'. I emailed them back saying:

> If *Bayya' al-Khawatem*, *Bint al-Hariss* or *Safar Barlik* did not invoke nostalgia, then no other Lebanese film will. If you want to invoke nostalgia, mention something like *Ma'boudat al-Gamahir*, or *al-Warda al-Bayda'*, or any Faten Hamama film ... yes, these are Egyptian films, and this is what our parents grew up watching. They did not grow up watching Lebanese films. Sorry to disappoint you, but we are a people detached from our own cinema.

Andrew Higson's third element links national cinema to issues of cultural specificity. He states:

> such a perspective will privilege particular film movements or directors felt to have some connection with the national culture, where the latter is defined in high cultural terms. From this perspective, popular cinema generally becomes something quite separate from national cinema, hardly worthy of appreciation.[11]

He goes on to quote Geoffrey Nowell-Smith who has said that there has been a consistent struggle to allow 'the recognition of popular forms as a legitimate part of national cultural life'.[12] Higson's third definition examines national cinema as an element of high culture which is separate from the mainstream. Again, Lebanese cinema complicates this definition through the majority of its products being somewhere between high art and the popular (examples include Maroun Baghadi's, Samir Habchi's, Jocelyne Saab's, and Randa Chahal's films, among others), and with its popular products being in turn divided into highly-regarded 'quality' popular products like the Rahbani films and films by Ziad Doueiri and Danielle Arbid, and 'commercial' films like those of Samir al-Ghoussaini and Youssef Charaf ed-Din. In other words, Lebanese cinema does not fit the definition because it resists the high/low culture binary.

Higson's final definition of national cinema is one about representation. He writes:

This time, the concern is with what the films are about. Do they share a common style or world-view? Do they share common themes, motifs, or preoccupations? How do they project the national character? How do they dramatize the fantasies of national identity? Are they concerned with questions of nationhood? What role do they play in constructing the sense or the image of a nation? ... Probably the most common version of this view of national cinema is the argument that 'a nation's films reflect a nation's thoughts', implying that cinema simply reflects or expresses a pre-existing national identity, consciousness, or culture... An alternative view is that national identity is constructed in and through representation: 'a nation does not express itself through its culture: it is culture that produces "the nation"'.[13]

This book has attempted to answer the questions presented by Higson under this definition. However, the book did not address the questions to probe whether Lebanese cinema is a national cinema or not; rather, the questions were used to reveal the role of cinema in commenting on and reflecting social malaise and trauma. By reflecting, the assumption is not, as Higson puts it, 'that cinema simply reflects or expresses a pre-existing national identity'.[14] Rather, the case of Lebanese cinema highlights the oversimplification of such a view. Instead of reflecting national identity, Lebanese cinema reveals the difficulty of asserting its existence in the case of Lebanon. A similar complication occurs when examining the alternative view, that it is culture that produces the nation. To assume that a culture is capable of that, the culture in question has to be created, consumed and accepted as belonging to the Self by a number of people who can then use this commonality to establish a nation. Lebanon differs by being a place that has been differently imagined by its different inhabitants since before its inception. Lebanon, as stated earlier in this book, is difficult to categorize as a nation.

However, perhaps ironically, what seems to unite the films of Lebanese cinema is the Civil War itself. The Civil War is the most visible element of films made over the last 30 years, and does not seem to be going away any time soon. With the vast majority of Lebanese films over the last three decades being about the war in one way or another, one can go far as saying that the Civil War has become *the* defining feature of Lebanese cinema.

Endnotes

1 Smith, Anthony (1991). *National Identity*, London: Penguin Books.
2 Hjort, Mette and Mackenzie, Scott (2000). 'Introduction', in Hjort, Mette and Scott Mackenzie (eds), *Cinema and Nation*, London: Routledge, p.1.

3 Anderson, Benedict (1983). *Imagined Communities: Reflections on the Origin and Spread of Nationalism*, London: Verso.
4 Hobsbawm, Eric (1990). *Nations and Nationalism Since 1780*, Cambridge: Cambridge University Press.
5 Gellner, Ernest (2006). *Nations and Nationalism*, London: Blackwell (2nd edition), p. 122, emphasis in original.
6 Hastings, Adrian (1997). *The Construction of Nationhood: Ethnicity, Religion and Nationalism*, Cambridge: Cambridge University Press, p.27.
7 Anderson: *Imagined Communities*, p.7.
8 Anderson: *Imagined Communities*.
9 Higson, Andrew (1995). *Waving the Flag: Constructing a National Cinema in Britain*, Oxford: Clarendon, p.4.
10 Higson: *Waving the Flag*, p.5.
11 Ibid.
12 Nowell-Smith, Geoffrey (1987). 'Popular culture', *New Formations* (2), p.80.
13 Higson: *Waving the Flag*, pp.5–6.
14 Higson: *Waving the Flag*, p.6.

BIBLIOGRAPHY

Abu Khalil, As'ad (2005). 'The ugly (real) face of Lebanon', *The Angry Arab News Service* (Thursday August 18) [Online]. Available: http://angryarab.blogspot.com/2005/08/sushar-rosky-lest-she-dies-namelessly.html

Abu Mrad, Ilham (1979). 'Why the new film theaters?', *As-Safir*, January 28 (Arabic).

Agamben, Giorgio (1998). *Homo Sacer: Sovereign Power and Bare Life*, translated by Daniel Heller-Roazen, Stanford: Stanford University Press.

Ahmed, Sara (2000). 'Embodying strangers', in Horner, Avril and Angela Keane (eds), *Body Matters: Feminism, Textuality, Corporeality*, Manchester: Manchester University Press, pp.85–96.

Ahmed, Sara (2002). 'Racialized Bodies', in Evans, Mary and Ellie Lee (eds), *Real Bodies: A Sociological Introduction*, New York: Palgrave, pp.46–63.

Ahmed, Sara et al (2003). 'Introduction: uprootings/regroundings: questions of home and migration', in Ahmed, Sara et al (eds), *Uprootings/Regroundings: Questions of Home and Migration*, Oxford: Berg, pp.1–19.

Al-Ahrar (1984). *Proposed Law to Impose Taxes on Home Videos*, April 14 (Arabic).

Al-Ariss, Ibrahim (1984). 'Reflections on Lebanese cinema and its history', *Al-Anwar*, March 5 (Arabic).

Al-Ariss, Ibrahim (1998). 'A panoramic representation of the history of Lebanese cinema at l'Institut du Monde Arabe', *Al-Hayat*, October 9 (Arabic).

Al-Ariss, Ibrahim (2000). 'A look into Lebanese war cinema on the civil war's twenty-fifth anniversary', *Al-Hayat*, April 14 (Arabic).

Al-Ariss, Ibrahim (2006). *Interview with the author*, Beirut, April.

Alawiyeh, Borhan (2004). *Interview with the author*, Beirut, April.

Al-Hajj, Nada (2002). 'Carole Abboud on her cinema, television and theater experiences', *An-Nahar*, December 22 (Arabic).

Al-Kassan, Jean (1982). 'Lebanese cinema from a critical historical perspective', *Al-Anwar*, April 22 (Arabic).

Alter, Peter (1985). *Nationalism*, London: Edward Arnold.
Anderson, Benedict (1983). *Imagined Communities: Reflections on the Origin and Spread of Nationalism*, London: Verso.
Anderson, Benedict (1999). 'The opening of Screen 6 at Cinema Empire: exclusive to European cinema', *An-Nahar*, May 5 (Arabic).
Anthias, Floya and Yuval-Davis, Nira (1989). 'Introduction', in Yuval-Davis, Nira and Floya Anthias (eds), *Woman-Nation-State*, London: Macmillan, pp.1–15.
Aractingi, Philippe (2006). *Interview with the author*, Beirut, April.
Arbid, Danielle (2006). *Interview with the author*, Paris, April.
Ardener, Shirley (1993). 'Ground rules and social maps for women: an introduction', in Ardener, Shirley (ed), *Women and Space: Ground Rules and Social Maps*, Oxford: Berg, pp.1–30.
Armitage, John (2003). 'Militarized bodies: an introduction', *Body & Society*, 9(4): pp.1–12.
Ashkal Alwan (2007). 'What we do', *Ashkal Alwan Official Website*. Available: http://www.ashkalalwan.org/
Assaf, Leyla (2007). *Interview with the author*, London, April.
Assaf, Roger (2006). *Interview with the author*, Beirut, April.
Atallah, Bshara (2006). *Interview with the author*, Beirut, April.
Bacha, Abido (1995). *Lebanese Cinema 1929–1995*, Beirut: Lebanese Ministry of Culture (Arabic).
Baghdadi, Maroun (1992). 'Interview with Mohamad Soueid', *An-Nahar*, September 5.
Baghdadi, Maroun (1993). 'Republished 1992 interview with Mohamad Soueid', *An-Nahar*, December 18.
Ball-Rokeach, S.J. (1980). 'Normative and deviant violence from a normative perspective', *Social Problems*, 28(1): pp.45–62.
Barrett, Frank J. (2001). 'The organizational construction of hegemonic masculinity: the case of the US Navy', in Whitehead, Stephen and Frank J. Barrett (eds), *The Masculinities Reader*, Cambridge: Polity Press, pp.77–99.
Barthes, Roland (1997). 'Semiology and the urban', in Leach, Neil (ed), *Rethinking Architecture: A Reader in Cultural Theory*, London: Routledge, pp.166–72.
Baubock, Rainer (1996). 'Social and cultural integration in a civil society', in Baubock, Rainer, Agnes Heller and Aristide R. Zolberg (eds), *The Challenge of Diversity: Integration and Pluralism in Societies of Immigration*, Aldershot: Avebury, pp.67–132.
Baudrillard, Jean (2006). 'War porn', *Journal of Visual Culture*, 5(1), p.86.
Bauman, Zygmunt (1996). 'From pilgrim to tourist – or a Short History of Identity', in Hall, Stuart and Paul du Gay (eds), *Questions of Cultural Identity*, London: Sage, pp.18–36.

Beirut DC (2007). 'About us', *Beirut DC Official Website*. Available: http://www.beirutdc.org/template.php?menu=1&temp=1&table=submenu&id=1&EF=About

Ben-Rafael, Eliezer (1996). 'Multiculturalism in a sociological perspective', in Bubock, Rainer, Agnes Heller and Aristide R. Zolberg (eds), *The Challenge of Diversity: Integration and Pluralism in Societies of Immigration*, Aldershot: Avebury, pp.133–54.

Benton, Sarah (1998). 'Founding fathers and earth mothers: women's place at the "birth' of nations", in Charles, Nickie and Helen Hintjens (eds), *Gender, Ethnicity and Political Ideologies*, London: Routledge, pp.27–45.

Berger, Peter L. (1967). *The Sacred Canopy*, New York: Anchor.

Beydoun, Ahmad (2005). *The Adventures of Adversity: The Lebanese – Sects, Arabs, and Phoenicians*, Beirut: Dar An-Nahar (Arabic).

Bhabha, Homi (1990). 'DissemiNation: time, narrative, and the margins of the modern nation', in Bhabha, Homi (ed), *Nation and Narration*, London: Routledge, pp.291–322.

Billig, Michael (1995). *Banal Nationalism*, London: Sage.

Bollens, Scott A. (2000). *On Narrow Ground: Urban Policy and Ethnic Conflict in Jerusalem and Belfast*, Albany: State University of New York Press.

Boltanski, Luke (1999). *Distant Suffering: Morality, Media and Politics*, Cambridge: Cambridge University Press.

Bouzid, Nouri (1995). 'New realism in Arab Cinema: Defeat Conscious Cinema', *Alif: Journal of Comparative Poetics*, Number 15, Arab Cinematics, pp.242–50.

Bowen, Jeremy (2006). *War Stories*, London: Simon and Schuster.

Boyer, M. Christine (1995). 'The great frame-up: fantastic appearances in contemporary spatial politics', in Liggett, Helen and David C. Perry (eds), *Spatial Practices*, London: Sage, pp.81–109.

Boym, Svetlana (2001). *The Future of Nostalgia*, New York: Basic Books.

Bradley, Richard (2003). 'The Translation of Time', in Van Dyke, Ruth M. and Susan E. Alcock (eds), *Archaeologies of Memory*, Oxford: Blackwell, pp.221–7.

Brittan, Arthur (1989). *Masculinity and Power*, Oxford: Basil Blackwell.

Burgoyne, Robert (2003). 'From contested to consensual memory: the Rock and Roll Hall of Fame and Museum', in Hodgkin, Katharine and Susannah Radstone (eds), *Contested Pasts: The Politics of Memory*, London: Routledge, pp.208–20.

Chahal, Randa (2006). *Interview with the author*, Paris, April.

Chambers, Iain (1994). *Migrancy, Culture, Identity*, London: Routledge.

Chamoun, Jean (2004). *Interview with the author*, Beirut, April.

Charles, Nickie and Hintjens, Helen (1998). 'Gender, ethnicity and women's identity: women's "places"', in Charles, Nickie and Helen Hintjens (eds), *Gender, Ethnicity and Political Ideologies*, London: Routledge, pp.1–26.

Clark Mitchell, Lee (1996). *Westerns: Making the Man in Fiction and Film*, London: University of Chicago Press.

Codsi, Jean-Claude (2004). *Interview with the author*, Beirut, April.

Cohan, Steven (1997). *Masked Men: Masculinity and the Movies in the Fifties*, Bloomington: Indiana University Press.

Cohen, Abner (1969). *Custom and Politics in Urban Africa*, Berkeley: University of California Press.

Connell, R.W. (1995). *Masculinities*, Oxford: Polity Press.

Connell, R.W. (2001). 'The social organization of masculinity', in Whitehead, Stephen and Frank J. Barrett (eds), *The Masculinities Reader*, Cambridge, Polity Press, pp.30–50.

Connor, Walker (1994). *Ethnonationalism: The Quest for Understanding*, New Jersey: Princeton University Press.

Cooke, Miriam (1996). *Women and the War Story*, Berkeley: University of California Press.

Crighton, Elizabeth and Iver, Martha Abele Mac (1991). 'The evolution of protracted ethnic conflict: group dominance and political underdevelopment in Northern Ireland and Lebanon', *Comparative Politics*, 23(2): pp.127–42.

Custen, George (1992). *Bio/Pics: How Hollywood Constructed Public History*, New Brunswick, New Jersey: Rutgers University Press.

Daoud, Hassan (2003). 'The final scene in the cinema of life', *BabelMed* [Online]. Available: http://www.babelmed.net/index.php?menu=162&cont=534&lingua=en

De Klerk, Vivian (1997). 'The role of expletives in the construction of masculinity', in Johnson, Sally and Ulrika Hanna Meinhof (eds), *Language and Masculinity*, London: Blackwell, pp.144–58.

Deleuze, Gilles (1994). *Difference and Repetition*, London: The Athlone Press.

Deleuze, Gilles and Guattari, Félix (1987). *A Thousand Plateaus: Capitalism and Schizophrenia*, Minneapolis: University of Minnesota Press.

Donald, Ralph R. (2001). 'Masculinity and machismo in Hollywood's war films', in Whitehead, Stephen and Frank J. Barrett (eds), *The Masculinities Reader*, Cambridge: Polity Press, pp.170–83.

Doueiri, Ziad (2004). *Interview with the author*, London, April.

Easthope, Antony (1997). 'Cinecities in the sixties', in Clarke, David B. (ed), *The Cinematic City*, London: Routledge, pp.129–39.

Edensor, Tim (2002). *National Identity, Popular Culture and Everyday Life*, Oxford: Berg.

Eley, Geoff (1997). 'Foreword', in Evans, Martin and Kenneth Lunn (eds), *War and Memory in the Twentieth Century*, Oxford: Berg, pp.vii-xiii.

Entelis, John P. (1974). *Pluralism and Party Transformation in Lebanon: Al-Kataeb 1936–1970*, Leiden: E.J. Brill.

Fanon, Frantz (1991). *Black Skin White Masks*, New York: Grove Press.
Farah, Joseph (1979). 'Thirteen new film theaters in the Eastern area', *Al-Anwar*, September 3 (Arabic).
Fawaz, Leila (1997). '*Once Upon a Time, Beirut; A Suspended Life; The Tornado; Time Has Come*', *The American Historical Review* (February) 102(1), pp.252–3.
Ferguson, Russell (1990). 'Introduction: invisible center', in Ferguson, Russell, Martha Gever, Trinh Minh-ha and Cornel West (eds), *Out There: Marginalization and Contemporary Culture*, Cambridge, MA: MIT Press, pp.9–14.
Forty, Adrian and Susanne Kuchler (eds) (1999). *The Art of Forgetting*, Oxford: Berg.
Foucault, Michel (1980). *Power/Knowledge*, London: The Harvester Press.
Fouladkar, Assad (2006). *Interview with the author*, Beirut, April.
Gabriel, Teshome H. (1989). 'Third cinema as guardian of popular memory: towards a third aesthetics', in Pines, Jim and Paul Willemen (eds), *Questions of Third Cinema*, London: BFI, pp.53–64.
Gavin, Angus and Maluf, Ramez (1996). *Beirut Reborn: The Restoration and Development of the Central District*, London: Academy.
Gellner, Ernest (2006). *Nations and Nationalism*, London: Blackwell (2nd edition).
Greene, Naomi (1999). *Landscapes of Loss: The National Past in Postwar French Cinema*, Princeton, New Jersey: Princeton University Press.
Grew, Raymond (1986). 'The construction of national identity', in Boerner, Peter (ed), *Concepts of National Identity: An Interdisciplinary Dialogue*, Baden-Baden: Nomos Verlagsgesellschaft.
Grosz, Elizabeth (1998). 'Bodies-cities', in Pile, Steve and Heidi Nast (eds), *Places Through the Body*, London: Routledge, pp.42–51.
Habchi, Samir (2005). *Interview with the author*, Beirut, April.
Habib, Vicky (2005). 'Where is Lebanese cinema after the last few years' achievements of its ambitious innovators?' *Al-Hayat*, November 18 (Arabic).
HadjiThomas, Joana (2006). *Interview with the author*, Beirut, April.
Hajjar, Ghassan (2002). 'The cinematheque is national cinema's home in Lebanon', *An-Nahar*, February 19 (Arabic).
Hall, Stuart (1996). 'Introduction: who needs "Identity"?', in Hall, Stuart and Paul du Gay (eds), *Questions of Cultural Identity*, London: Sage, pp.1–17.
Hamam, Iman (2005). 'Shooting for real', *Al-Ahram Weekly* [Online]. Available: http://weekly.ahram.org.eg/2005/740/cu5.htm
Hamilton, Paula (2003). 'Sale of the century? Memory and historical consciousness in Australia', in Hodgkin, Katharine and Susannah Radstone (eds), *Contested Pasts: The Politics of Memory*, London: Routledge, pp.136–52.

Hamza, Radwan (1997). 'Al-Kifah al-Arabi opens the Lebanese cinema file', *Al-Kifah A-Arabi*, April 29 (Arabic).
Harper, Sue (1997). 'Popular film, popular memory: the case of the Second World War', in Evans, Martin and Kenneth Lunn (eds), *War and Memory in the Twentieth Century*, Oxford: Berg, pp.163–76.
Hastings, Adrian (1997). *The Construction of Nationhood: Ethnicity, Religion and Nationalism*, Cambridge: Cambridge University Press.
Hayden, Dolores (1999). 'Landscapes of loss and remembrance: the case of Little Tokyo in Los Angeles', in Winter, Jay and Emmanuel Sivan (eds), *War and Remembrance in the Twentieth Century*, Cambridge: Cambridge University Press, pp.42–160.
Healy, Chris (2003). 'Dead man: film, colonialism and memory', in Hodgkin, Katharine and Susannah Radstone (eds), *Contested Pasts: The Politics of Memory*, London: Routledge, pp.221–36.
Heller, Agnes (1996). 'The many faces of multiculturalism', in Bubock, Rainer, Agnes Heller and Aristide R. Zolberg (eds), *The Challenge of Diversity: Integration and Pluralism in Societies of Immigration*, Aldershot: Avebury, pp.25–42.
Hellmann, John (1997). 'The Vietnam film and American memory', in Evans, Martin and Kenneth Lunn (eds), *War and Memory in the Twentieth Century*, Oxford: Berg, pp.177–88.
Herbert, David T. and Thomas, Colin J. (1997). *Cities in Space, City as Place*, London: David Fulton Publishers.
Herzfeld, Michael (2004). *Cultural Intimacy: Social Poetics in the Nation-State*, New York: Routledge.
Higson, Andrew (1995). *Waving the Flag: Constructing a National Cinema in Britain*, Oxford: Clarendon.
Hirsch, Marianne and Spitzer, Leo (2003). ' "We would never have come without you": generations of nostalgia', in Hodgkin, Katharine and Susannah Radstone (eds), *Contested Pasts: The Politics of Memory*, London: Routledge, pp.79–95.
Hjort, Mette and Scott Mackenzie (2000). 'Introduction', in Hjort, Mette and Scott Mackenzie (eds), *Cinema and Nation*, London: Routledge, pp.1–16.
Hoang, Mai (2004). 'Lebanese filmmaker: Randa Chahal Sabbag', *World Press Review*, 51:3 (March) [Online]. Available: http://www.worldpress.org/Mideast/1803.cfm
Hobsbawm, Eric and Terence Ranger (eds) (1983). *The Invention of Tradition*, Cambridge: Cambridge University Press.
Hobsbawm, Eric (1990). *Nations and Nationalism since 1780*, Cambridge: Cambridge University Press.

Hockstader, Lee (1999). 'Lebanon's Forgotten Civil War', *Washington Post Foreign Service* (Monday December 20) [Online]. Available: http://www.library.cornell.edu/colldev/mideast/civwr1.htm

Hodgkin, Katharine and Radstone, Susannah (2003a). 'Introduction: contested pasts', in Hodgkin, Katharine and Susannah Radstone (eds), *Contested Pasts: The Politics of Memory*, London: Routledge, pp.1–21.

Hodgkin, Katharine and Radstone, Susannah (2003b). 'Patterning the national past', in Hodgkin, Katharine and Susannah Radstone (eds), *Contested Pasts: The Politics of Memory*, London: Routledge, pp.169–74.

Hodgkin, Katharine and Radstone, Susannah (2003c). 'Remembering suffering: trauma and history', in Hodgkin, Katharine and Susannah Radstone (eds), *Contested Pasts: The Politics of Memory*, London: Routledge, pp.97–103.

Hojeij, Bahij (2005). *Interview with the author*, Beirut, April.

Holt, Maria (1996). 'Palestinian women and the Intifada: an exploration of images and realities', in Afshar, Haleh (ed), *Women and Politics in the Third World*, London: Routledge, pp.186–203.

hooks, bell (1990). *Yearning: Race, Gender, and Cultural Politics*, Boston: South End Press.

Höpfl, Heather J. (2003). 'Becoming a (virile) member: women and the military body', *Body & Society*, 9(4): pp.13–30.

Hynes, Samuel (1999). 'Personal narratives and commemoration', in Winter, Jay and Emmanuel Sivan (eds), *War and Remembrance in the Twentieth Century*, Cambridge: Cambridge University Press, pp.205–20.

Inness, Sherrie A. (1999). *Tough Girls: Women Warriors and Wonder Women in Popular Culture*, Philadelphia: University of Pennsylvania Press.

Jaafar, Ali (2004). 'Domestic battlefields: Danielle Arbid on *Maarek Hob*', *Bidoun*, issue 2 (Fall: We Are Old) [Online]. Available: http://www.bidoun.com/issues/issue_2/02_all.html#article

Jabre, Farid (1966). 'The industry in Lebanon 1958–1965', in Sadoul, George (ed), *The Cinema on the Arab Countries*, Beirut: Interarab Centre of Cinema and Television, pp.172–8.

Jarjoura, Nadim (2000). 'The Lebanese cinema file', *Al-Itihad*, June 29 (Arabic).

Jeffords, Susan (1993). 'Can masculinity be terminated?', in Cohan, Steven and Ina Rae Hark (eds), *Screening the Male: Exploring Masculinities in Hollywood Cinema*, London: Routledge, pp.245–62.

Jones, Vivien (2000). 'Eighteenth-Century prostitution: feminist debates and the writing of histories', in Horner, Avril and Angela Keane (eds), *Body Matters: Feminism, Textuality, Corporeality*, Manchester: Manchester University Press, pp.127–42.

Joreige, Khalil (2005). Introduction to the screening of *A Perfect Day*, London Film Festival, October 26.
Joyce, Rosemary A. (2003). 'Concrete memories: fragments of the classic Maya past (500–1000AD)', in Van Dyke, Ruth M. and Susan E. Alcock (eds), *Archaeologies of Memory*, Oxford: Blackwell, pp.104–25.
Kahly, Marie (1993). 'Samir Habchi: the Lebanese Civil War was a nightmare and the pain increased when we woke up', *Al-Hayat*, February 12.
Kammoun, Michel (2006). 'Falafel', *Michel Kammoun Official Website*. Available: http://www.michelkammoun.com
Kaplan, Danny (2000). 'The military as a second Bar Mitzvah: combat service as initiation to Zionist masculinity', in Ghoussoub, Mai and Emma Sinclair-Webb (eds), *Imagined Masculinities: Male Identity and Culture in the Modern Middle East*, London: Saqi Books, pp.127–46.
Kennedy-Day, Kiki (2001). 'Cinema in Lebanon, Syria, Iraq and Kuwait', in Leaman, Oliver (ed), *Companion Encyclopedia of Middle Eastern and North African Film*, London: Routledge, pp.364–406.
Khalaf, Ghazi (1994). 'Documentary cinema: a true human testimony to the harshness of war', *Ad-Deyar*, October 18 (Arabic).
Khalaf, Samir (1993). *Beirut Reclaimed: Reflections on Urban Design and the Restoration of Civility*, Beirut: Dar An-Nahar.
Khalaf, Samir (2002). *Civil and Uncivil Violence in Lebanon: A History of the Internationalization of Communal Conflict*, New York: Columbia University Press.
Khatib, Lina (2006). *Filming the Modern Middle East: Politics in the Cinemas of Hollywood and the Arab World*, London: I.B.Tauris.
Ki'di, George (1991a). 'The file: Emile Chahine, Mohammad Soueid', *An-Nahar*, October 21 (Arabic).
Ki'di, George (1991b). 'The file: Houssam Khayat, Khaled Itani', *An-Nahar*, October 28 (Arabic).
Ki'di, George (1995a). 'Graduates write the image and we are in light and darkness', *An-Nahar*, June 26 (Arabic).
Ki'di, George (1995b). 'The centenary of cinema reaches Lebanon too', *An-Nahar*, August 14 (Arabic).
Ki'di, George (1997a). 'An-Nahar opens the file of the disappeared Lebanese cinema and its possible horizons 1', *An-Nahar*, January 20 (Arabic).
Ki'di, George (1997b). 'An-Nahar opens the file of the disappeared Lebanese cinema and its possible horizons 2', *An-Nahar*, January 21 (Arabic).
Ki'di, George (2006). 'Falafel', *Al-Balad*, December (Arabic).
Kimmel, Michael S. (2001). 'Masculinity as homophobia: fear, shame, and silence in the construction of gender identity', in Whitehead, Stephen and Frank J. Barrett (eds), *The Masculinities Reader*, Cambridge: Polity Press, pp.266–87.

King, Nicola (2000). *Memory, Narrative, Identity: Remembering the Self*, Edinburgh: Edinburgh University Press.
Kristeva, Julia (1982). *Powers of Horror: An Essay on Abjection*, New York: Columbia University Press.
Kristeva, Julia (1991). *Strangers to Ourselves*, London: Harvester Wheatsheaf.
'Lebanese cinema between the past and the present: a mysterious future?', *Al-Amal* (1982), December 10 (Arabic).
'Lebanese Cinema in its New Season', *An-Nida'* (1983), August 9 (Arabic).
Ledwith, Sue, Woods, Roberta and Jane Darke (2000). 'Women and the city', in Ledwith, Sue, Roberta Woods and Darke, Jane (eds), *Women and the City: Visibility and Voice in Urban Space*, Basingstoke: Palgrave, pp.1–10.
Lentin, Ronit (1997). 'Introduction: (en)gendering genocides', in Lentin, Ronit (ed), *Gender and Catastrophe*, London: Zed Books, pp.2–17.
Lowenthal, David (1985). *The Past is a Foreign Country*, Cambridge: Cambridge University Press.
Maalouf, Amin (2000). *On Identity*, London: The Harvill Press.
Macdonald, Sharon (1987). 'Drawing the lines: gender, peace and war: an introduction', in Macdonald, Sharon, Pat Holden and Shirley Ardener (eds), *Images of Women in Peace and War: Cross-Cultural and Historical Perspectives*, London: Macmillan Education, pp.1–26.
Mackey, Sandra (2006). *Lebanon: A House Divided*, New York: W.W. Norton and Company.
Madanat, Adnan (2004). 'Transformations in contemporary Arab cinema: issues and films', Damascus: Kanaan Press (Arabic).
Mahoney, Elisabeth (1997). '"The people in parentheses": space under pressure in the postmodern city', in Clarke, David B. (ed), *The Cinematic City*, London: Routledge, pp. 168–85.
McAllister, Ian (2002). 'The devil, miracles and the afterlife: the political sociology of religion in Northern Ireland', *British Journal of Sociology*, 33(3), pp.330–47.
McArthur, Colin (1997). 'Chinese boxes and Russian dolls: tracking the elusive cinematic city', in Clarke, David B. (ed), *The Cinematic City*, London: Routledge, pp.19–45.
Mellen, Joan (1978). *Big Bad Wolves: Masculinity in the American Film*, London: Elm Tree.
Melling, Phil (1997). 'War and memory in the new world order', in Evans, Martin and Kenneth Lunn (eds), *War and Memory in the Twentieth Century*, Oxford: Berg, pp.255–67.
Merridale, Catherine (1999). 'War, death, and remembrance in Soviet Russia', in Winter, Jay and Emmanuel Sivan (eds), *War and Remembrance in the Twentieth Century*, Cambridge: Cambridge University Press, pp.61–83.

Meskell, Lynn (2003). 'Memory's materiality: ancestral presence, commemorative practice and disjunctive locales', in Van Dyke, Ruth M. and Susan E. Alcock (eds), *Archaeologies of Memory*, Oxford: Blackwell, pp.34–55.

Moghadam, Valentine (2000). 'Economic restructuring and the gender contract: a case study of Jordan', in Marchand, Marianne and Anne Sisson Runyan (eds), *Gender and Global Restructuring*, London: Routledge, pp.99–115.

Morgan, Michael and Susan Leggett (1996). 'Introduction', in Morgan, Michael and Susan Leggett (eds), *Mainstreams(s) and Margins: Cultural Politics in the 90s*, Westport, Connecticut: Greenwood Press, pp.vii–xi.

Morokvasic, Mirjana (1998). 'The logics of exclusion: nationalism, sexism and the Yugoslav war', in Charles, Nickie and Helen Hintjens (eds), *Gender, Ethnicity and Political Ideologies*, London: Routledge, pp.65–90.

Moufarrej, Nada (1985). 'Home video: people's best companion', *Al-Anwar*, March 24 (Arabic).

Murshed, S. Mansoob (2002). 'Conflict, civil war and underdevelopment: an introduction', *Journal of Peace Research*, 39(4), pp.387–93.

Na'ouss, Nadine (2000). 'Lebanese cinema is fine despite war, poverty, and governmental neglect', *Al-Hayat*, January 14 (Arabic).

Narkunas, J. Paul (2001). 'Streetwalking in the cinema of the city: capital flows through Saigon', in Shiel, Mark and Tony Fitzmaurice (eds), *Cinema and the City: Film and Urban Societies in a Global Context*, Oxford: Blackwell, pp.147–57.

Nasri, Samir (1982). 'The Lebanese filmmakers' excuse is that they are passionate', *An-Nahar*, December 30 (Arabic).

Nasri, Samir (1985a). '*Ma'raka* in South Beirut, Nabatieh and South Lebanon', *An-Nahar*, November 18 (Arabic).

Nasri, Samir (1985b). 'Soueid, Birjaoui, Qaboos: a matter of enlightenment and critical knowledge', *An-Nahar*, December 3 (Arabic).

Nast, Heidi J. and Pile, Steve (1998). 'Introduction: MakingPlacesBodies', in Nast, Heidi J. and Steve Pile (eds), *Places through the Body*, London: Routledge, pp.1–20.

Né à Beyrouth (2007). *Official Website*. Available: http://www.neabeyrouth.org/index_english.html

Neale, Steve (1993). 'Prologue: masculinity as spectacle: reflections on men and mainstream cinema', in Cohan, Steven and Ina Rae Hark (eds), *Screening the Male: Exploring Masculinities in Hollywood Cinema*, London: Routledge, pp.9–22.

Newsinger, John (1993). ' "Do you walk the walk?": aspects of masculinity in some Vietnam War films', in Kirkham, Pat and Janet Thumim (eds), *You Tarzan: Masculinity, Movies and Men*, London: Lawrence and Wishart, pp.126–36.

Nietzche, Friedrich (1983). *Untimely Meditation*, Cambridge: Cambridge University Press.
Nowell-Smith, Geoffrey (1987). 'Popular culture', *New Formations*, issue 2, pp.79–90.
Oberschall, Anthony (1978). 'Theories of social conflict', *American Review of Sociology*, 4, pp.291–315.
Olkowski, Dorothea (1998). *Gilles Deleuze and the Ruin of Representation*, Berkeley: University of California Press.
Page, Ken (1993). 'Going solo: performance and identity in *New York, New York* and *Taxi Driver*', in Kirkham, Pat and Janet Thumim (eds), *You Tarzan: Masculinity, Movies and Men*, London: Lawrence and Wishart, pp.137–43.
Passerini, Luissa (2003). 'Memories between silence and oblivion', in Hodgskin, Katharine and Susannah Radstone (eds), *Contested Pasts: The Politics of Memory*, London: Routledge, pp.238–54.
Peteet, Julie (2000). 'Male gender and rituals of resistance in the Palestinian Intifada: a cultural politics of violence', in Ghoussoub, Mai and Emma Sinclair-Webb (eds), *Imagined Masculinities: Male Identity and Culture in the Modern Middle East*, London: Saqi Books, pp.92–102.
Pillai, Poonam (1996). 'Notes on centers and margins', in Morgan, Michael and Susan Leggett (eds), *Mainstream(s) and Margins: Cultural Politics in the 90s*, Westport, Connecticut: Greenwood Press, pp.3–13.
Plano, Jack C. and Roy Olton (1969). *The International Relations Dictionary*, New York: Holt, Rinehart & Winston.
Portelli, Alessandro (2003). 'The massacre at the Fosse Ardeatine: history, myth, ritual and symbol', in Hodgkin, Katharine and Susannah Radstone (eds), *Contested Pasts: The Politics of Memory*, London: Routledge, pp.29–41.
'Proposed law to impose taxes on home videos', *Al-Ahrar* (1984), April 14 (Arabic).
Qirdahi, Joseph (1985). 'Lebanese cinema has been searching for an identity for six decades', *As-Sayyad*, November 27 (Arabic).
Reading, Anna (2002). *The Social Inheritance of the Holocaust: Gender, Culture and Memory*, New York: Palgrave.
Riding, Alan (2000). 'A filmmaker without honor or outlets in her own land', *The New York Times* (Wednesday June 14) [Online]. Available: http://www.library.cornell.edu/colldev/mideast/chahal.htm
Rizk, Bahjat Edmond (2006). *Lebanese Plurality in Identity and Government*, Beirut: Bahjat Edmond Rizk (Arabic).
Roach Pierson, Ruth (1987). '"Did your mother wear Army boots?": feminist theory and women's relation to war, peace and revolution', in Macdonald, Sharon, Pat Holden and Shirley Ardener (eds), *Images of Women in Peace*

and War: Cross-Cultural and Historical Perspectives, London: Macmillan Education, pp.205–27.

Rosen, Miriam (1989). 'The uprooted cinema: Arab filmmakers abroad', Middle East Report, Number 159 (July/August), 'Popular Culture', pp.34–7.

Rykwert, Joseph (2000). The Seduction of Place: The City in the Twentieth-First Century, London: Weidenfeld & Nicolson.

Rzouk, Giselle (2004). 'Ayoub: two hundred and fifty ads are made in Lebanon every year', Al-Anwar, July 19 (Arabic).

Saab, Jocelyne (2006). Interview with the author, Paris, April.

Salhab, Ghassan (2004). Interview with the author, Beirut, April.

Salibi, Kamal (2005). A House of Many Mansions: The History of Lebanon Reconsidered, London: I.B.Tauris.

Samuel, Raphael (1994). Theatres of Memory, London: Verso.

Sarkis, Hashim (1993). 'Territorial claims: architecture and post-war attitudes toward the built environment', in Khalaf, Samir and Philip S. Khoury (ed), Recovering Beirut: Urban Design and Post-War Reconstruction, Leiden: E.J. Brill, pp.101–27.

Sarkis, Hashim (2005). 'A vital void: reconstructions of Downtown Beirut', in Vale, Lawrence J. and Thomas J. Campanella (eds), The Resilient City: How Modern Cities Recover from Disaster, Oxford: Oxford University Press, pp.281–98.

Seton-Watson, Hugh (1977). Nations and States: An Enquiry into the Origins of Nations and the Politics of Nationalism, London: Westview Press.

Seul, Jeffrey R. (1999). '"Ours is the Way of God": religion, identity and intergroup conflict', Journal of Peace Research, 36(5), pp.553–69.

Shaviro, Steven (1993). The Cinematic Body, Minneapolis: University of Minnesota Press.

Shaw, Martin (1997). 'Past wars and present conflicts: from the Second World War to the Gulf War', in Evans, Martin and Kenneth Lunn (eds), War and Memory in the Twentieth Century, Oxford: Berg, pp.191–204.

Shiel, Mark (2001). 'Cinema and the city in history and theory', in Shiel, Mark and Tony Fitzmaurice (eds), Cinema and the City: Film and Urban Societies in a Global Context, Oxford: Blackwell, pp.1–18.

Smith, Anna (1996). Julia Kristeva: Readings of Exile and Estrangement, London: Macmillan.

Smith, Anthony (1986). The Ethnic Origins of Nations, Oxford: Blackwell.

Smith, Anthony (1991). National Identity, London: Penguin Books.

Sorlin, Pierre (1999). 'Children as war victims in postwar European cinema', in Winter, Jay and Emmanuel Sivan (eds), War and Remembrance in the Twentieth Century, Cambridge: Cambridge University Press, pp.104–24.

Soueid, Mohamad (1982). 'The condition of filmmakers according to the head of their Union', As-Safir, October 18 (Arabic).

Soueid, Mohamad (1983a). 'At the start of the new round of film productions: on which edge does production stand?', *As-Safir*, June 20 (Arabic).
Soueid, Mohamad (1983b). 'Stories from cinematic production in Lebanon', *As-Safir*, September 12 (Arabic).
Soueid, Mohamad (1986). *The Postponed Cinema: Films of the Lebanese Civil War*, Beirut: The Arab Research Organization (Arabic).
Soueid, Mohamad (1989). 'Lebanese expat cinema: war, exile and the French Revolution', *Al-Hayat*, December 6 (Arabic).
Soueid, Mohamad (1990a). 'Sixty years since the establishment of cinema in Lebanon', Part 1, *Al-Hayat*, August 28 (Arabic).
Soueid, Mohamad (1990b). 'Sixty years since the establishment of cinema in Lebanon', Part 2, *Al-Hayat*, August 30 (Arabic).
Soueid, Mohamad (1990c). 'Sixty years since the establishment of cinema in Lebanon', Part 3, *Al-Hayat*, August 31 (Arabic).
Soueid, Mohamad (1990d). 'Sixty years since the establishment of cinema in Lebanon', Part 5, *Al-Hayat*, September 2 (Arabic).
Soueid, Mohamad (1990e). 'Sixty years since the establishment of cinema in Lebanon', Part 6, *Al-Hayat*, September 4 (Arabic).
Soueid, Mohamad (1991). 'Beirut's film theaters on the eve of the war', *Al-Hayat*, August 2 (Arabic).
Soueid, Mohamad (1992). 'Maroun Baghdadi', *An-Nahar newspaper supplement*, 5 September.
Soueid, Mohamad (1998). 'Lebanese cinema: the migrant image', *An-Nahar Culture Supplement*, October 3 (Arabic).
Soueid, Mohamad (1999). 'Lebanese cinema in the hands of the censors', *An-Nahar*, October 30 (Arabic).
Soueid, Mohamad (2000). 'The cinema industry in Lebanon', *Al-Hiwar*, April 15 (Arabic).
Soueid, Mohamad (2006). *Interview with the author*, Beirut, April.
Spike Peterson, V. (1996). 'Shifting ground(s): epistemological and territorial remapping in the context of globalization(s)', in Kofman, Eleonore and Gillian Youngs (eds), *Globalization: Theory and Practice*, London: Pinter, pp.11–27.
Spike Peterson, V. (1999). 'Sexing political identities/nationalism as heterosexism', *International Feminist Journal of Politics*, 1(1): pp.34–65.
Stein, Janet Gross (1996). 'Image, identity and conflict resolution', in Crocker, Chester, Fen Hampson and Pamela Aall (eds), *Managing Global Chaos*, Washington DC: USIP Press, pp.93–111.
Studlar, Gaylyn and Desser, David (1988). 'Never having to say you're sorry: *Rambo*'s rewriting of the Vietnam War', *Film Quarterly* (Autumn) 42(1), pp.9–16.
Tasker, Yvonne (1993). 'Dumb movies for dumb people: masculinity, the body, and the voice in contemporary action cinema', in Cohan, Steven and Ina

Rae Hark (eds), *Screening the Male: Exploring Masculinities in Hollywood Cinema*, London: Routledge, pp.230–44.
Tawfiq, Mohamad (1982). 'The war and Lebanese cinema', *As-Safir*, March 28 (Arabic).
Taylor, Diana (2003). *Performing Cultural Memory in the Americas*, Durham: Duke University Press.
Taylor, Gary and Spencer, Steve (2004). 'Introduction', in Taylor, Gary and Steve Spencer (eds), *Social Identities: Multidisciplinary Approaches*, London: Routledge, pp.1–13.
'The Lebanese General Security bans *The Civilized* and distributes a proof of insults... and scenes', *Al-Hayat* (1999), October 21 (Arabic).
'The opening of Screen 6 at Cinema Empire: exclusive to European cinema', *An-Hahar* (1999), May 5 (Arabic).
Tonkiss, Fran (2003). 'The ethics of indifference: community and solitude in the city', *International Journal of Cultural Studies*, 6(3), pp.297–311.
Traboulsi, Fawwaz (2006). *A History of Modern Lebanon*, London: Pluto Press.
Van Dyke, Ruth M. and Susan E. Alcock (2003). 'Archaeologies of memory: an introduction, in Van Dyke, Ruth M. and Susan E. Alcock (eds), *Archaeologies of Memory*, Oxford: Blackwell, pp.1–13.
Variety (2007). *Falafel*, January 5 [Online]. Available: http://www.variety.com/review/VE1117932397.html?categoryid=1270&cs=1
Walker, Janet (2003). 'The traumatic paradox: autobiographical documentary and the psychology of memory', in Hodgkin, Katharine and Susannah Radstone (eds), *Contested Pasts: The Politics of Memory*, London: Routledge, pp.104–19.
Walsh, David (2000). 'War and peace', *World Socialist Web Site* [Online]. Available: http://www.wsws.org/articles/2000/may2000/sff3–m26.shtml
Warshaw, Robert (1962). *The Immediate Experience: Movies, Comics, Theater and Other Aspects of Popular Culture*, Garden City, New York: Doubleday.
Wassaf, Abir (2000). 'Half a million dollars for the first post-war comedy film', *Al-Afkar*, October 30 (Arabic).
Waylen, Georgina (1996). *Gender in Third World Politics*, Buckingham: Open University Press.
Wazen, Abdo (1995). 'War as subject for cinema', translated by Ferial J. Ghazoul, *Alif: Journal of Comparative Poetics*, 15, pp.229–34.
Weber, Eugen (1977). *Peasants into Frenchmen*, London: Chatto and Windus.
Westmoreland, Mark (2002). 'Cinematic dreaming: on phantom poetics and the longing for a Lebanese national cinema', *Text, Practice, Performance*, issue IV, pp.33–50.
Wettig, Hannah (2004). 'Lebanese authorities ban "The Da Vinci Code" ', *The Daily Star* (Thursday September 16) [Online]. Available: http://www.dailystar.com.lb/article.asp?edition_ID=1&article_ID=8424&categ_id=2

White, Hayden (1988). 'Historiography and historiophoty', *The American Historical Review* (December), 95(5), pp.1193–9.

Widder, Nathan (2002). *Genealogies of Difference*, Urbana and Chicago: University of Illinois Press.

Williams, Doug (1991). 'Concealment and disclosure: from *Birth of a Nation* to the Vietnam War film', *International Political Science Review* (January), 12(1), pp.29–47.

Willis, Sharon (1993). 'Disputed territories: masculinity and social space', in Penley, Constance and Sharon Willis (eds), *Male Trouble*, Minneapolis: University of Minnesota Press, pp.263–82.

Winter, Jay and Sivan, Emmanuel (1999). 'Setting the framework', in Winter, Jay and Emmanuel Sivan (eds), *War and Remembrance in the Twentieth Century*, Cambridge: Cambridge University Press, pp.6–39.

Yahya, Maha (1993). 'Reconstituting space: the aberration of the arban in Beirut', in Khalaf, Samir and Philip S. Khoury (eds), *Recovering Beirut: Urban Design and Post-War Reconstruction*, Leiden: E.J. Brill, pp.128–65.

Young, James (2003). 'Between history and memory: the voice of the eye witness', in Douglass, Ana and Thomas A. Vogler (eds), *Witness and Memory: The Discourse of Trauma*, London: Routledge, pp.275–84.

FILMOGRAPHY

Around the Pink House (Al-Beit al-Zahr). Joana HadjiThomas and Khalil Joreige. 1998.
Beirut, The Encounter (Beirut al-Liqa'). Borhan Alawiyeh. 1981.
Beirut Phantoms (Ashbah Beirut). Ghassan Salhab. 1998.
Beirut ya Beirut. Maroun Baghdadi. 1975.
The Belt of Fire (Zinnar al-Nar). Bahij Hojeij. 2003.
Bosta [The Bus] (Al-Bosta). Philippe Aractingi. 2005.
The Civilized (Moutahaddirat). Randa Chahal Sabbagh. 1998.
A Country above Wounds (Watan Fawq al-Jirah). Sobhi Saif ed-Din. 1983.
The Explosion (Al-Infijar). Rafic Hajjar. 1982.
Falafel. Michel Kammoun. 2006.
In the Battlefields (Maarik Hob). Danielle Arbid. 2004.
In the Shadows of the City (Tayf al-Madina). Jean Chamoun. 2000.
Kite (Tayyara min Waraq). Randa Chahal Sabbagh. 2003.
(Lebanon) Land of Honey and Incense (Loubnan Balad al-Assal wal Bakhour). Maroun Baghdadi. 1987.
Lebanon in Spite of Everything (Loubnan Roghma Kulla Shai'). André Ged'oun. 1982.
Letter from a Time of Exile (Risala min Zaman al-Manfa). Borhan Alawiyeh. 1988.
Little Wars (Houroub Saghira). Maroun Baghdadi. 1982.
Ma'raka. Roger Assaf. 1985.
Martyrs. Leyla Assaf-Tengroth. 1988.
Once Upon a Time, Beirut (Kan ya ma Kan, Beirut). Jocelyne Saab. 1994.
Outside Life (Kharij al-Hayat). Maroun Baghdadi. 1991.
A Perfect Day (Yawm Akhar). Khalil Joreige and Joana HadjiThomas. 2005.
Al-Sheikha. Leyla Assaf-Tengroth. 1994.
The Shelter (Al-Malja'). Rafic Hajjar. 1980.
A Suspended Life (Ghazl al-Banat). Jocelyne Saab. 1984.
Terra Incognita (Al-Ard al-Majhoula). Ghassan Salhab. 2002.

A Time Has Come (An al-Awan). Jean-Claude Codsi. 1994.
To you wherever you are (Ilayk Aynama Takoun). Borhan Alawiyeh. 2001.
The Tornado (Al-I'sar). Samir Habchi. 1992.
The Veiled Man (L'Homme Voilé). Maroun Baghdadi. 1987.
West Beyrouth (Beirut al-Gharbiyah). Ziad Doueiri. 1998.
When Maryam Spoke Out (Lamma Hikyit Maryam). Assad Fouladkar. 2002.
Zozo. Josef Fares. 2005.

INDEX

Agamben, Giorgio 100, 101
Amal 6
America (see also United States)
    xx, xxiii, 10, 26, 36, 38, 49, 59,
    101, 102, 106, 116, 117, 118,
    125, 138, 165, 174, 186
Ambivalence xvii, 12, 60, 66
Amnesia (see also Forgetting) xix,
    10, 11, 58, 74, 77, 171, 176
Arab (Arabia, Arabic, Arabian)
    xiv, xvii, xx, 3, 4, 8, 9, 10, 12,
    14, 21, 22, 23, 24, 25, 28, 29, 34,
    35, 39, 40, 42, 43, 44, 48, 49, 59,
    70, 86, 111, 114, 117, 135, 145,
    169, 171, 175
Arab-Israeli conflict xx, 9, 59,
    171
Army xvi, 13, 34, 85, 108, 134,
    146

Beirut xiii, xvi, xix, xxi, xxiv, 7, 8,
    11, 12, 13, 21, 22, 25, 26, 27, 28,
    30, 31, 35, 48, 49, 50, 57, 58, 59,
    60, 61, 62, 63, 64, 65, 66, 67, 69,
    70, 71, 72, 73, 74, 75, 76, 77, 78,
    84, 85, 86, 87, 88, 92, 93, 94, 96,
    97, 99, 110, 112, 113, 133, 134,
    136, 142, 143, 144, 145, 146,
    147, 157, 160, 161, 162, 163,
    164, 165, 169, 170, 171, 172,
    173, 177

Binary 10, 83, 96, 99, 129, 140,
    148, 187
Blame (see also Guilt) 95, 138,
    140, 155, 171, 175, 176, 177
Body (Bodies) 44, 61, 62, 69, 84,
    97, 105, 106, 107, 113, 118, 122,
    123, 125, 132, 137, 141, 142,
    143, 144, 145, 146, 147, 163
Border 8, 13, 16, 65, 146, 171
Boundary 8, 67, 96, 105, 130, 132,
    143, 144, 145

Cedar Revolution xix, 11, 12, 165,
    168
Censor (censorship) 23, 29, 34, 35,
    36, 43, 44, 46, 96
Christian (Christianity) 4, 5, 6, 8,
    12, 16, 35, 36, 58, 65, 66, 68, 72,
    86, 91, 92, 93, 94, 95, 96, 122,
    136, 137, 142, 144, 145, 146,
    147, 160, 170, 173, 175, 177
Class xx, 7, 8, 31, 64, 66, 90, 139,
    140, 142
Collective xviii, 58, 67, 71, 74, 75,
    83, 105, 153, 154, 155, 157, 158,
    178, 179, 185
Colonial (colonize) 10, 59, 75, 76,
    125, 143
Contest (contestation) xiii, xvii,
    xx, xxi, 3, 13, 14, 16, 60, 65, 67,
    75, 83, 89, 154, 155, 166, 179

Control 6, 14, 41, 67, 72, 75, 84, 85, 87, 95, 96, 100, 120, 122, 123, 125, 131, 132, 144, 145, 169, 174, 186

Culture (Cultural) xvii, xviii, xix, 4, 5, 8, 10, 14, 15, 17, 24, 25, 28, 29, 30, 31, 32, 33, 36, 38, 40, 44, 45, 46, 48, 57, 63, 67, 76, 89, 94, 95, 99, 130, 140, 143, 154, 157, 177, 179, 186, 187, 188

Diversity (Diverse) xvii, 6, 12, 14, 44, 160

Divide (Division) 4, 5, 6, 7, 8, 10, 12, 13, 14, 15, 17, 25, 26, 31, 34, 39, 49, 57, 59, 60, 65, 66, 77, 89, 90, 91, 92, 93, 95, 120, 121, 140, 141, 142, 143, 144, 145, 157, 170, 172, 175, 177, 187

Dominance (Dominant, Dominate) xvi, xviii, 4, 7, 15, 23, 29, 31, 60, 77, 99, 100, 106, 114, 118, 120, 121, 129, 130, 140, 154, 169

Druze 6, 9, 160, 173

Economic (Economy) 6, 7, 8, 23, 29, 34, 45, 57, 75, 76, 84, 85, 90, 130, 185, 186

Egypt (Egyptian) xiii, xiv, 21, 22, 23, 24, 26, 27, 29, 32, 35, 41, 48, 59, 135, 142, 143, 171, 186, 187

Enemy 66, 84, 106, 114, 115, 122, 135

Essential (-ist, -ism) 70, 73, 95, 98, 100, 106, 130, 140, 145, 148, 186

Ethnic (ethnicity) 7, 14, 16, 17, 66, 67, 75, 78, 96, 99, 130, 139, 140, 145, 147, 179

Exclusion (Exclude) 12, 13, 45, 60, 64, 66, 67, 75, 84, 98, 100, 105, 122, 134, 144, 185

Exile xvii, 11, 13, 68, 69, 70, 71, 88, 135

Fear 6, 28, 66, 71, 84, 98, 106, 109, 110, 118, 120, 123, 130, 131, 135, 145, 157, 175, 178

Foreign xiv, 9, 10, 11, 12, 13, 14, 24, 30, 38, 39, 41, 59, 85, 91, 92, 115, 142, 143, 144, 155, 174, 177, 186

Forget (see also Amnesia) 58, 60, 61, 70, 78, 169, 171, 173, 176, 178, 179

France 9, 10, 13, 22, 27, 35, 38, 39, 40, 46, 50, 65, 68, 70, 106, 111, 112, 114, 143, 158

French xxiii, 9, 10, 22, 35, 37, 38, 39, 40, 41, 46, 49, 50, 59, 91, 106, 110, 111, 113, 114, 115, 118, 122, 143, 159, 174, 186

Future xv, xviii, xxiii, xxiv, 3, 13, 23, 30, 31, 47, 61, 77, 110, 155, 158, 160, 161, 163, 166, 168, 174, 177

Gaze 62, 87, 106, 117, 120, 123

Guilt (see also Blame) xix, 59, 95, 169, 177

Hegemony (Hegemonic) xxii, 121, 122

History (Historical) xv, xvii, xviii, xix, xxiii, xxiv, 3, 4, 5, 6, 8, 10, 11, 13, 16, 17, 21, 28, 29, 44, 59, 72, 74, 76, 95, 99, 117, 124, 130, 144, 153, 154, 155, 156, 157, 158, 166, 169, 171, 174, 176, 177, 178, 179

Hizbullah xvi, 6, 11, 13

Hollywood xiii, xiv, 26, 41, 45, 105, 106, 118, 124

Homogeneity (Homogenous) 13, 15, 17, 60, 64, 67, 73, 84, 100

Ideal (Idealize) 92, 119, 122, 130, 148, 155, 169, 170

Identity (see also National Identity) xvii, xxii, 5, 8, 9, 10, 13, 14, 15, 16, 24, 59, 60, 61, 62, 65, 70, 71, 72, 75, 76, 83, 84, 90, 95, 96, 99,

INDEX

109, 113, 119, 120, 130, 137, 144, 145, 148, 154, 160, 162, 166, 169, 173, 177, 185
Ideology (Ideological) xviii, 5, 9, 10, 13, 16, 17, 28, 121, 125, 130, 154, 172, 174
International xviii, 13, 14, 21, 22, 24, 30, 39, 43, 175
Innocence (Innocent) xviii, 92, 107, 114, 140, 165, 176
Islam (see Muslim)
Israel (Israeli) xvi, xx, 9, 10, 11, 13, 16, 28, 36, 59, 65, 111, 129, 135, 136, 137, 138, 143, 163, 166, 171, 172, 177

Language 4, 22, 29, 35, 37, 40, 41, 48, 63, 70, 108, 114, 143, 175, 177, 186

Margin (see also Periphery) xviii, 8, 41, 71, 84, 99, 109, 122, 130, 140, 142, 147, 148, 158, 160, 165, 171
Maronite 5, 6, 9, 10
Martyr 61, 62, 67, 74, 97, 136, 137, 138, 139, 160, 172
Military (Militant, Militia -man) xiii, xvii, xx, 8, 9, 11, 13, 33, 34, 35, 40, 57, 58, 60, 65, 66, 67, 68, 71, 72, 73, 84, 85, 86, 87, 88, 89, 91, 92, 95, 96, 97, 100, 107, 108, 109, 110, 111, 112, 113, 114, 115, 116, 117, 118, 122, 124, 129, 130, 132, 133, 135, 136, 137, 138, 142, 144, 145, 146, 147, 160, 161, 169, 170, 176, 177
Moral (morality) 5, 35, 36, 62, 90, 113, 147, 185
Muslim 5, 6, 8, 9, 12, 35, 58, 64, 65, 66, 68, 86, 89, 91, 92, 93, 95, 96, 110, 111, 122, 134, 137, 144, 145, 146, 147, 160, 170, 173, 175, 177
Myth xix, 4, 7, 10, 22, 58, 65, 66, 99, 154, 155, 158, 169, 174, 176, 179, 185

Nation (Nationalism, Nationalist) xix, 3, 4, 5, 6, 9, 10, 11, 12, 13, 14, 15, 16, 17, 22, 23, 24, 25, 29, 32, 34, 40, 45, 46, 48, 50, 58, 59, 66, 67, 69, 70, 71, 75, 76, 77, 83, 84, 87, 88, 90, 130, 134, 135, 139, 140, 143, 144, 145, 146, 147, 148, 153, 154, 155, 156, 158, 160, 166, 168, 169, 170, 174, 175, 178, 179, 185, 186, 187, 188
National identity xvii, xxiv, 3, 5, 13, 15, 16, 89, 188
Nostalgia xiv, 58, 60, 63, 70, 166, 167, 168, 169, 186, 187

Other (Otherness) xviii, xx, 6, 10, 11, 65, 66, 67, 83, 84, 90, 91, 93, 95, 96, 98, 99, 100, 101, 105, 112, 114, 117, 122, 123, 125, 140, 141, 142, 143, 144, 145, 146, 155, 175, 175, 176, 177, 179

Palestine (Palestinian) 8, 9, 10, 16, 24, 64, 65, 135, 138, 163, 171, 175, 177
Past xvii, xviii, xix, xxii, xxiii, 3, 4, 7, 10, 11, 27, 49, 59, 60, 74, 75, 76, 77, 93, 137, 143, 153, 154, 155, 156, 158, 159, 160, 161, 162, 163, 166, 167, 168, 169, 174, 176, 177, 178, 179
Peace xv, xxiii, 7, 9, 34, 129, 130, 134, 139, 142, 167
Periphery (see also Margin) 84
Phoenicia 4
Pluralism 14, 15
Power xviii, 4, 5, 7, 9, 10, 12, 15, 57, 76, 90, 95, 96, 99, 100, 105, 114, 115, 125, 134, 136, 147
Present xiv, xv, xvii, xviii, xix, xxii, xxiii, xxiv, 4, 10, 28, 49, 59, 60, 63, 74, 76, 77, 93, 110, 143, 157, 158, 162, 163, 166, 167, 168, 169, 174, 176, 178

Refugee 8, 71, 86, 91, 136, 171, 172, 173
Religion (Religious) xx, 5, 6, 7, 13, 14, 15, 17, 34, 57, 60, 66, 67, 84, 89, 90, 91, 92, 93, 94, 95, 96, 98, 100, 108, 140, 141, 143, 145, 147, 163, 164, 172, 173, 177, 179
Resist (Resistance, Resistant) 11, 24, 28, 65, 67, 74, 77, 107, 129, 135, 136, 139, 140, 147, 155, 156, 169, 171, 172, 177, 187
Responsibility xix, 10, 30, 46, 99, 111, 134, 140, 155, 171, 174

Saudi Arabia 9, 11, 12
Sectarian (Sectarianism) xvi, xvii, xx, xxiv, 5, 6, 7, 13, 15, 17, 34, 59, 60, 64, 65, 84, 89, 90, 91, 92, 93, 94, 95, 96, 98, 100, 175, 177, 179
Secular 6, 90
Self xviii, xix, 10, 14, 67, 78, 83, 84, 95, 100, 105, 110, 115, 123, 125, 137, 141, 143, 144, 145, 146, 147, 155, 169, 188
Sexuality (Sexual) 27, 31, 61, 96, 121, 122, 130, 139, 140, 142, 143, 145, 146, 160
Shiite 5, 6, 8, 9, 28, 36, 135, 172
Silence (Silent) xix, 11, 22, 59, 68, 70, 84, 106, 114, 122, 129, 130, 132, 133, 146, 169, 176, 179
South [Lebanon] 6, 8, 28, 36, 37, 70, 71, 72, 89, 91, 129, 135, 136, 138, 145, 171, 172, 173

State xvii, 3, 6, 8, 9, 10, 14, 15, 16, 29, 30, 31, 32, 46, 47, 76, 84, 100, 154, 155, 175, 186
Sunni 5, 6, 7, 8, 9
Syria (Syrian) 8, 9, 10, 11, 12, 14, 23, 24, 136, 138, 142, 144, 165, 169
Syrian Social Nationalist Party 136, 137, 172

Terror (Terrorism) xvi, 88, 90, 105, 111, 112, 113, 114, 118, 165, 174, 175
Tradition xviii, 3, 4, 7, 8, 14, 35, 48, 57, 75, 76, 97, 105, 106, 110, 111, 114, 118, 129, 130, 135, 136, 143, 146, 147, 154, 160, 176, 177
Trauma xviii, xix, 60, 178, 179, 188
Truth xix, 11, 12, 154, 174, 176, 178

United States (see also America) 10, 11, 12, 42, 45, 46
Unity 5, 10, 11, 12, 84, 87, 147, 154, 155, 158, 174, 179, 188

Victim (Victimization) xviii, xx, 10, 11, 59, 73, 84, 86, 87, 98, 99, 107, 111, 112, 113, 115, 117, 118, 123, 125, 129, 130, 131, 132, 133, 134, 139, 144, 155, 174, 175

'War of others on our land' 10, 11, 65, 155, 176

INDEX OF FILMS

Around the Pink House 30, 37, 39, 63, 64, 74, 75, 76, 77, 160
Beirut, The Encounter 27, 38, 39, 40, 68, 72, 73, 85, 92, 93, 171, 172
Beirut Phantoms 30, 37, 39, 74, 87, 88, 161, 162, 167, 171, 175
Beirut ya Beirut 28, 50, 172
The Belt of Fire xix, xxii, 38, 39, 42, 43, 47, 72, 86, 87, 88, 123, 132, 173
Bosta xviii, 31, 36, 37, 39, 40, 42, 43, 46, 92, 93, 156, 160, 161, 164, 172
The Civilized 31, 35, 36, 39, 40, 42, 43, 87, 89, 92, 93, 96, 98, 112, 129, 140, 142, 144, 145, 147
A Country above Wounds 68, 85, 87, 89, 157, 169, 173, 174, 177
The Explosion 26, 27, 68, 85, 87, 91, 92, 93, 94, 171, 175, 177
Falafel xx, 31, 161, 163, 165
In the Battlefields xx, xxiii, 31, 33, 36, 38, 39, 42, 43, 61, 66, 67, 68, 87, 91, 92, 93, 96, 115, 129, 132, 141, 170
In the Shadows of the City xx, 39, 42, 61, 71, 85, 87, 92, 107, 157, 170, 171, 176, 178
Kite 39, 40, 145, 146
(Lebanon) Land of Honey and Incense 40, 85, 106, 110, 113, 115, 116, 122, 156

Lebanon in Spite of Everything 36, 68, 71, 85, 87, 89, 91, 107, 169, 171, 175
Letter from a Time of Exile 39, 68, 69, 129
Little Wars 27, 38, 61, 62, 63, 68, 96, 106, 107, 108, 109, 110, 113, 116, 117, 122, 129, 133, 134, 162, 165, 166, 173
Ma'raka 28, 36, 39, 50, 129, 135, 136, 172, 173
Martyrs 42, 49, 92, 93, 129, 136, 139, 169, 171
Once Upon a Time, Beirut 28, 40, 42, 59, 62, 88, 171, 174
Outside Life 40, 85, 106, 110, 111, 112, 113, 115, 117, 118, 119, 120, 122, 129, 134
A Perfect Day xx, xxii, 39, 43, 74, 76, 161
The Shelter 87, 92, 96, 130, 131, 132, 133, 171, 173
Al-Sheikha 28, 91, 158, 159
A Suspended Life xx, xxi, 38, 40, 42, 71, 87, 89, 96, 112, 171, 174
Terra Incognita 42, 161, 162, 163, 172
A Time Has Come 28, 39, 42, 85, 91, 93, 96, 107, 170, 174
To you wherever you are xvi, 62, 64, 75

The Tornado xiv, xix, xx, 28, 34, 38, 39, 42, 44, 96, 97, 98, 107, 108, 112, 174
The Veiled Man 40, 50, 156
West Beyrouth xv, xix, xxiii, 21, 30, 34, 35, 37, 38, 42, 43, 61, 63, 64, 65, 66, 67, 68, 92, 93, 94, 129, 140, 143, 144, 146, 147, 156, 168, 169, 170, 171, 175, 176, 178
When Maryam Spoke Out xxi, 31, 33, 36, 37, 39, 42, 43, 47
Zozo 43, 68, 87, 88

www.ingramcontent.com/pod-product-compliance
Lightning Source LLC
Chambersburg PA
CBHW070311230426
43663CB00011B/2089